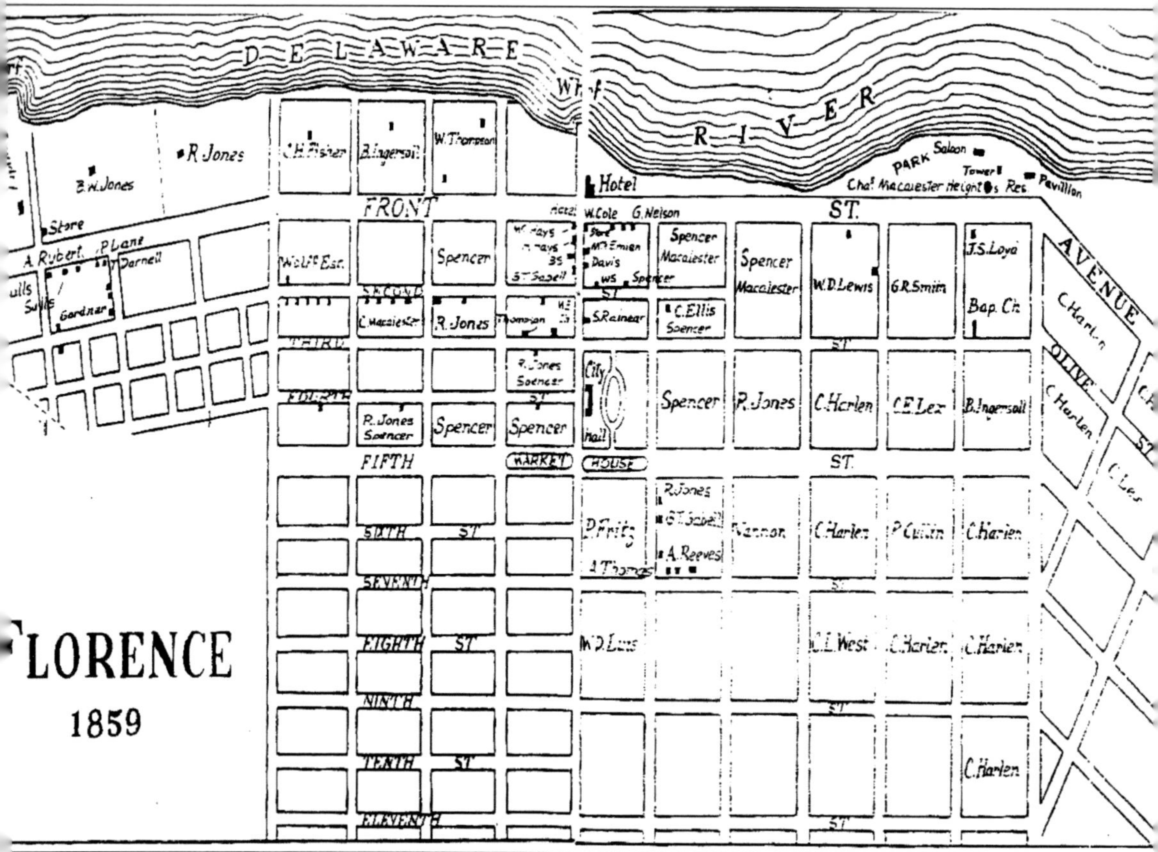

A map of Florence dated 1859 gives the basic layout of the town before side streets were named. As far as we know, the market house on Fifth Street never materialized, nor did the city hall on the eastern side of Broad Street in the third block. Also, many of the large tracts of land owned by Schuyler, Durell, and Rainier had been sold to the Jones family for construction of the foundry on West Front Street.

IMAGES
of America

FLORENCE

Florence Historical Society Book Committee

ARCADIA
PUBLISHING

IISBN 978-0-7385-1295-2

Published by Arcadia Publishing
Charleston, South Carolina

Printed in the United States of America

For all general information, please contact Arcadia Publishing:
Telephone 843-853-2070
Fax 843-853-0044
E-mail sales@arcadiapublishing.com
For customer service and orders:
Toll-Free 1-888-313-2665

Visit us on the Internet at www.arcadiapublishing.com

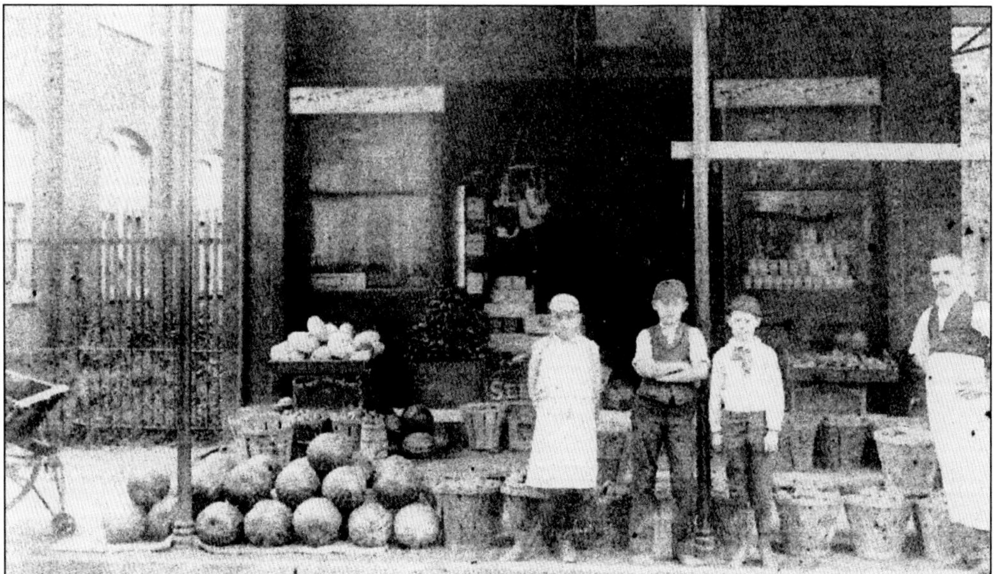

The R.D. Wood company store offered an assortment of food and staples for homes. Shown is what appears to be the company's first store (wood frame), which was destroyed by fire and replaced with a brick structure. Mr. Foulks (right), likely the manager, stands outside the store with three young helpers. (Courtesy of Barbara Bishop Durham.)

Contents

Acknowledgments		6
Introduction		7
1.	The Early Days	9
2.	Around Town	37
3.	Churches	57
4.	Business and Industry	63
5.	Monuments and Celebrations	83
6.	The Police, Fire Company, and Beach Patrol	89
7.	The River	93
8.	Schools	101
9.	Social Organizations	113
10.	Sports	123

ACKNOWLEDGMENTS

The Florence Historical Society Book Committee dedicates this book to Wayne Campbell (1924–2003), who shared his passion for Florence history in photographs, stories, and artifacts. He was the inspiration for starting the Florence Historical Society and for the completion of this book.

Our appreciation as a group is expressed to Stanley Fayer for his excellent photographs of our large documents and images. His expertise and advanced computer skills were critical to the success of this project.

We also appreciate the equally proficient computer skills of Jim Roache, who copied many photographs for preservation and publication before the collection deteriorated. His knowledge of town history and family trees was shared with and appreciated by us.

Not to be overlooked is Robyn Alton, daughter of Helen Panaro Henderson; we are grateful for her editorial expertise in assembling our materials for this book. Her background in publishing has proven invaluable.

Information was obtained from past issues of the *Mount Holly Herald*, the *Florence Township News*, and *Scott's 1876 Atlas*, as well as census information and the Slack Funeral Home death records. Other important sources were the *History of Burlington County*, by Woodward and Hageman, dated 1883; the 1910 *Boyd's Business Directory*; *The Genealogical and Memorial History of the State of New Jersey*, by Francis Bazley Lee, dated 1910; the *Biographical Review of Camden and Burlington Counties*, dated 1897; *Howe's Business Directory* of 1899; and the *History of Baseball in Burlington County*, dated 1948.

Finally, the individual authors would like to extend their thanks to the following people:

> To my husband, Albert L. King, and his family, who have taught me patience, good humor, and grace under trying circumstances. Their encouragement is greatly appreciated.
>
> —Judith L. King

> To the memory of my mother-in-law, Lydia Brown Tapper, whose great interest in Florence history and vast collection of memorabilia inspired me to follow that same interest.
>
> —Mary Tapper

> To my family and the people living in Florence who have made this town on the Delaware River such a great place to live.
>
> —Helen Panaro Henderson

> To Jamie, who shares my interest in genealogy, history, and historic preservation.
>
> —Deborah J. Hartshorn

> To Norman P. Hamilton and Charles "Scoots" Adams, because their stories aroused my interest in Florence's history, and to Judy King for being the driving force behind this book.
>
> —Jack Ulmer

INTRODUCTION

According to *The History of Burlington County*, prepared by Woodward and Hageman in 1883, Florence is a small but well-settled town located within easy and direct reach of Philadelphia by both rail and water. The Amboy division of the Pennsylvania Railroad crosses the township, with many of its trains stopping at Florence Station. Originally, Florence was part of Mansfield Township, but it became separate when it incorporated in 1872.

According to old records, the first resident was Henry Kale, who began farming in 1743. Other early family names were Ashby, Richardson, Gaskill, Taylor, Jackson, Durell, James, Spachius, Griffith, Schuyler, English, and Rainier.

In the mid-1800s, Florence was a summer resort for Philadelphians who came up the Delaware River by steamboat to spend the season. When the town was laid out in 1849 by the Florence City Company, a large hotel was erected on the banks of the Delaware, and a large rooming house was built in Florence Heights to accommodate tourists. Several double brick homes were also built, and streets were laid out much like those in Philadelphia. The area was known at that time as High Banks. Local farmers shipped produce by boat to the Florence Hotel, and shad fishermen in the area supplied the hotels in season. Various religious groups held week-long revival meetings in the Heights, an area that was also popular for its dance pavilion and picnic grove with swings and food stands.

When the Florence City Company experienced financial problems, Charles Macalester of Philadelphia bought the controlling interest in the town properties. Most of the existing deeds were conveyed by him.

In 1857, the Florence Iron Works was established on land bought from Schuyler Rainier and Edward Durell, two local farmers with large holdings. This enterprise employed generations of Irish, and later, Italian, immigrants. The ironworks erected homes to rent and a general store for employees, and it donated land for a library and several churches. Iron pipe from the ironworks—later known as R.D. Wood Company—was shipped by boat all over the world. Fire hydrants, lampposts, gas machinery equipment, turbines, hydraulic machinery, valves for water and gas, and machine castings, gearing, and shafting were also produced here. These items were manufactured in 47 buildings located on more than 60 acres. Two turbines from R.D. Wood are still in use at Niagara Falls.

A division of the 1st New Jersey Cavalry from Florence, led by Capt. William W. Gray, fought at Gettysburg during the Civil War. Along with Captain Gray, the names of the Florence men in the Civil War were Cpl. Charles Lynche; Pvts. Albert Harkins, Richard Earley, William Earley, Charles Eckslery, Stewart Henry, and Thomas Henry; and soldiers John H. Stratton, James D. Craig, Benjamin F. Horner, Benjamin Robbins, Joseph E. Mead , Richard Hamilton, Erasmus Webb, William Lanning, Charles E. Baker, Elwood Durell, Edward S. Dorsey, Edward Stewart, George W. Hobbs, Cortenas Patterson, Miles Lucas Jr., George H. Emlen, Patrick Christy, John Adams, Jason Cox, Charles D. Wilkie, Jacob Miller, Carr Ivins, George Wispert, Reuben Anderson, Charles R. Allen, Joseph Flood, Thomas Lanning, James E. Johnson, George L. Aikins, Joseph Donnelly, Alfred Green, Michael Woolston, John F. Jones, Henry Strick, Eugene Delaroi, William Thacher, Peter Miles, Charles Woolston, James Killet, William Ireton

Sr., Alexander Whippy, and John S. Parker. Some of these men died in battle or did not survive the war.

There were four schools in the town of Florence in early days.

As the town grew, many signs of progress were apparent, such as trolleys running in 1898, the water works erected in 1930 (celebrated with a parade), and a sewer system built in 1937 by the Works Progress Administration. The town water system was fed by artesian wells. Streets were also improved over the years, as was the wharf. Gaslights arrived in early 1900, and electricity came in 1925. In 1902, the telephone exchange was installed on Broad Street.

Florence's social organizations included the Improved Order of Redmen, the Ancient Order of Foresters, the Florence Quoit Club, the American Legion, the Mohican Boat Club, the Beach Patrol, the Florence Rifle and Pistol Club, the Order of the Sons of Temperance, the Florence Gunning and Fishing Club, the Masonic Ladies' Golden Rule Lodge, Marconi Lodge, many church groups, and the ladies' auxiliary of the fire company. Picnics, carnivals, minstrel shows, and church suppers kept the townspeople busy with activities. Florence also had a roller rink and a bicycle path on Front Street. Summers meant swimming, boating, and fishing in the Delaware River and the arrival of steamboats, including the *Florence*, which brough vacationers to town.

Baseball was a popular sport in Florence, and special trains would arrive with out-of-town spectators to watch the games. A large field was cleared by R.D. Wood and a stadium and grandstand erected. Florence's R.D. Wood team won many championships in the county league over the years. All games came to an end when the train departed, regardless of the score or inning, for there were no further trains until the next day.

Charles Lindbergh's flight up the Delaware after his 1927 return from Paris inspired townspeople to erect a sign and name Lindywood Park—located on the river, northeast of the current Yacht Club—after him.

Many of the original homes still stand. Some reveal the remnants of storefronts where candy and cigars were sold or dress shops and other private enterprises were run.

People in early Florence were known for their good humor and generosity, and the town was one of the first to respond with donations to the victims of the Johnstown flood. Indeed, they were commended in local newspapers: "if the little town of Florence could send money, why couldn't larger towns in the county match their generosity?" Florence is a fine example of small-town America.

One

The Early Days

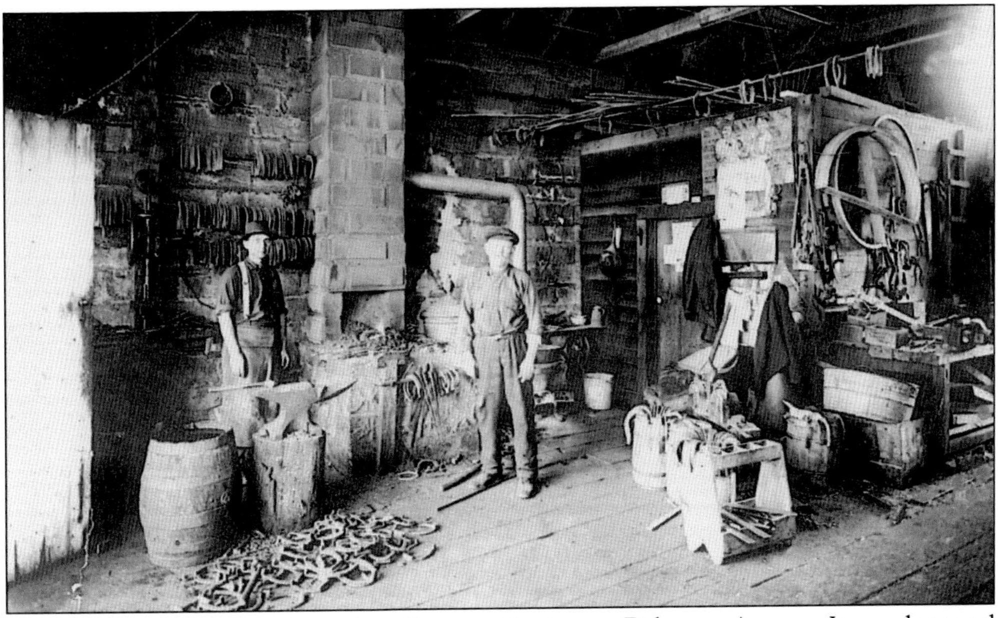

This blacksmith shop was located at Florence Station on Delaware Avenue. It was destroyed by fire many years ago and was replaced by the building that housed Wilson Chevrolet. This photograph appears to have been taken in the early 1900s. (Courtesy of Florence Historical Society; information from Carl Friday.)

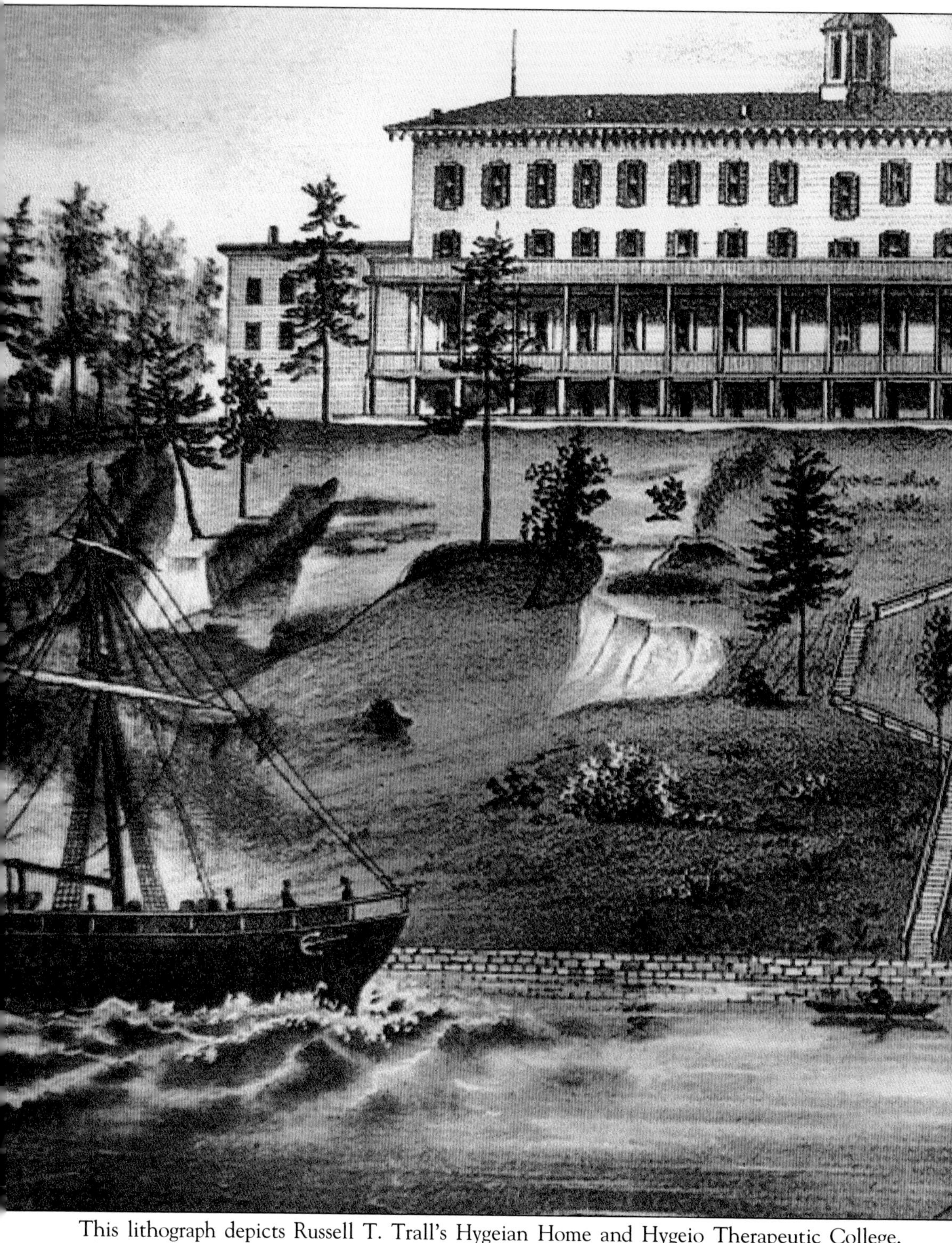

This lithograph depicts Russell T. Trall's Hygeian Home and Hygeio Therapeutic College, which was located in Florence Heights just northeast of the present-day high school. Originally built in 1850 by the Florence City Company as a boardinghouse, the college in 1862 became

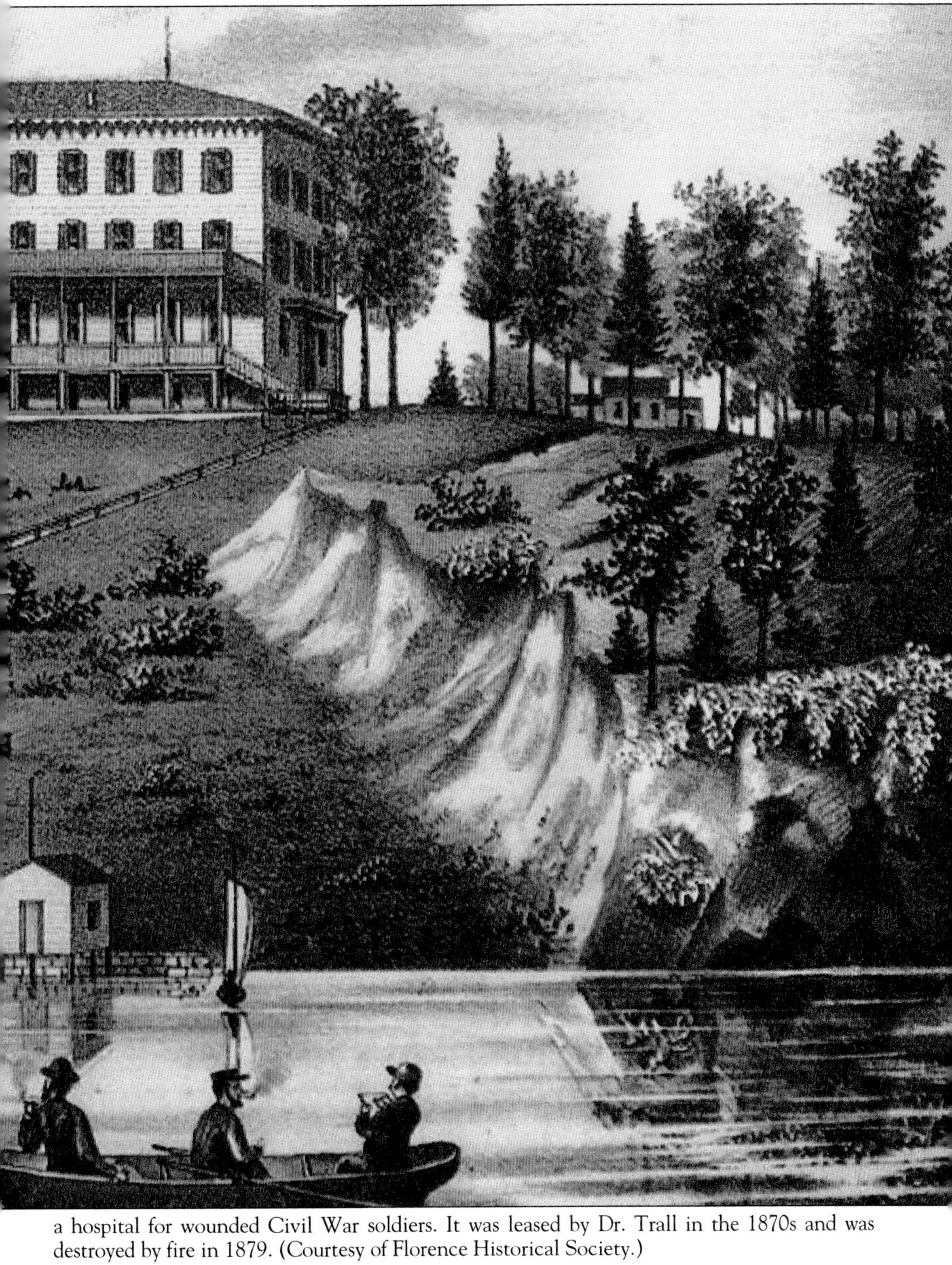

a hospital for wounded Civil War soldiers. It was leased by Dr. Trall in the 1870s and was destroyed by fire in 1879. (Courtesy of Florence Historical Society.)

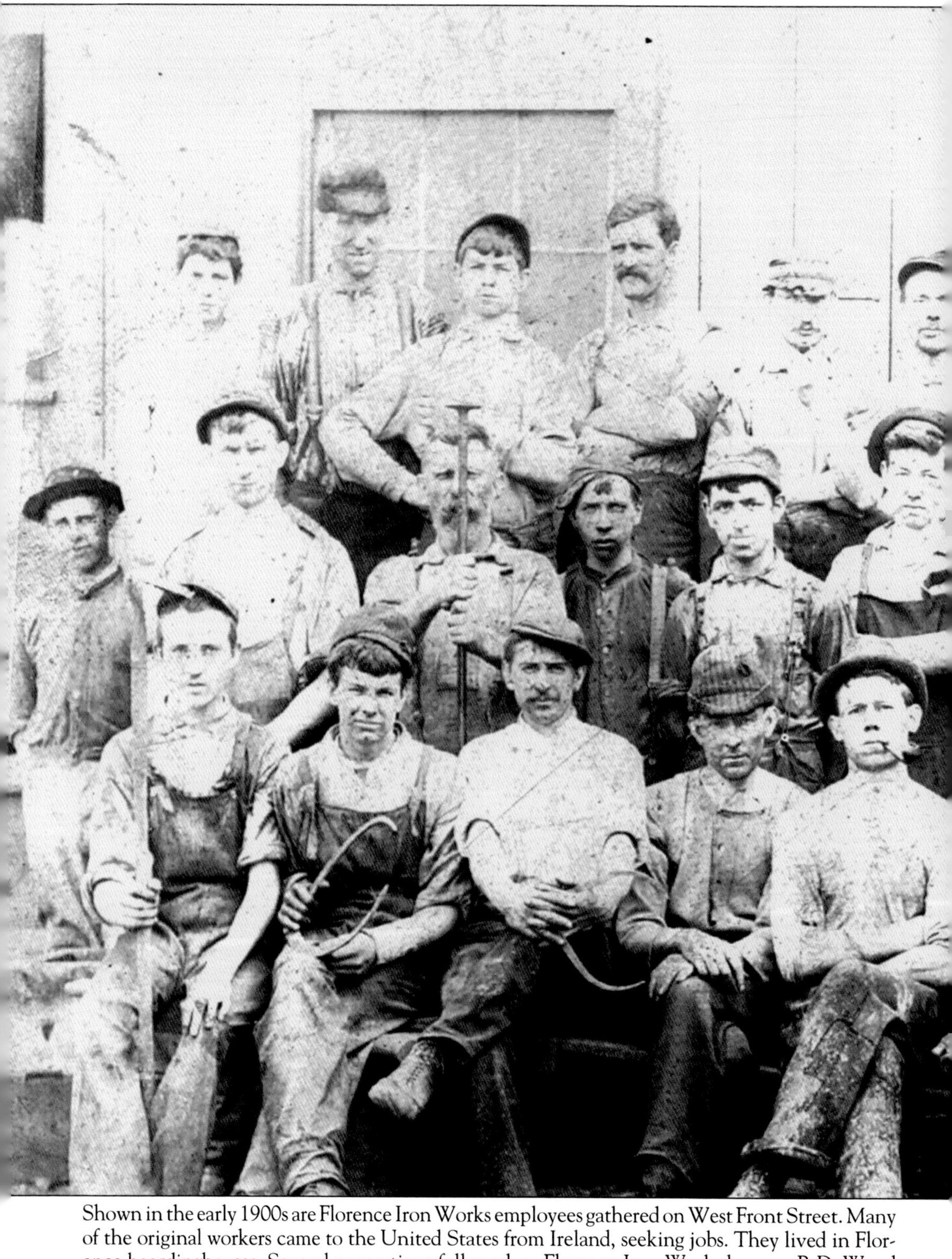

Shown in the early 1900s are Florence Iron Works employees gathered on West Front Street. Many of the original workers came to the United States from Ireland, seeking jobs. They lived in Florence boardinghouses. Several generations followed, as Florence Iron Works became R.D. Wood

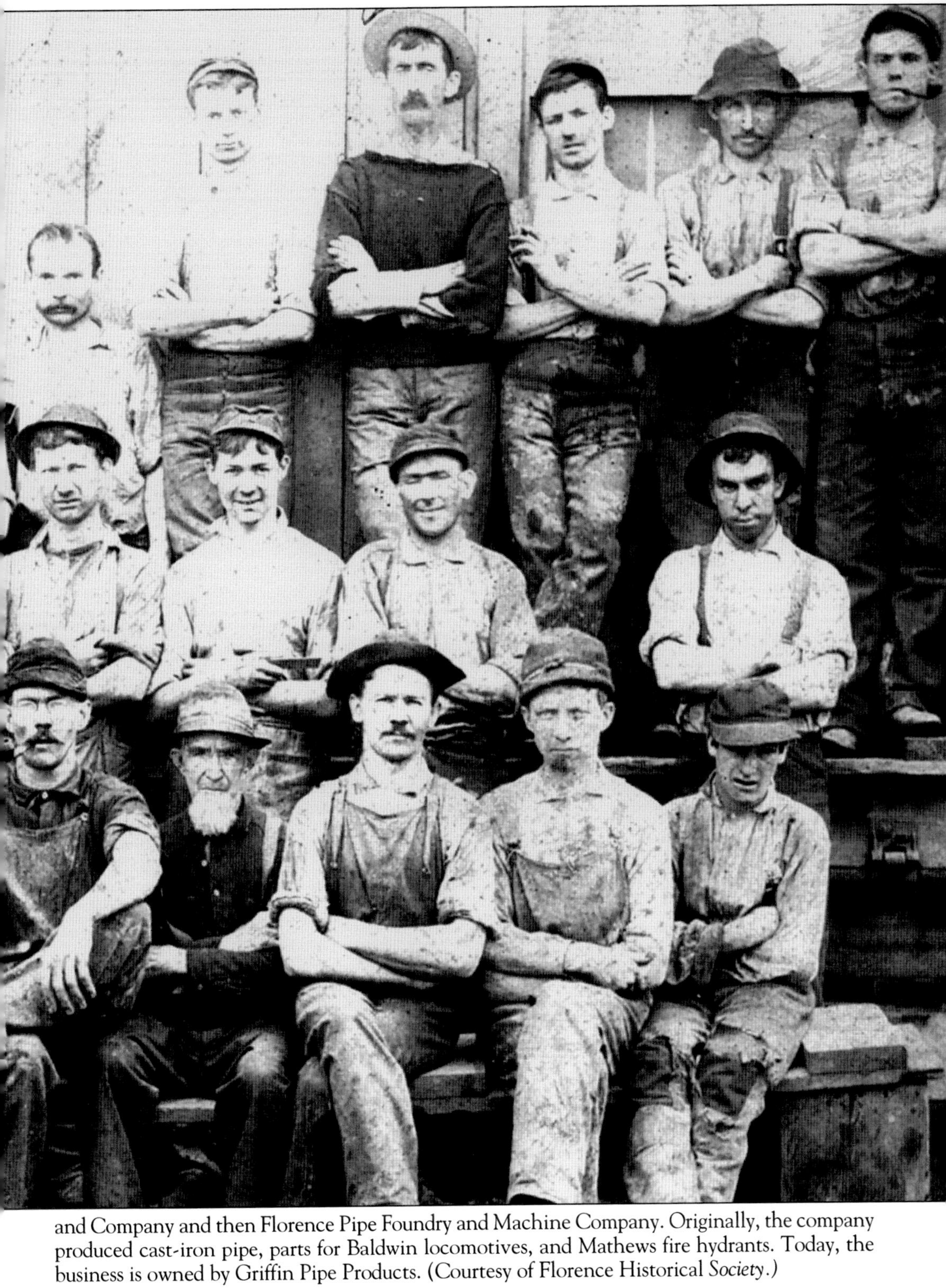

and Company and then Florence Pipe Foundry and Machine Company. Originally, the company produced cast-iron pipe, parts for Baldwin locomotives, and Mathews fire hydrants. Today, the business is owned by Griffin Pipe Products. (Courtesy of Florence Historical *Society*.)

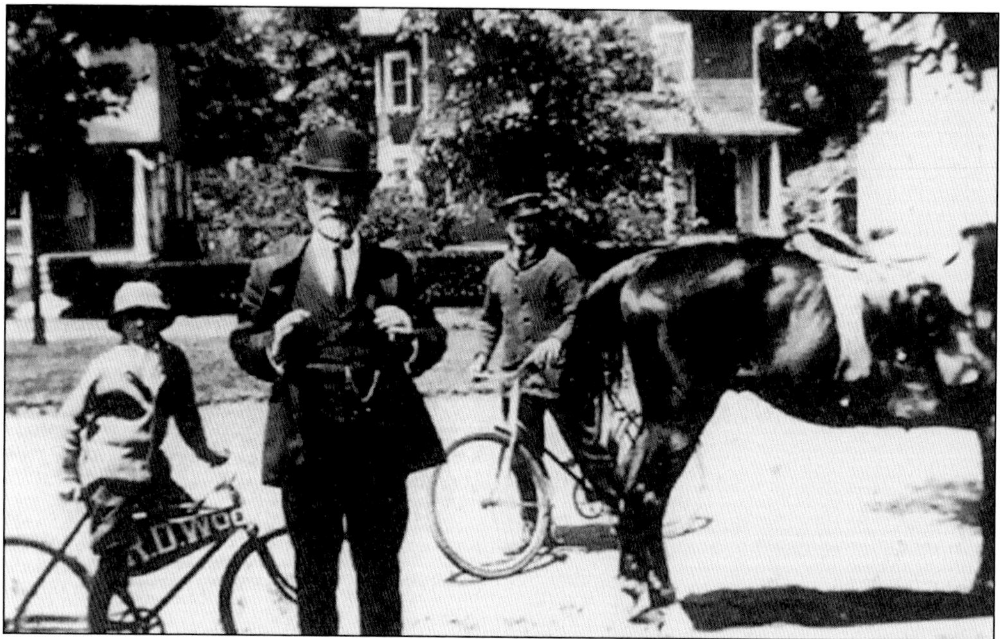

This view likely shows the Boulevard in the early 1900s. Despite the sign, the bicycle on the left was apparently not manufactured by R.D. Wood. The man in the foreground is identified as Dr. Baird, and the man on the bicycle appears to be a telegraph deliveryman. (Courtesy of Barbara Bishop Durham.)

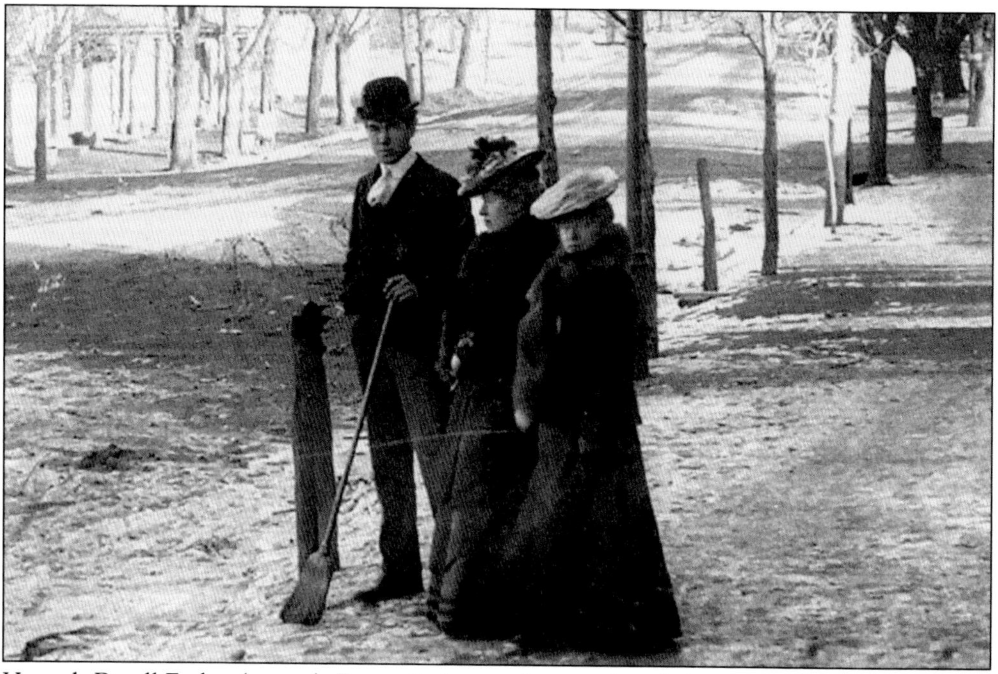

Hannah Durell Emlen (center), Emma Emlen, and an unidentified man stand on the southeast corner of Front and Broad Streets, across from the Florence Hotel *c.* 1905. The Emlens were the great-granddaughters of William and Jemima Emlen and the granddaughters of Hannah Quigley, whose daughter Jemima married Charles Emlen. (Courtesy of Jim and Hannah Roache.)

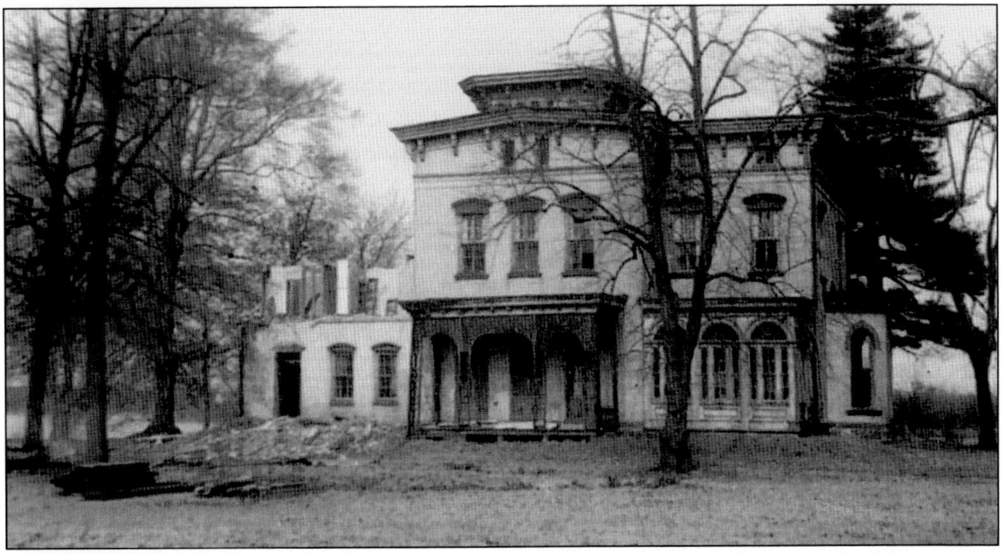

Wood's Mansion, built *c.* 1856, was located on West Front Street on the grounds of the present Wilkie Park. Built by Richard Jones, who also started the Jones Foundry (later Florence Iron Works), this 21-room home faced Front Street, as shown. Used as a summer home by the Wood family, subsequent owners of Florence Iron Works, it was razed in 1950, after sitting idle and falling into disrepair. (Courtesy of Florence Historical Society.)

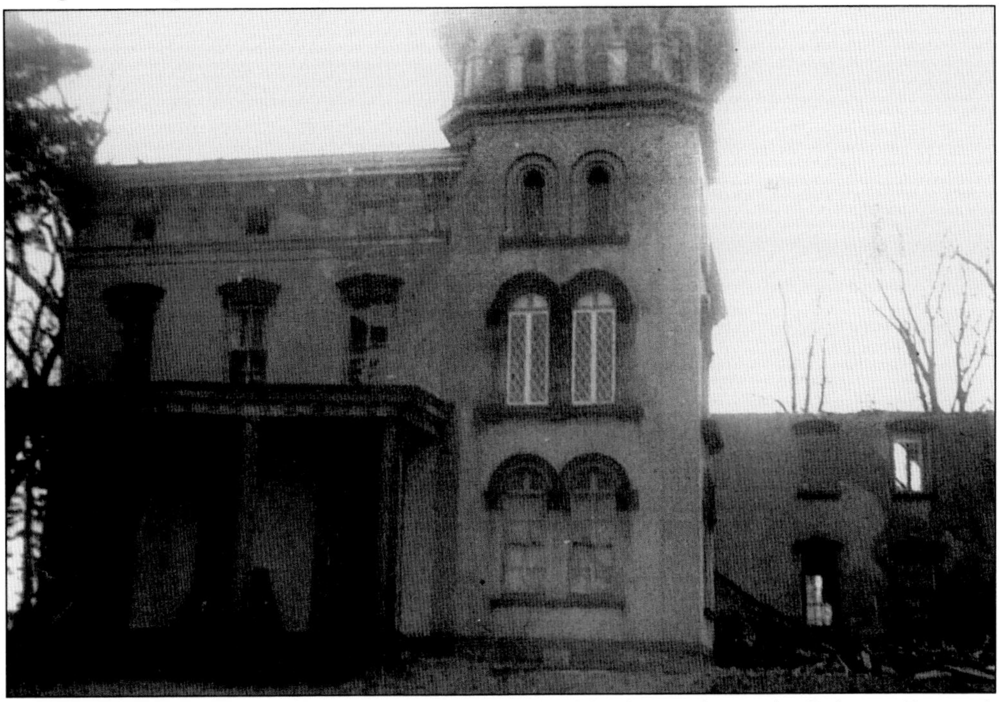

This photograph of Wood's Mansion shows the back of the house, facing the Delaware River. A wood frame and stucco dwelling, it used only gas fixtures for lighting and had cast-iron window sills and marble bathtubs. A large garden was located in front of the house near Church Street, and rare trees from all over the world—among them, horse chestnuts, a tulip poplar, and a large beech—were planted to enhance the grounds. (Courtesy of Florence Historical Society.)

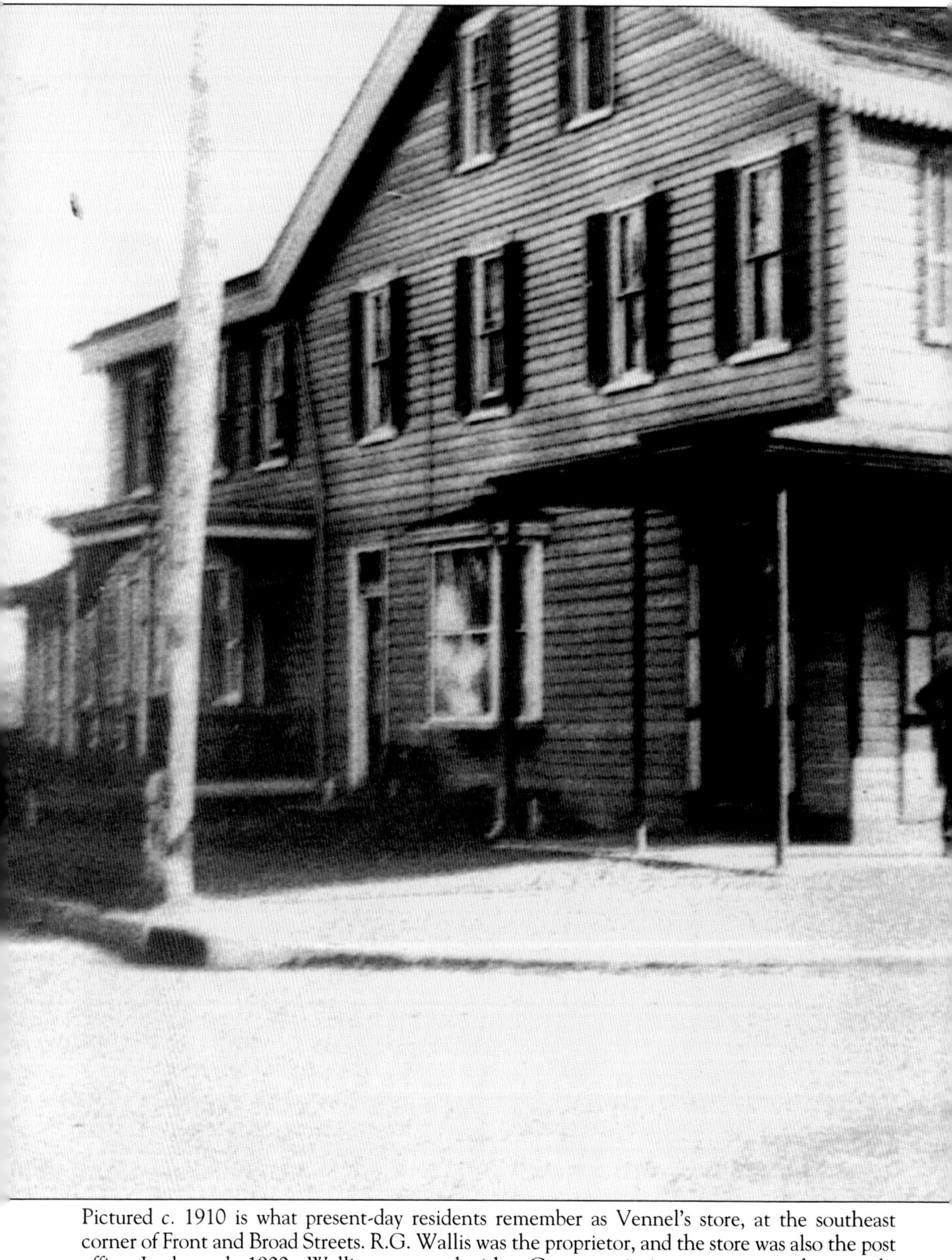

Pictured *c.* 1910 is what present-day residents remember as Vennel's store, at the southeast corner of Front and Broad Streets. R.G. Wallis was the proprietor, and the store was also the post office. In the early 1900s, Wallis contracted with a German printing company to photograph,

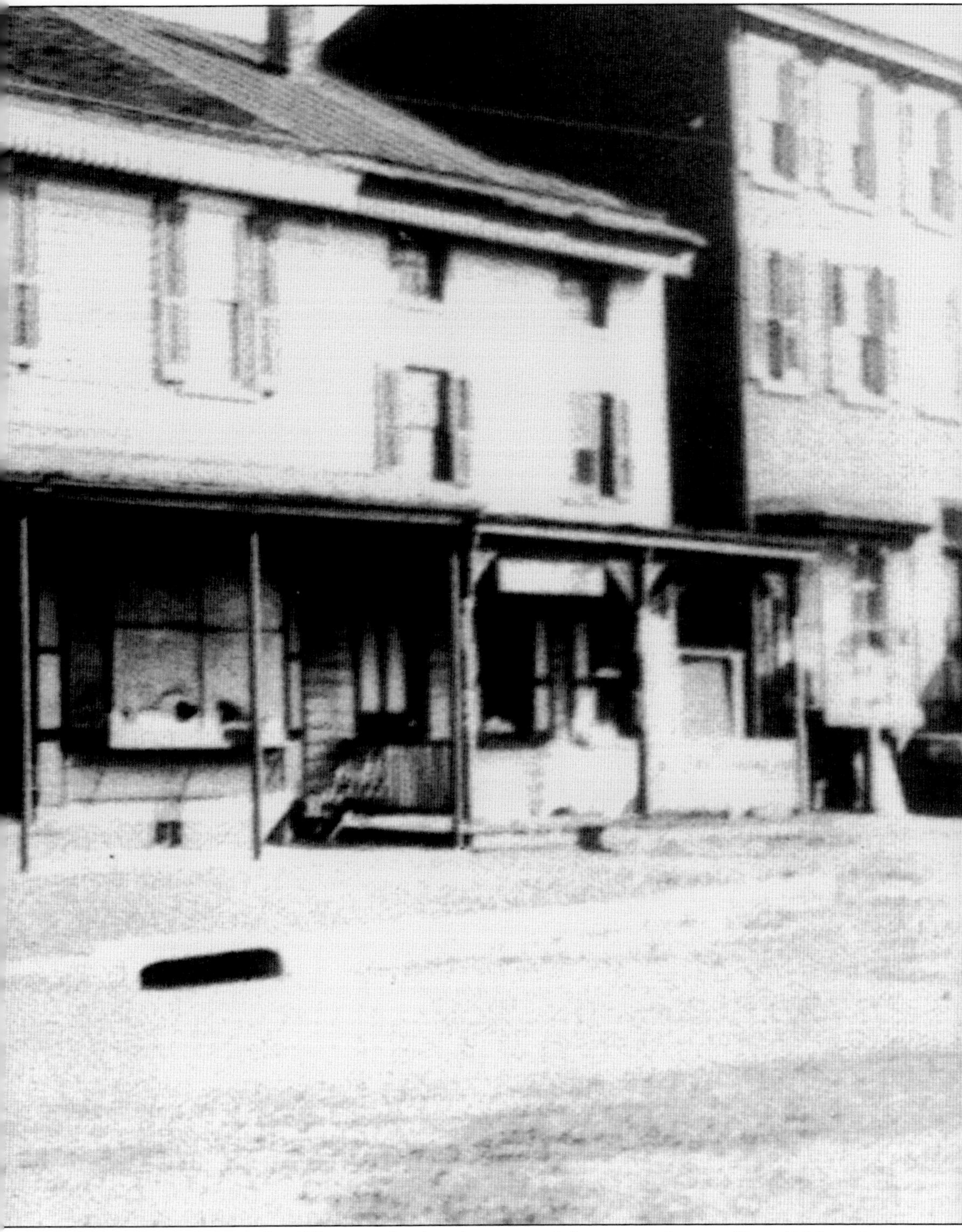

color, and print postcards of Florence landmarks; some of the postcards are still available today. The building was demolished in 1999, after becoming vacant and falling into disrepair. The site is now owned by the People's Bank. (Courtesy of Florence Historical Society.)

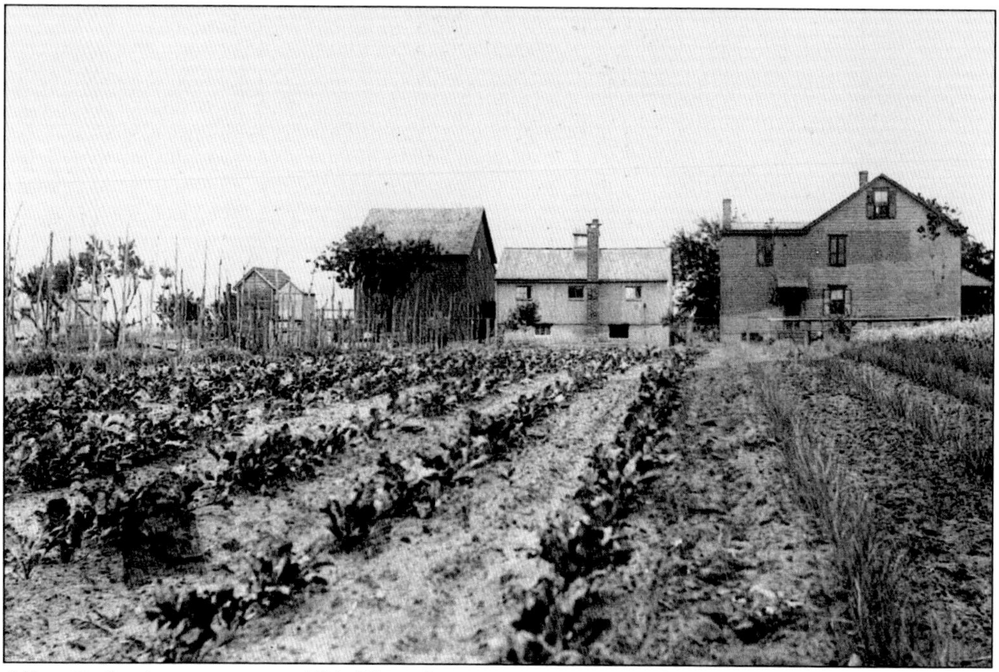

Allen Bodine's property, at 754 Olive Street intersecting Oak Street, is shown in the early 1900s. Today, the property is largely unchanged and is typical of small farms around Florence. (Courtesy of Florence Historical Society; donated by Thomas Adams.)

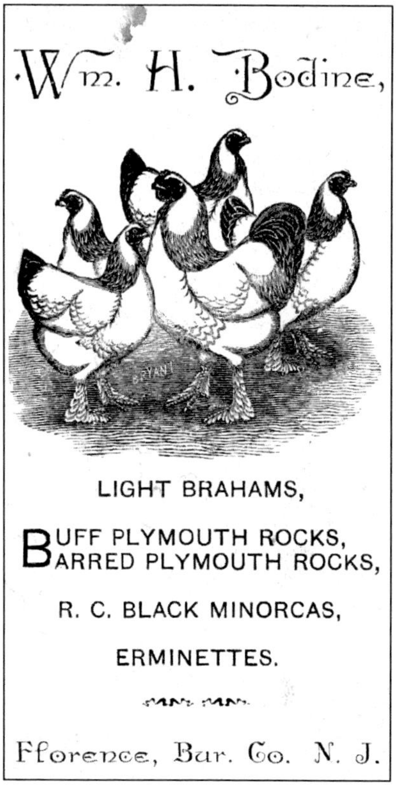

William H. Bodine's sales brochure advertises chickens—five different types of live chickens for breeding stock and egg production—which he sold around the country. Printed in this 1897 booklet are letters of commendation from customers. Bodine also sold eggs during the days when most households kept chickens in the backyard. (Courtesy of Florence Historical Society; donated by Thomas Adams.)

The children of Mary and Harry Abrams are pictured *c.* 1900. From left to right are James Abrams, born in 1896; Walter Abrams, born in 1894; Russell Abrams, born in 1899; and Katie Abrams, born in 1890. (Courtesy of Albert L. King.)

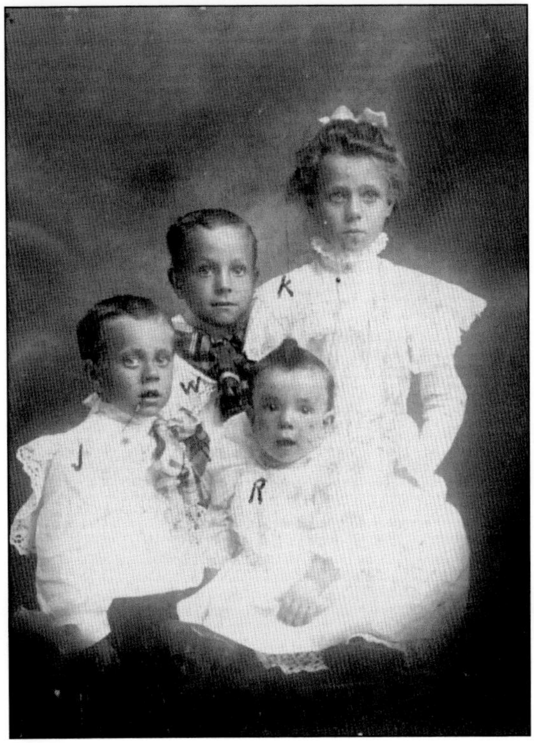

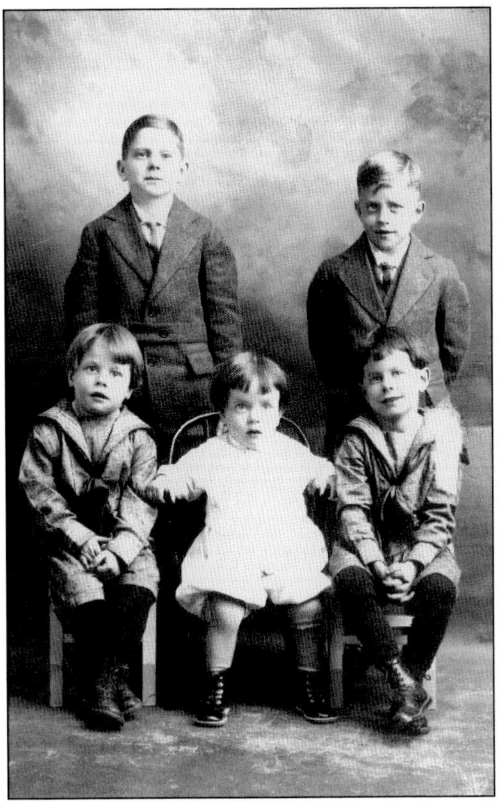

Large families were common in the early days. Shown *c.* 1924 are the children of James and Margaret Abrams, of Florence Station. From left to right are the following: (front row) George Abrams, born in 1921; Paul Abrams, born in 1923; and Orland Abrams, born in 1920; (back row) Arnold Abrams, born 1916; and Norman Abrams, born in 1919. (Courtesy of Albert L. King.)

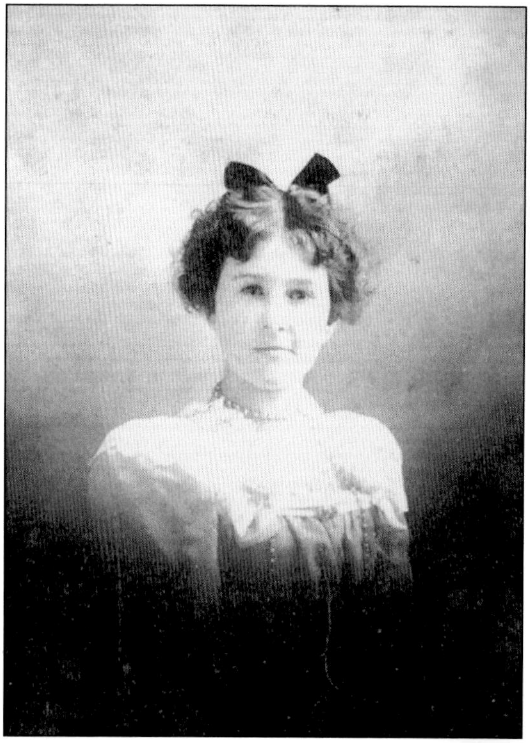

Ida Eliza Dubell, shown in the early 1900s, was a member of the George Dubell family. Born in 1883, she was involved in two train wrecks on the same day in November 1906 and survived both. She moved to Wilmington, Delaware, to work in Washington D.C. She died in 1972 at the age of 89 and was buried at Cedar Hill Cemetery. (Courtesy of Barbara Bishop Durham.)

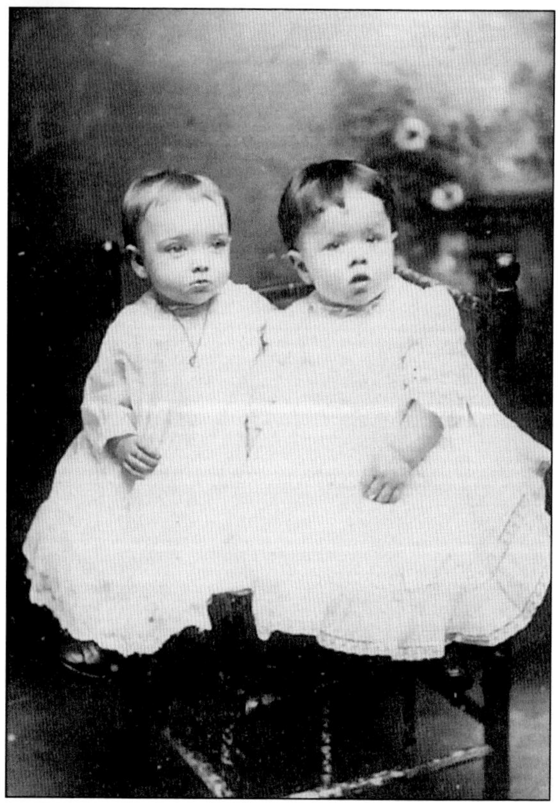

Frances Horton (left) and Florence Richardson are shown *c.* 1908. Born in 1907, Frances Horton served in the Army Air Force's Aircraft Warning Service Reserve during World War II. The wife of Harry Lutes, she died in 2001. (Courtesy of Barbara Bishop Durham.)

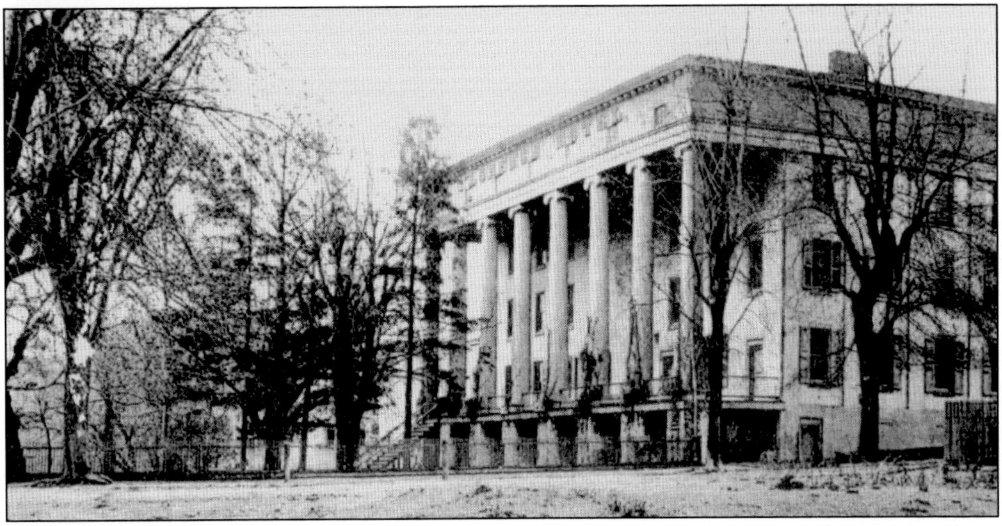

The Florence Hotel is pictured c. 1907, facing the Delaware River. It boasted a 100-foot-long wharf to accommodate steamships carrying tourists along the river. According to a vintage pamphlet, the hotel's dining room and a large veranda overlooked the river. "Hot water heat and sunparlors make this an all-season hotel." Closed as a hotel in the 1920s, it last served as the Florence Township Municipal Building until it was destroyed by fire in 1979. (Courtesy of Florence Historical Society.)

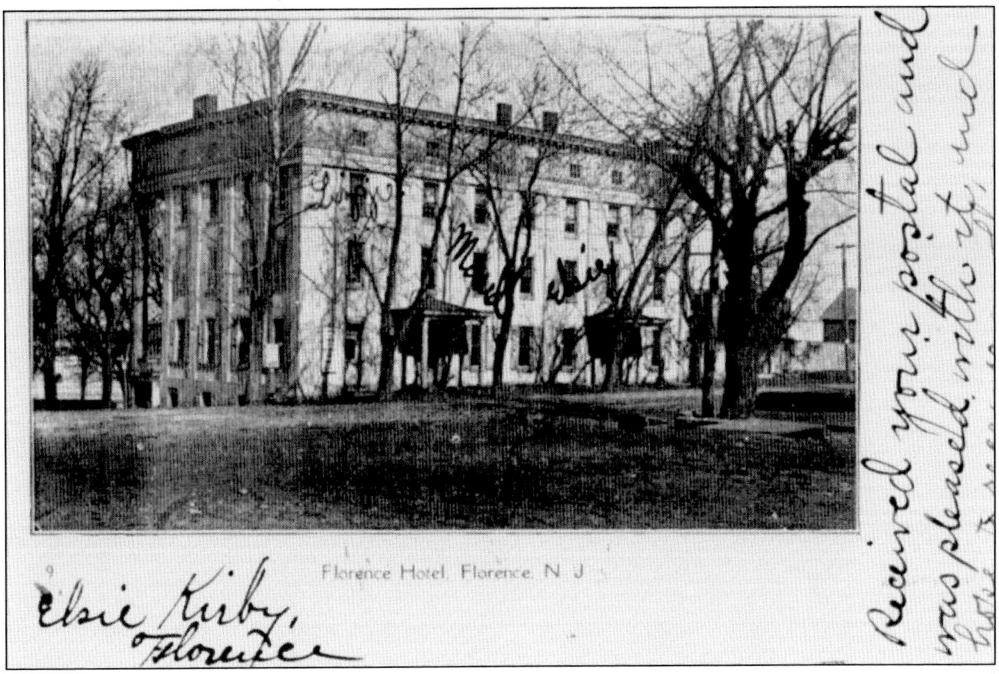

The Florence Hotel is pictured on a c. 1903 postcard, facing Front Street. It was constructed by the Florence City Company at Broad and Front Streets on the river in 1853, when Florence was a famous resort town. Originally six stories tall, it was built of brick covered in stucco to resemble brownstone, with 35 bedrooms and a bath on each floor. An 1867 advertising poster described guest room balconies—removed before this picture was taken. Plank shad dinners were available in season. (Courtesy of Florence Historical Society.)

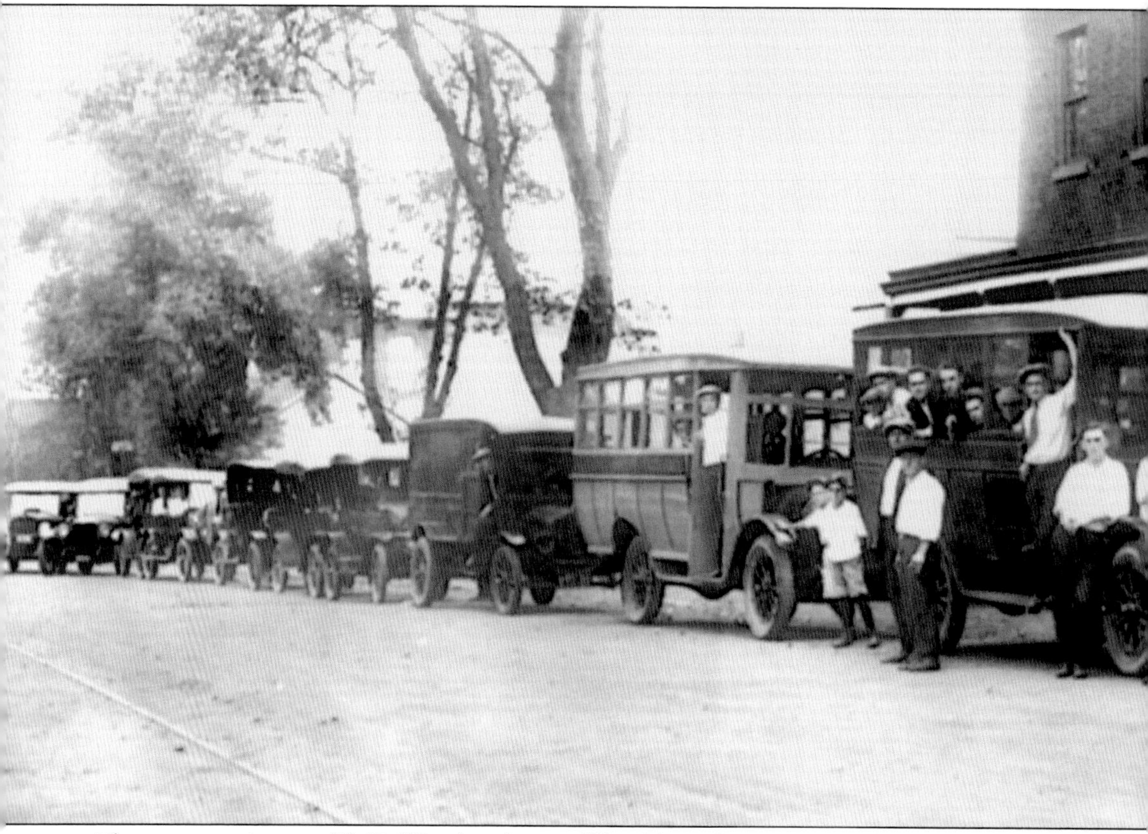

The crane engineers of R.D. Wood gather on West Front Street c. 1900 for their first annual picnic. The yearly event involved a brass band, a baseball game, and field games for all guests,

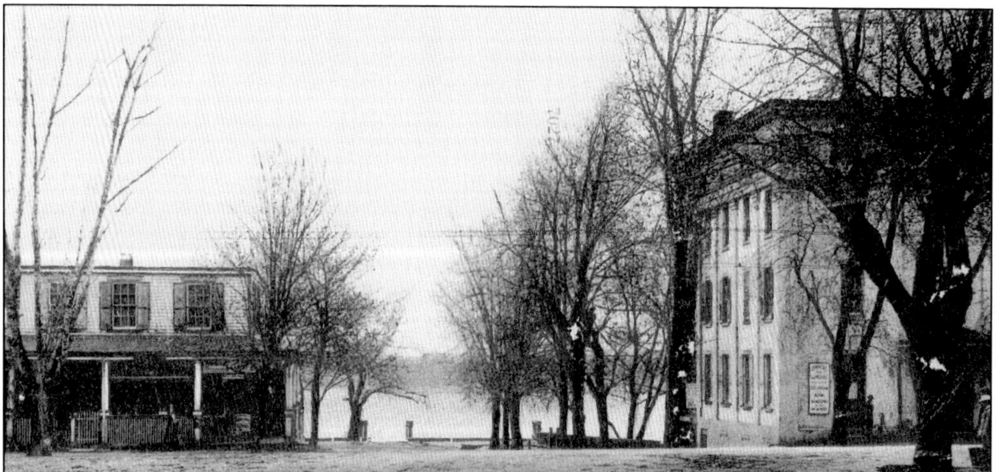

Pictured to the left of the Florence Hotel on the northwest corner of Front and Broad Street is a building which was, in Florence's early days, a steamboat waiting room. It subsequently became an Acme grocery store, c. 1918. The building was demolished in the 1940s. An early map of Florence shows many large mansions (no longer standing) along the river side of West Front Street. (Courtesy of Deborah J. Hartshorn.)

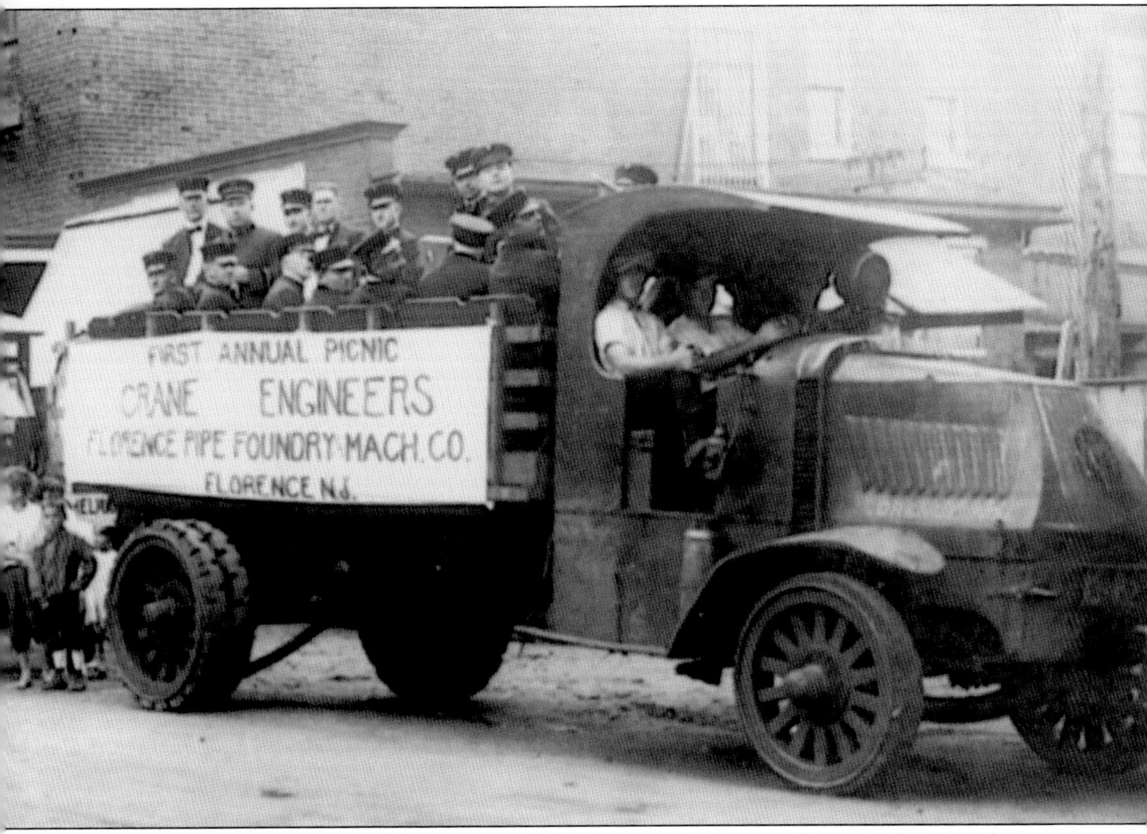

and the R.D. Wood foundry closed for the day. (Courtesy of Florence Historical Society.)

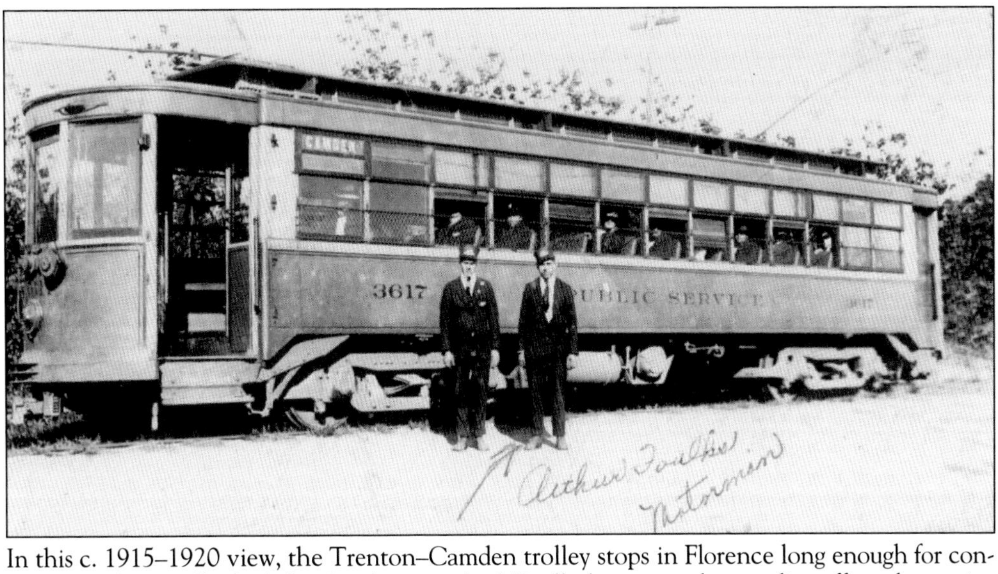

In this c. 1915–1920 view, the Trenton–Camden trolley stops in Florence long enough for conductor Arthur Foulks (right) to be photographed. Foulks later served as a police officer, becoming the first motorcycle patrolman in Florence. Pictured at left is the motorman, Jesse Smith, Father of Laura Smith Panaro. (Courtesy of Florence Historical Society.)

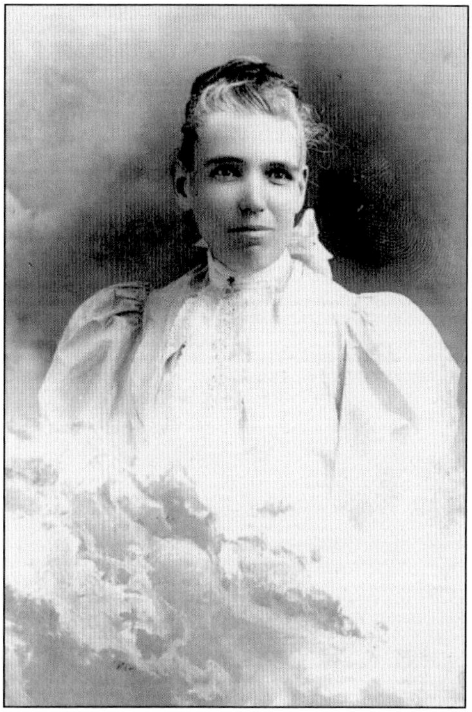

Sarah "Sallie" Marter was born in 1854 in Burlington Township. She owned the family farm on Broad Street, where the municipal building now stands. She died in 1944 at the age of 90. Notice the unusual cloud effect in the foreground of this *c.* 1880. studio portrait. (Courtesy of Mary Tapper.)

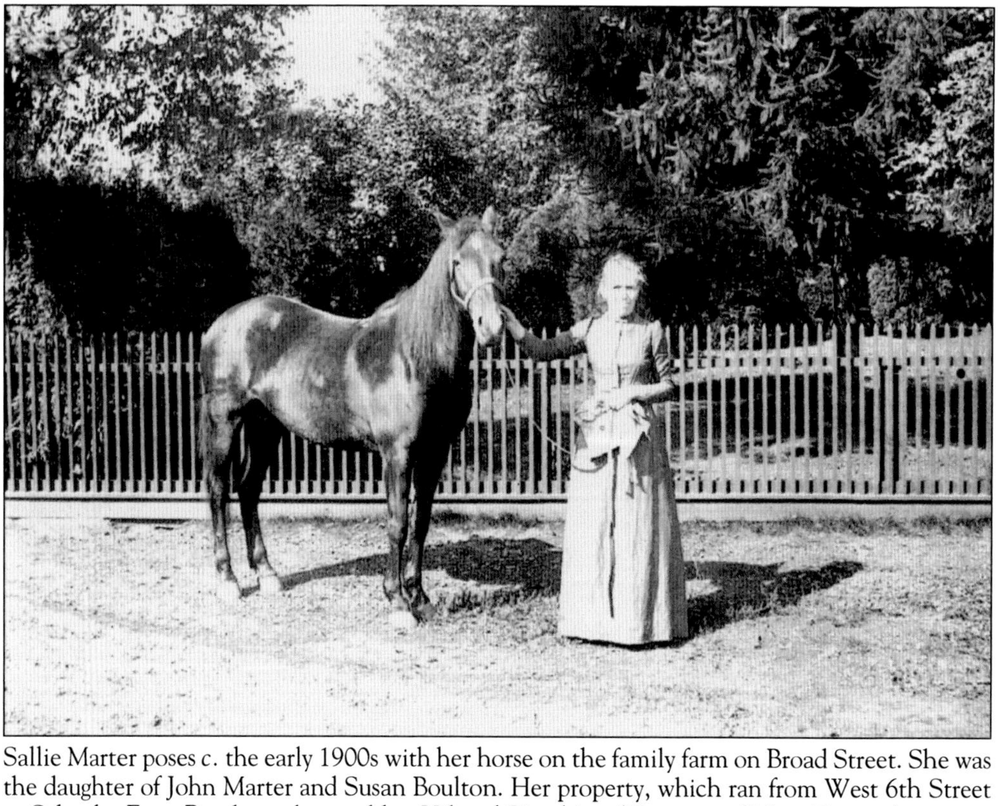

Sallie Marter poses *c.* the early 1900s with her horse on the family farm on Broad Street. She was the daughter of John Marter and Susan Boulton. Her property, which ran from West 6th Street to Schuyler Ferry Road, was later sold to Hilyard Simpkins. (Courtesy of Mary Tapper.)

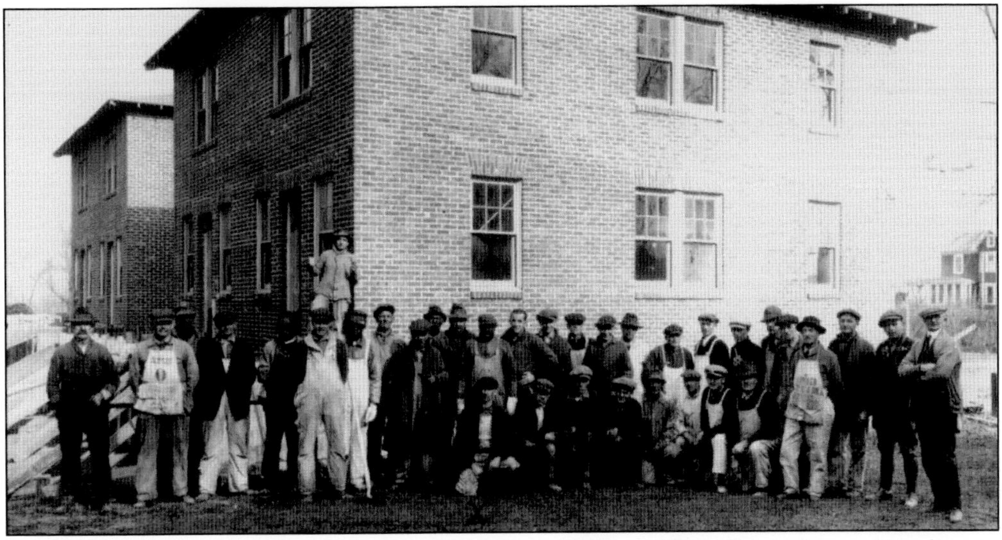

Construction of Laurel Avenue homes is shown *c.* 1920 on West Front Street. Kneeling in front with the "X" is Albert "Brandy" Ireland, who moved to the area from Allentown and also worked at the John A. Roebling mill. At the right is the Rigg house, on Riverview Avenue; the house now has many beautiful trees and a cast-iron fence on the property. (Courtesy of Albert King, grandson of Albert Ireland.)

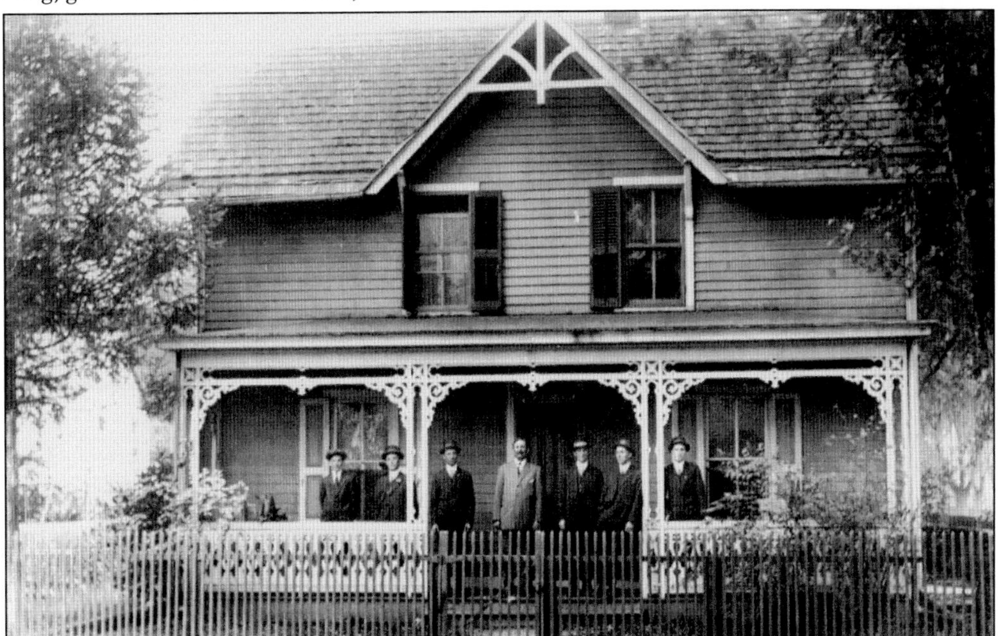

Father and sons in the McGrath family are pictured on the front porch of their home, at 612 West 2nd Street. The house is still standing. From left to right are Leo Carroll McGrath, born in 1899; William McGrath, born in 1885; Michael McGrath, born in 1881; Michael J. McGrath (father), born in 1850; James McGrath, born in 1876; Martin McGrath, born in 1893; and Philip McGrath, born in 1890. Not pictured are Mary McGrath (mother), born in 1854; and daughters Sarah, born in 1875; Mamie, born in 1884; and Nora, born in 1888. (Courtesy of John Williams.)

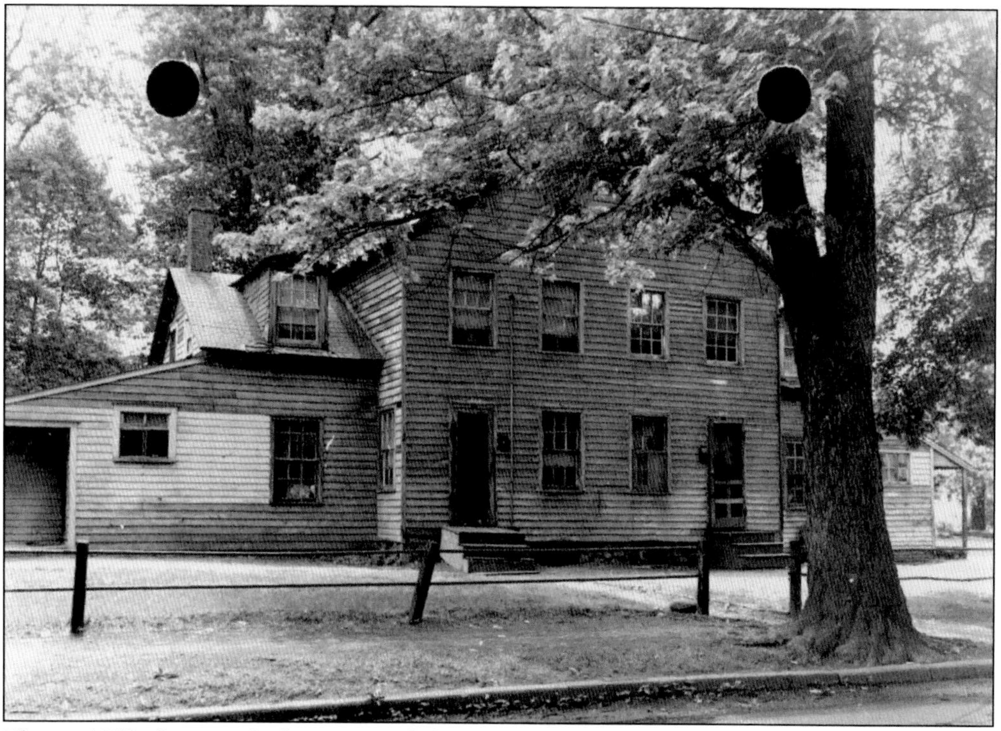

This *c.* 1952 photograph shows one of the remaining "bouquet" houses, built by R.D. Wood and demolished to make way for Maplewood Homes. The bouquet houses were four-family dwellings with a well in the middle of the house shared by all tenants. Among the town's earliest structures, they were located in an area commonly known as "Skunktown," at West 3rd Street, west of the Boulevard. (Courtesy of Florence Historical Society.)

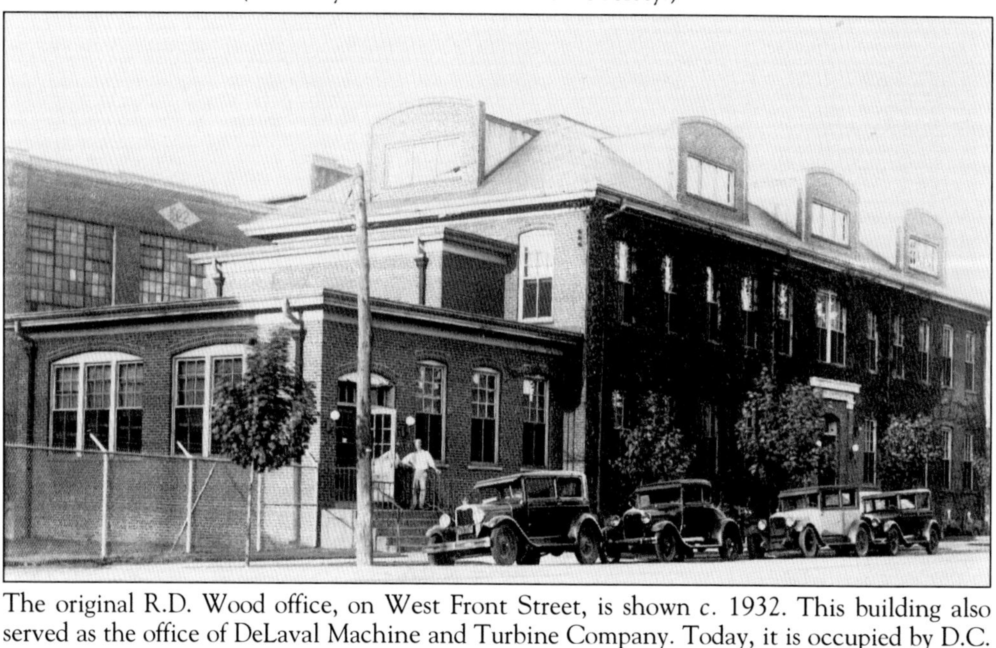

The original R.D. Wood office, on West Front Street, is shown *c.* 1932. This building also served as the office of DeLaval Machine and Turbine Company. Today, it is occupied by D.C. Fabricators. (Courtesy of Richard Glass.)

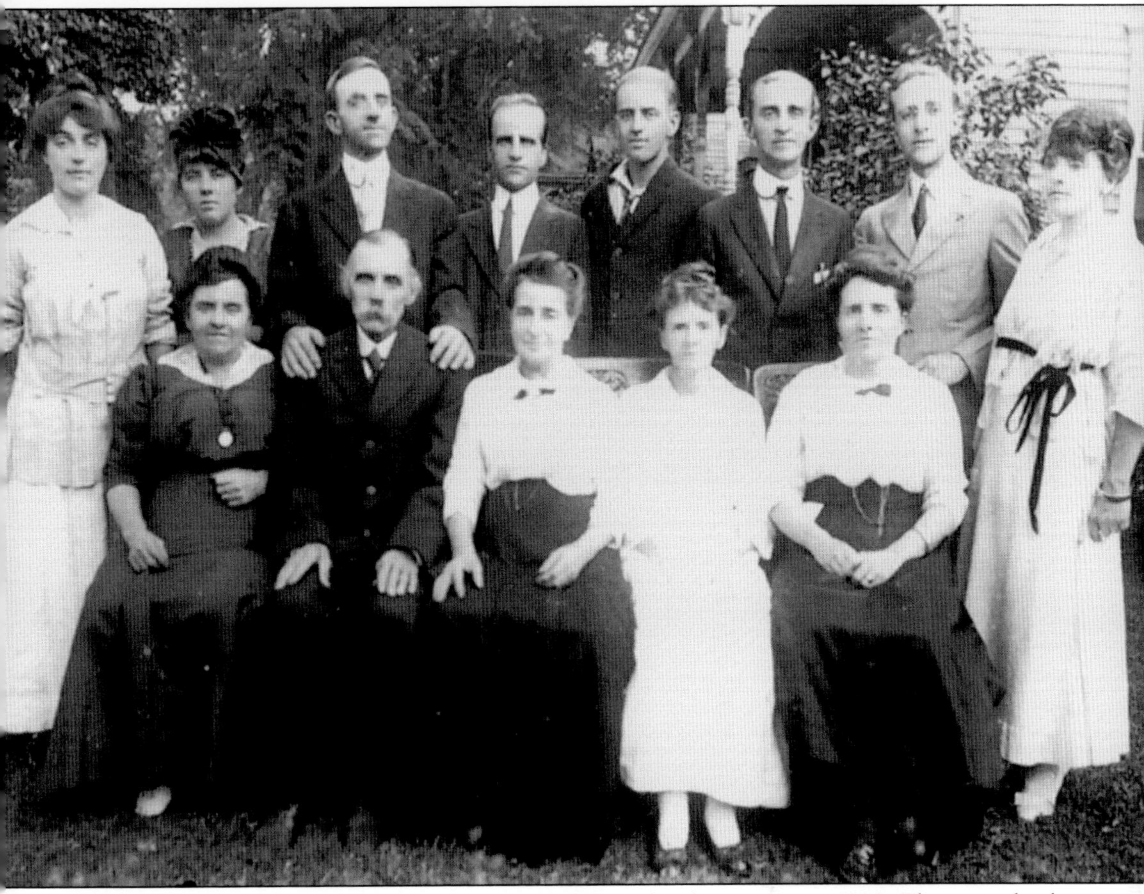

A group of 13 people assembles in the side yard for a family portrait c. 1900. The man third from the left in the back row is identified as William C. Foulks. (Courtesy of Barbara Bishop Durham.)

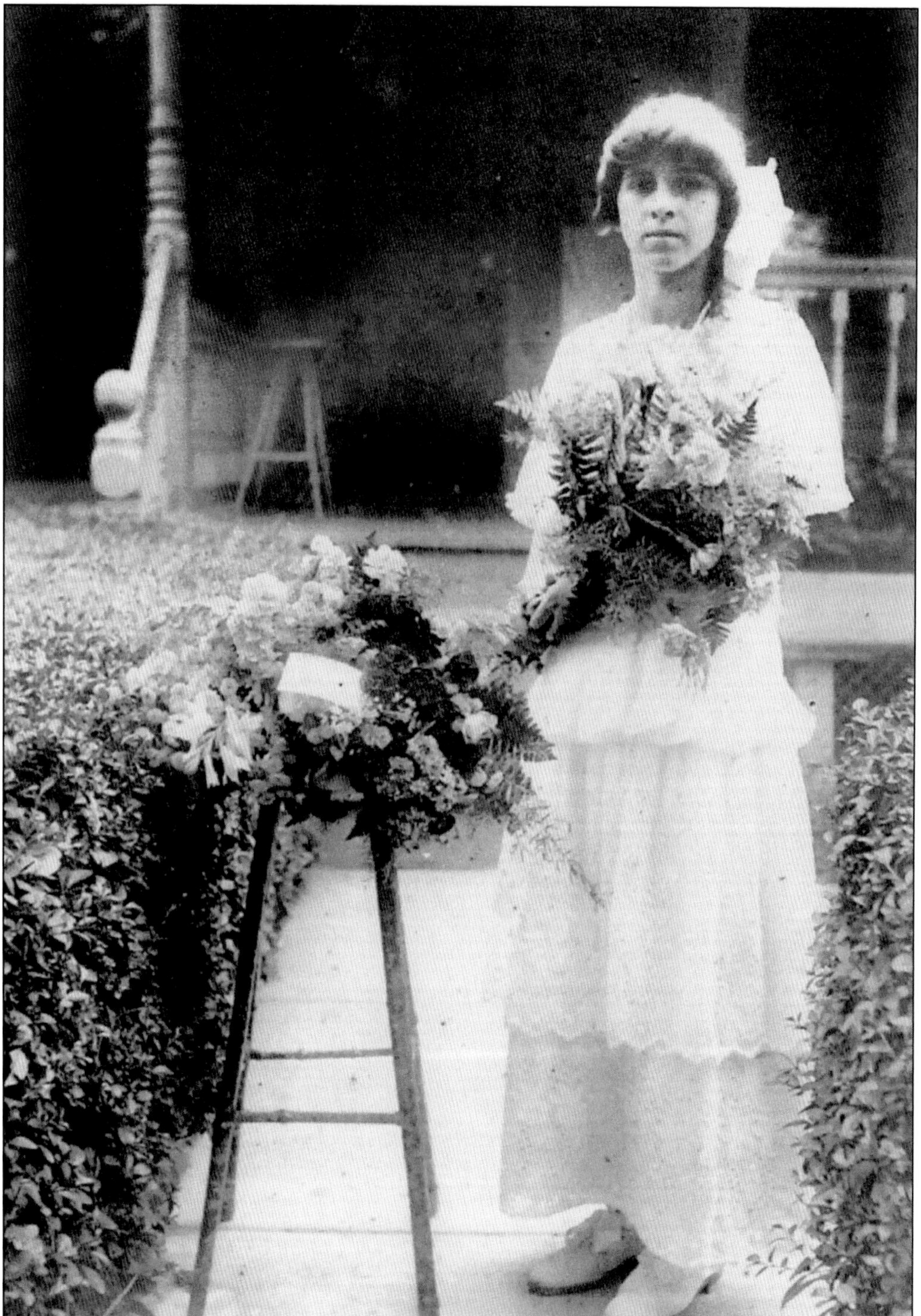

This young woman poses with flowers gathered for a wedding procession *c.* the early 1900s. She is probably a member of the Bishop family, who lived on the Boulevard. (Courtesy of Barbara Bishop Durham.)

Charles Alexander Elliott poses on an attractive wicker seat at a portrait studio *c.* 1912–1915. The son of Edward R. Elliott and Rebecca Virginia Woolman Elliott, he was born in 1897. He married Rhuhamah Hill, raised three daughters, and died in 1963. (Courtesy of Virginia Elliott Speed.)

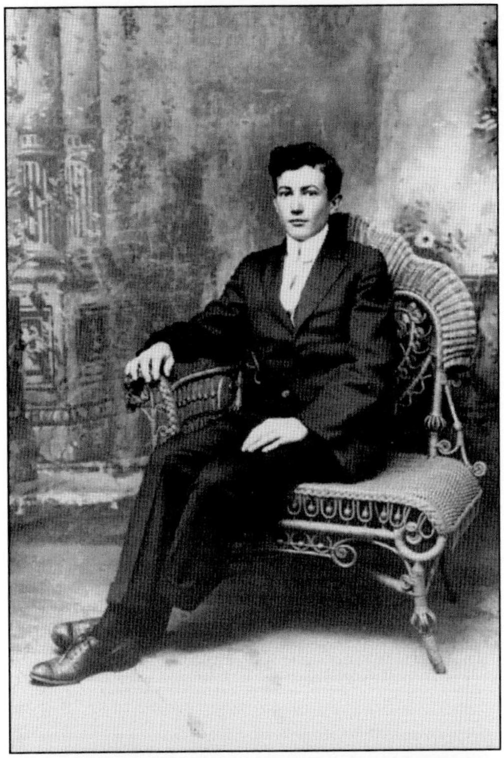

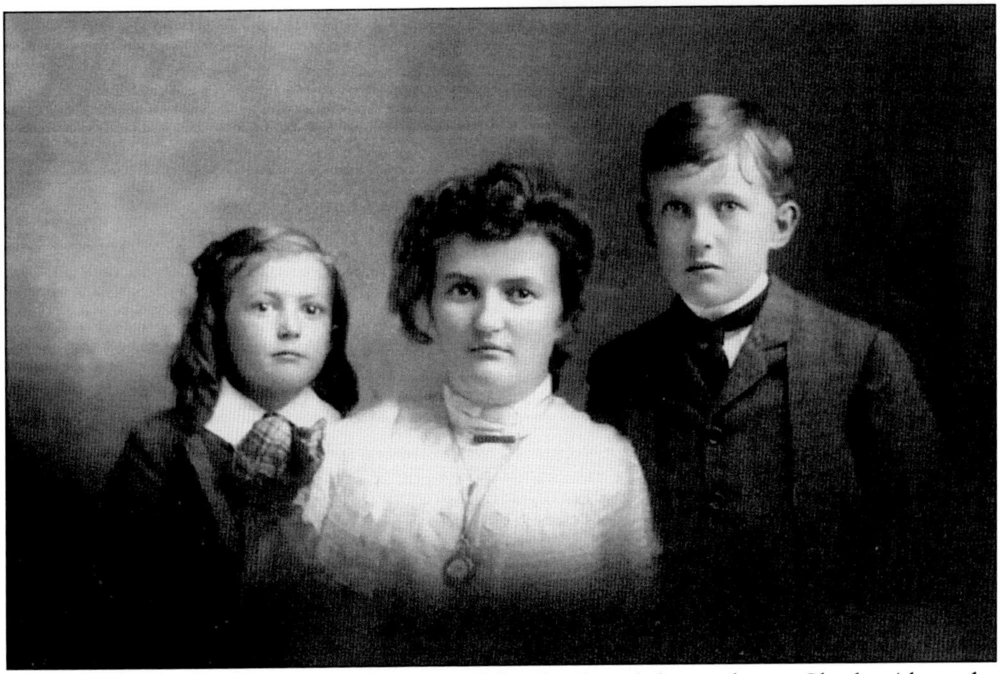

This *c.* 1908 portrait shows part of the Durell family. From left to right are Charles Alexander Elliott (with beautiful long curls, fashionable at the time), Kate Woolman Elliott Church, and Edward Rowland Elliott—children of Edward and Rebecca Virginia Elliott and grandchildren of Julia Durell Elliott. (Courtesy of Jim and Hannah Roache.)

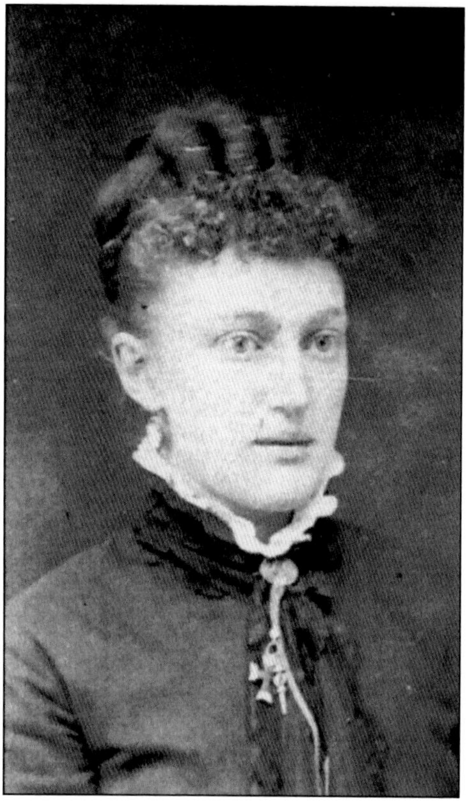

Julia Durell Elliott, a descendant of the Durell family, is pictured *c.* 1860. The watch key on the chatelaine around the high collar of her dress was used to wind pin watches, which were popular with women of the day. Early Florence residents, the Durells owned large tracts of land for farming and deeded property to the Wood family for the Florence Iron Works and to the Florence City Company for building lots. (Courtesy of Virginia Elliott Speed.)

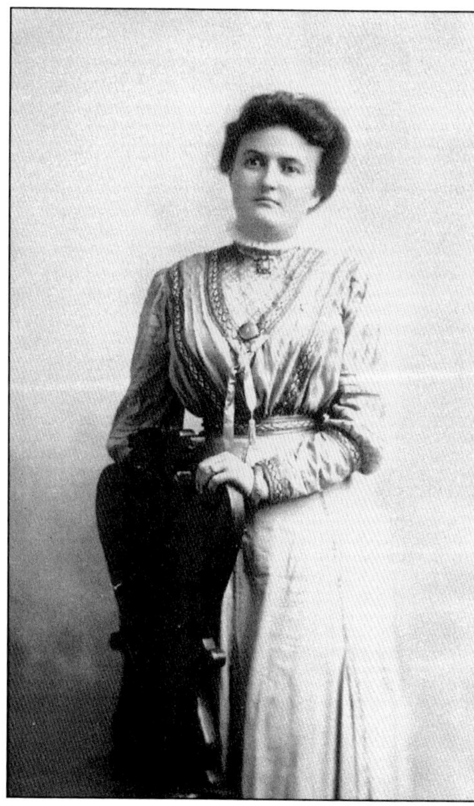

Katherine Elliott Church poses *c.* 1908 in a dress with ribbons and tucks—a good example of the beautiful art of dressmaking. (Courtesy of Dorothy Elliott Quenzel.)

The Lannings were among the earlier Florence families. Luman Lanning, shown *c.* 1880, was born in 1840 in Monmouth County. His occupation was listed as moulder. He died in Burlington in 1925 at the age of 84. Subsequent relatives included the Brown, Tapper, and Samson families of Florence. (Courtesy of Mary Tapper.)

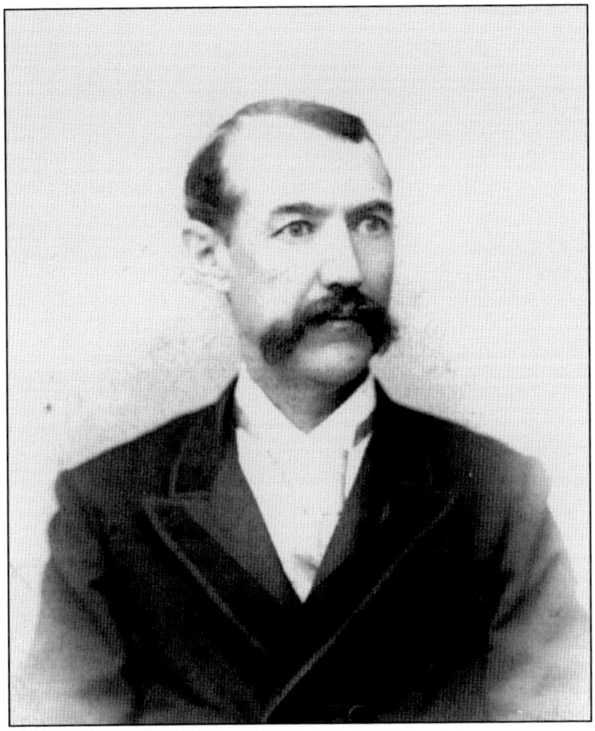

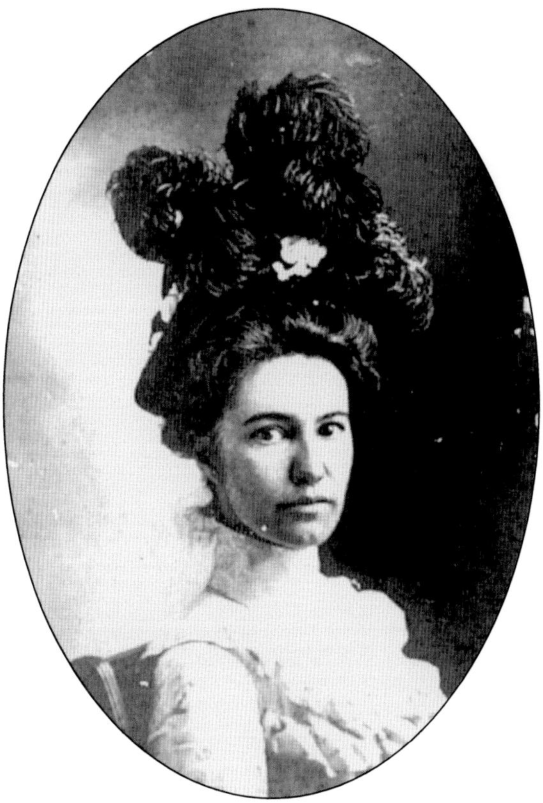

Georgie Lanning, daughter of Luman Lanning, is pictured wearing an ostrich feather hat *c.* 1900. One of her relatives, William Lanning, served in the Pennsylvania Cavalry during the Civil War and later built the home at the southwest corner of 2nd and Walnut Streets in Florence. (Courtesy of Mary Tapper.)

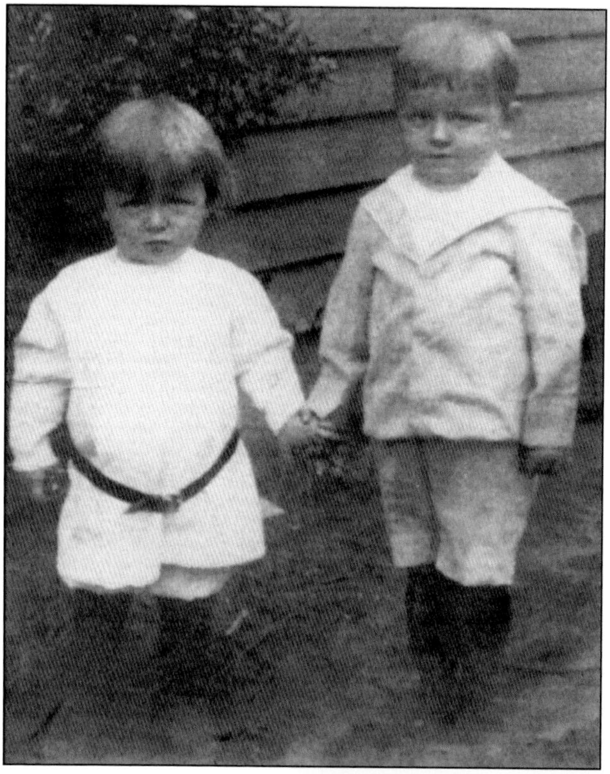

Wilber Bishop (left) was born in 1902. He died in 1952, and is buried at Odd Fellows Cemetery in Burlington. He and his brother, Allan Bishop, are shown c. 1904 in Florence. (Courtesy of Barbara Durham.)

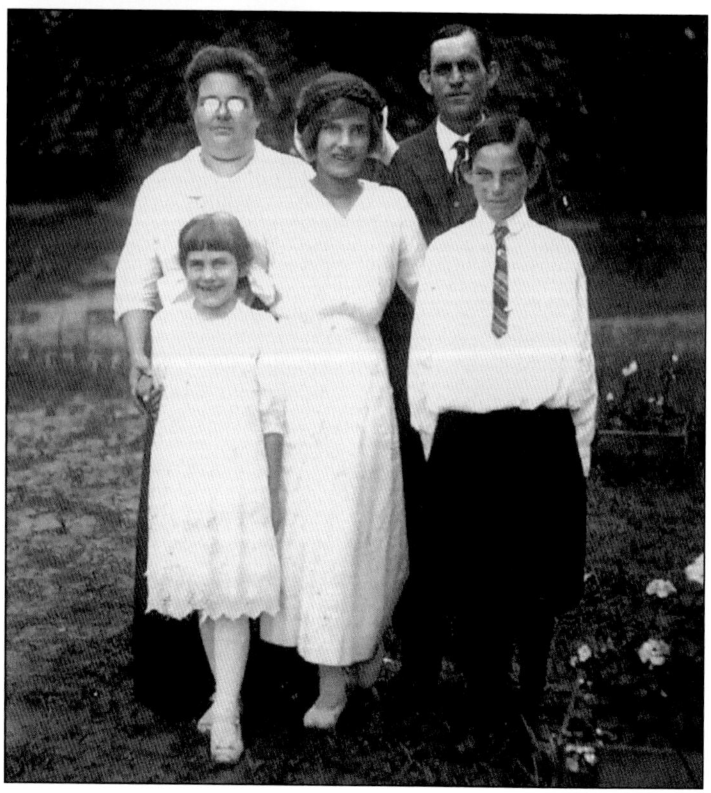

The Mitchells poses on their front lawn in the early 1900s. From left to right are the following: (front row) Margaret Mitchell Buck, Beatrice Mitchell Stiltz, and J. Everett Mitchell; (back row) Lillie Harker Mitchell and Harry Mitchell. (Courtesy of Jim and Hannah Roache.)

Edward Rowland, who later played on the R. D. Wood team in 1910, is shown around 1900. (Courtesy of Dorothy Elliott Quenzel.)

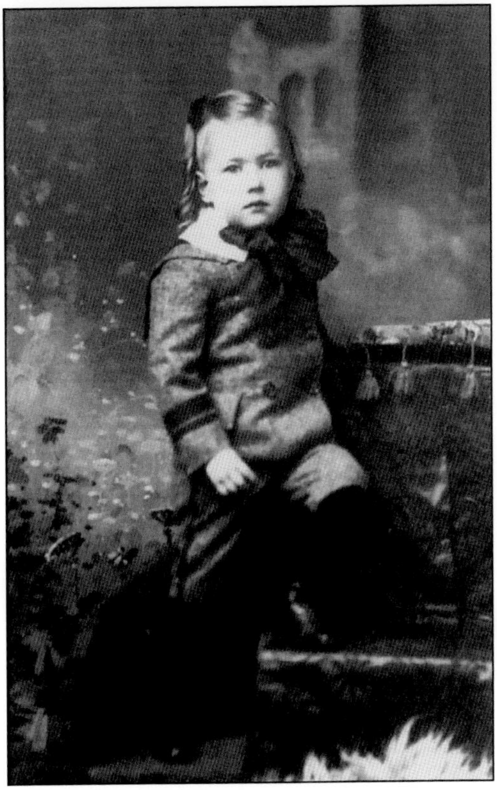

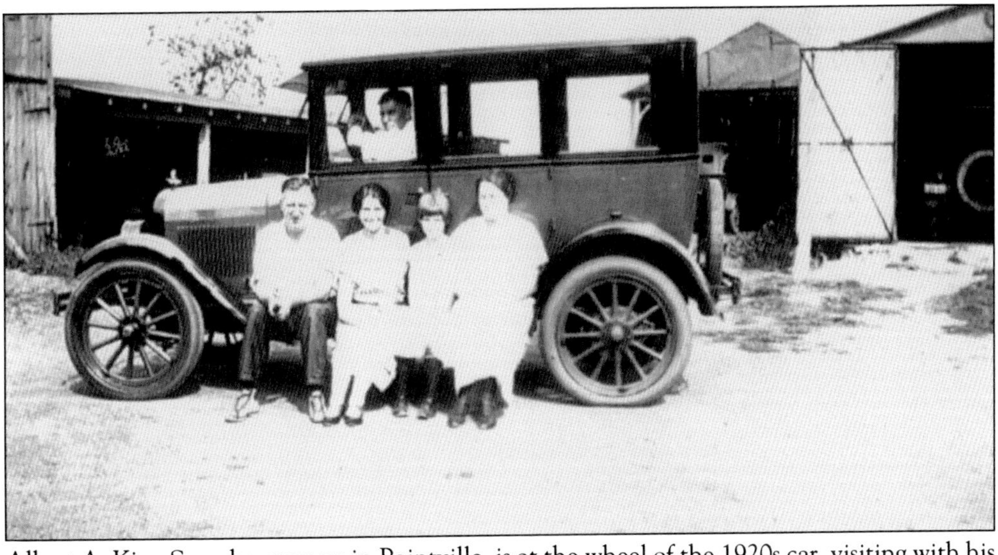

Albert A. King Sr., who grew up in Pointville, is at the wheel of the 1920s car, visiting with his family. On the running board, from left to right, are Harry and Lizzie Simpson, their daughter Florence Simpson, and Katie King, wife of Albert. (Courtesy of Florence Historical Society.)

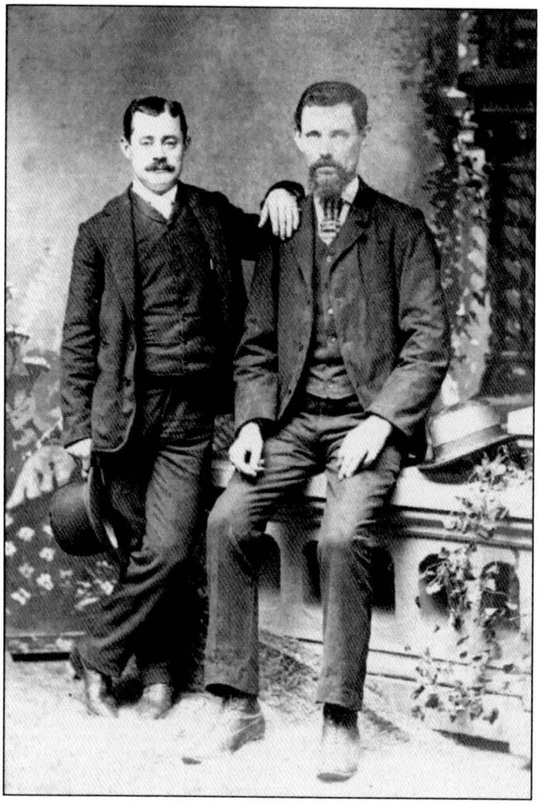

This *c*. 1890s portrait looks like the Smith Brothers cough drop advertisement. John Lukens Abrams (left) was born in 1861. He married, and with his wife, Mary Anna English, raised three sons—Walter, James, and Russell. He died in 1931 and was buried at Cedar Hill Cemetery. The man pictured with him is unidentified. (Courtesy of Albert L. King.)

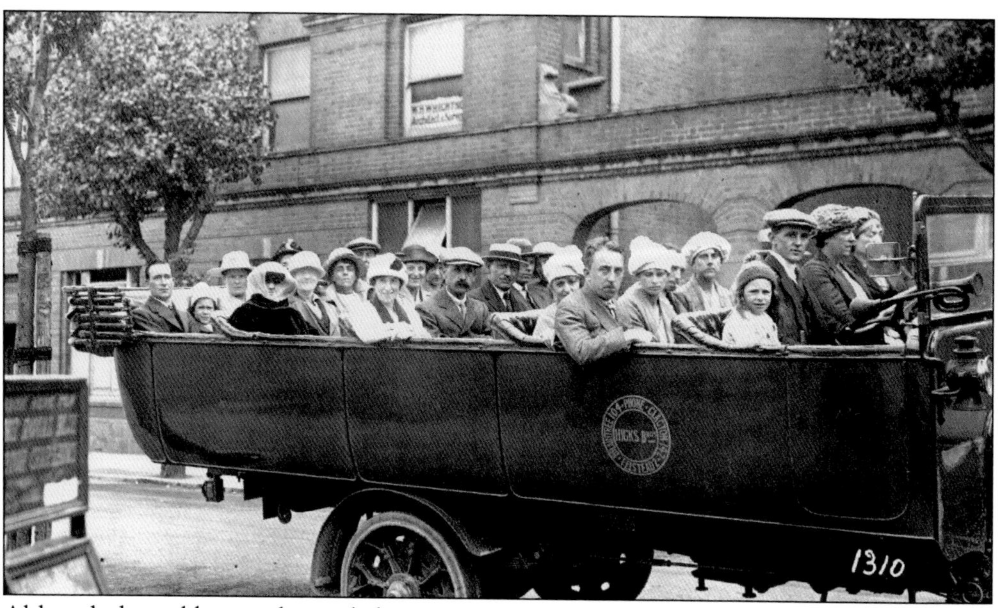

Although the emblem on the truck door says "Braintree, Mass.," the building in the background is identified as the Florence Foundry office, on West Front Street. These people may be here for a picnic or a tour of the town in the early 1900s. (Courtesy of Florence Historical Society.)

The funeral card of 1891 lists Levi Lower's death at the age of 33. These black-and-gold cards were popular for some time. They were addressed to family members with only the town indicated, as all mail was picked up at the post office. No home delivery was available at the time. (Courtesy of Albert L. King.)

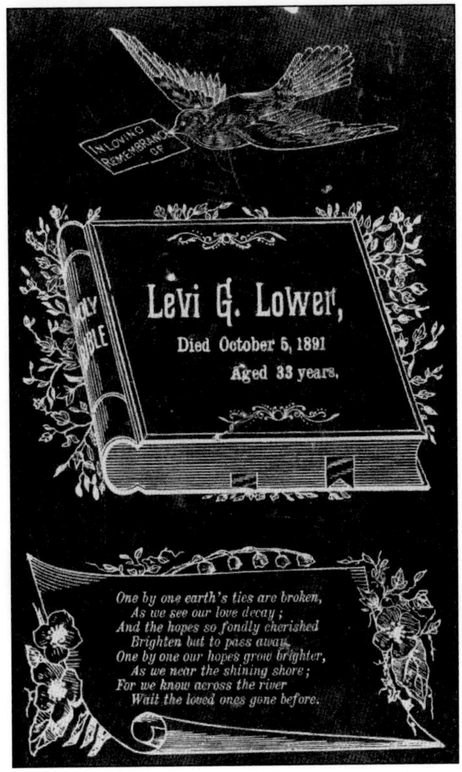

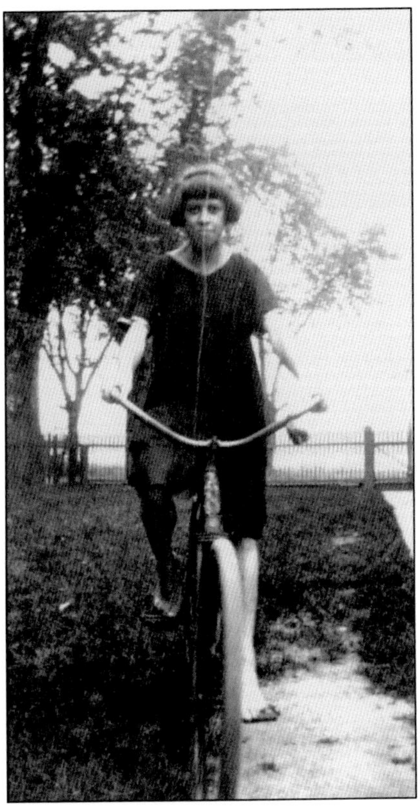

Verna Parker rides her bicycle in Florence *c.* 1918. She was the daughter of Joseph and Hannah Lower Parker and the sister of Minnie Parker. She died of nephritis in 1922 and was buried at Cedar Hill Cemetery. As automobiles were scarce in Florence at that time, a notice of appreciation for the loan of vehicles in the funeral procession was later printed in the local newspaper. (Courtesy of Albert L. King.)

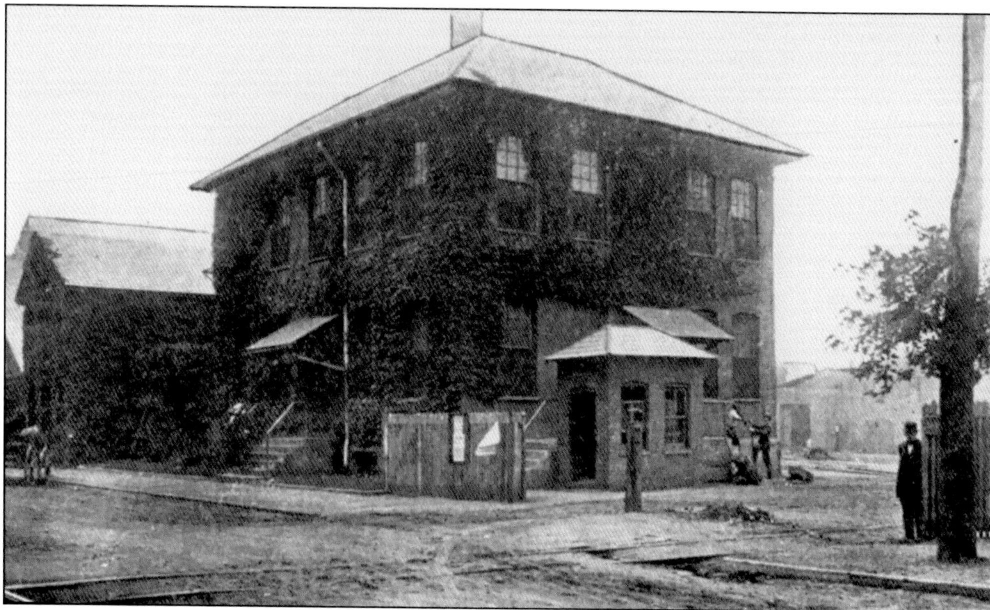

This early postcard shows the office of the Florence Iron Works. It was mailed by "James" (possibly an employee in town, writing home) to George Krom at Spillway, New York, in 1906. (Courtesy of Florence Historical Society.)

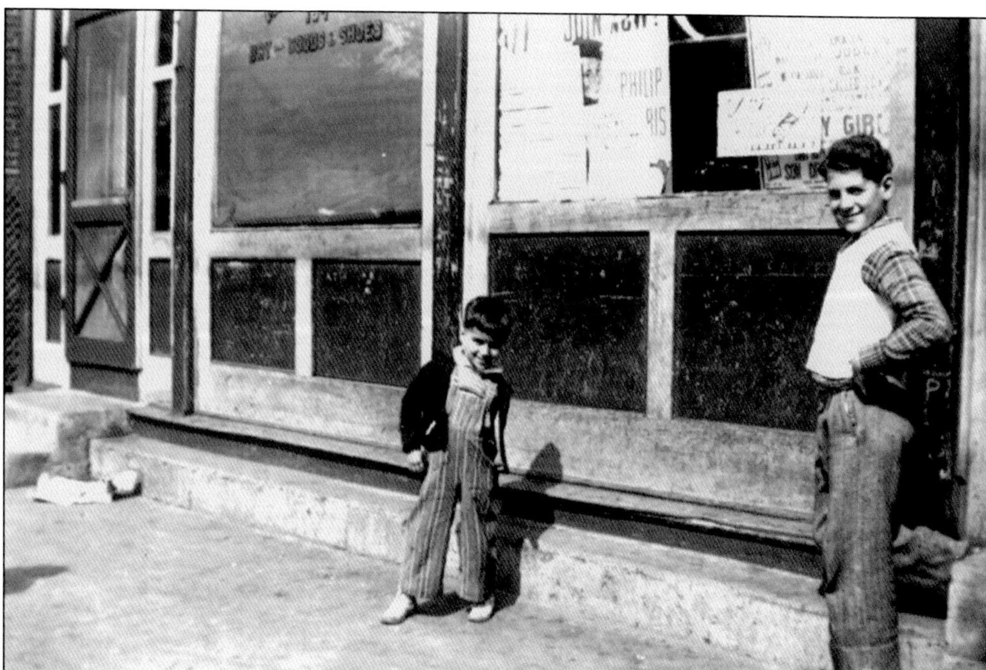

B. Travia (left) and M. Mocini stand in front of the Italian Cooperative Store, in downtown Florence c. 1940. (Courtesy of Florence Historical Society.)

Two

Around Town

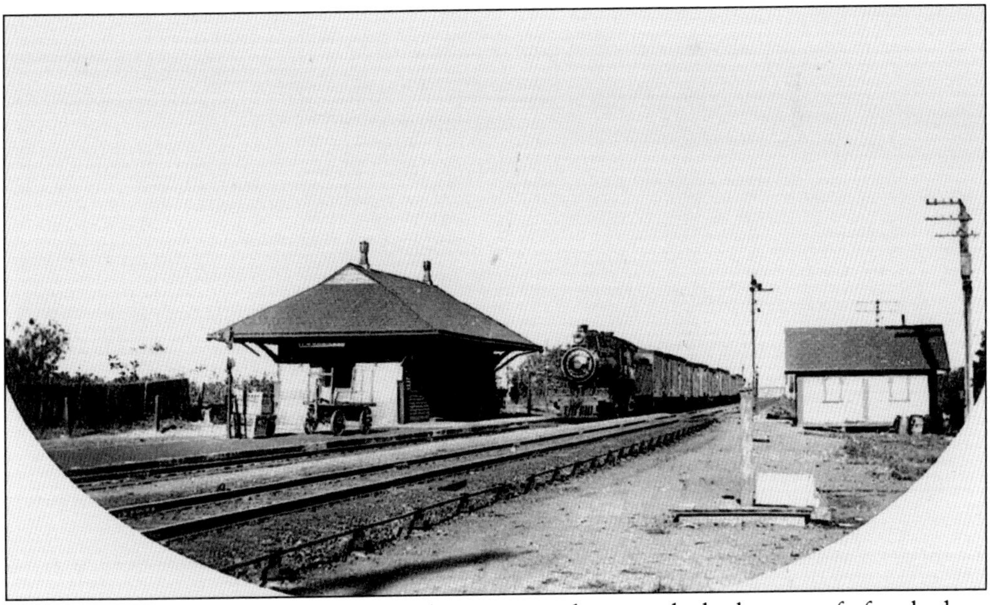

The Florence Train Station, on Railroad Avenue, is shown with the larger roof of early days, giving the building a Queen Anne appearance typical of the time. With the freight train approaching and no raised loading dock, it is likely that this view dates from the 1920s or 1930s. (Courtesy of Florence Historical Society.)

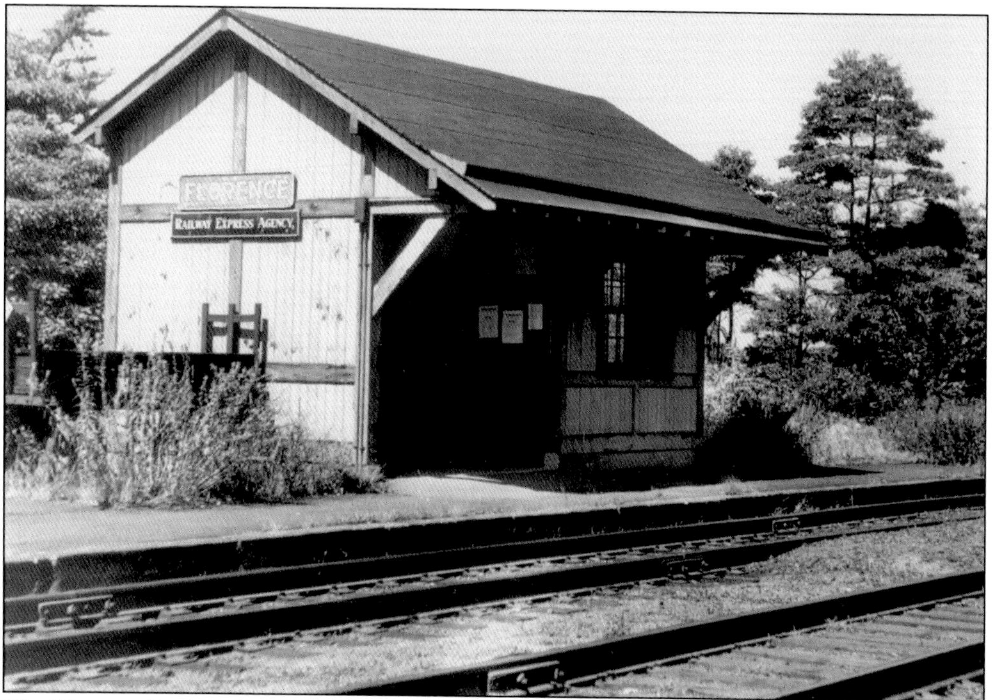

The Florence Railway Express Agency stood on the east side of Delaware Avenue. It serviced the rail line of the Camden and Amboy Division of the Pennsylvania Railroad. It was torn down many years ago. (Courtesy of Florence Historical Society.)

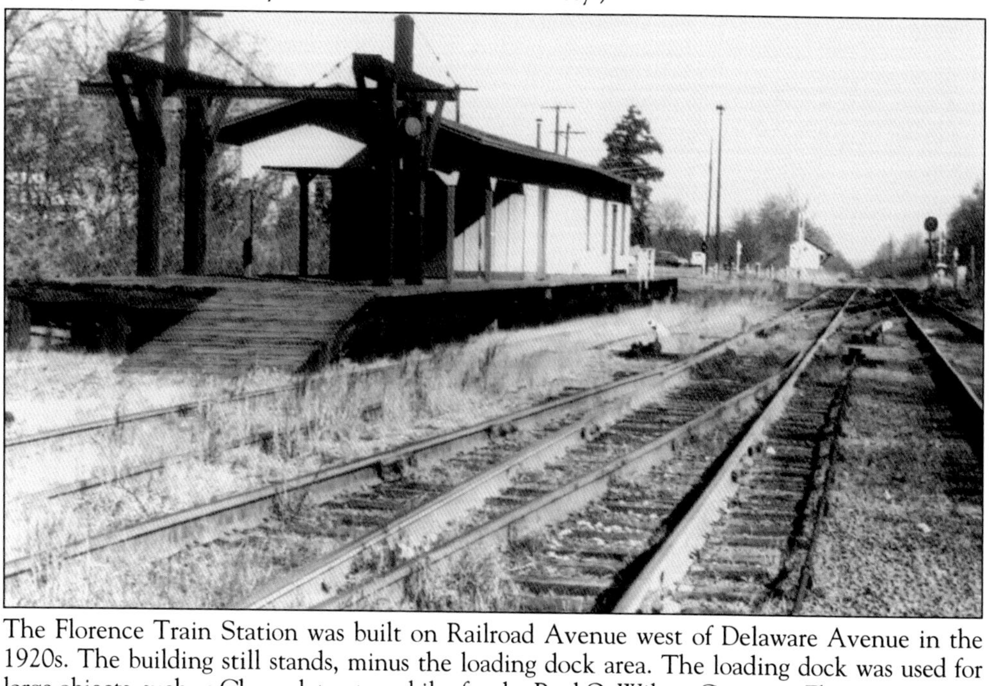

The Florence Train Station was built on Railroad Avenue west of Delaware Avenue in the 1920s. The building still stands, minus the loading dock area. The loading dock was used for large objects, such as Chevrolet automobiles for the Paul Q. Wilson Garage in Florence Station, which were hoisted from train cars to the platform and then driven to the dealership. (Courtesy of Florence Historical Society.)

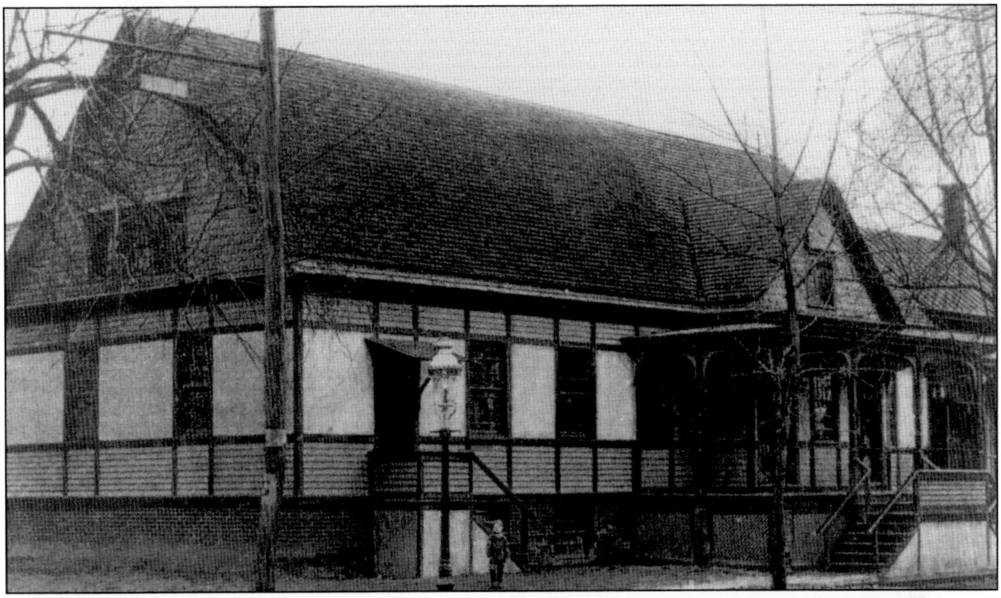

Library Hall, on West Front Street across from Wilkie Park, is the oldest public building still standing in Florence. Built by the Wood family in 1859, it was used originally as a library, later for cooking classes for school girls, and then as a meeting and social hall for town functions, including church suppers and election rallies. The Florence Rifle and Pistol Club met in the basement to use the target range, and the Boy Scouts held monthly meetings upstairs. It was last used as the Florence Nursing Home, which closed in the early 1990s. It is now being renovated to become a church. (Courtesy of Florence Historical Society.)

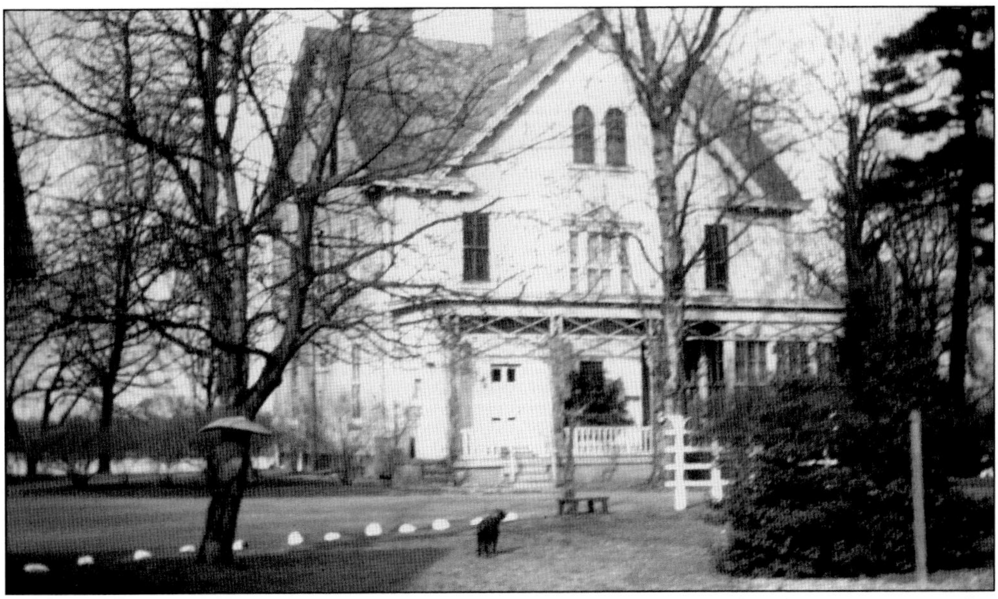

Built *c.* 1870, Iron House was situated on the foundry mansion grounds, where the present-day tennis court is located, at Wilkie Park on West Front Street. Note the iron dog on the lawn, cast at Florence Pipe Foundry. The house was the residence of foundry superintendent Douglas J. Peake and his family, and was the scene of many picnics and outings on the Delaware River by the Peake family and friends. It was razed *c.* 1950. (Courtesy of Florence Historical Society.)

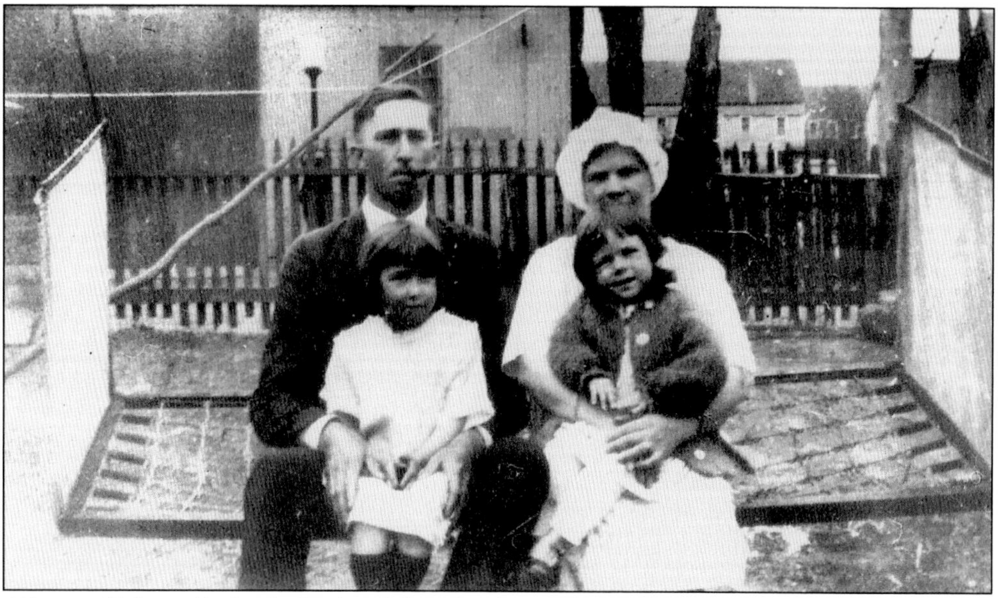

Albert and Minnie Parker Ireland and their daughters Alice and Evelyn Ireland sit on a makeshift glider in the yard behind Parker House Garage, on West Second Street, c. 1917. Minnie Parker's father, John S. Parker, fought in the Civil War with the 1st New Jersey Cavalry. He is buried in the Episcopal Cemetery, also on West Second Street. (Courtesy of Albert King.)

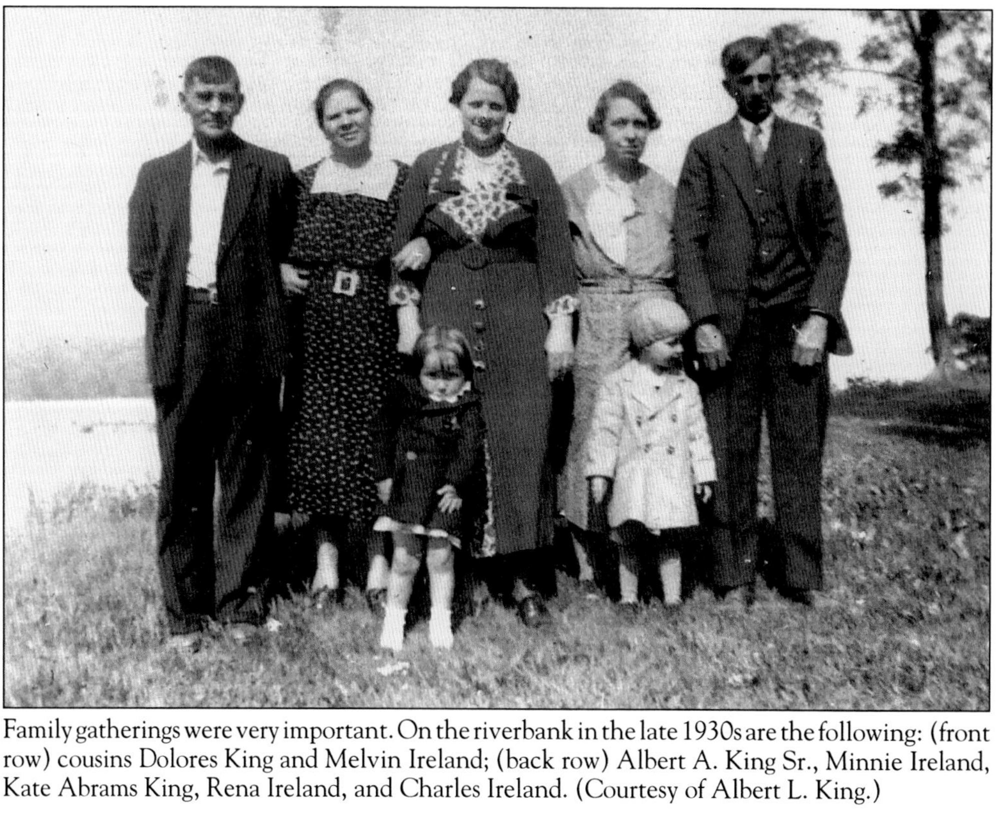

Family gatherings were very important. On the riverbank in the late 1930s are the following: (front row) cousins Dolores King and Melvin Ireland; (back row) Albert A. King Sr., Minnie Ireland, Kate Abrams King, Rena Ireland, and Charles Ireland. (Courtesy of Albert L. King.)

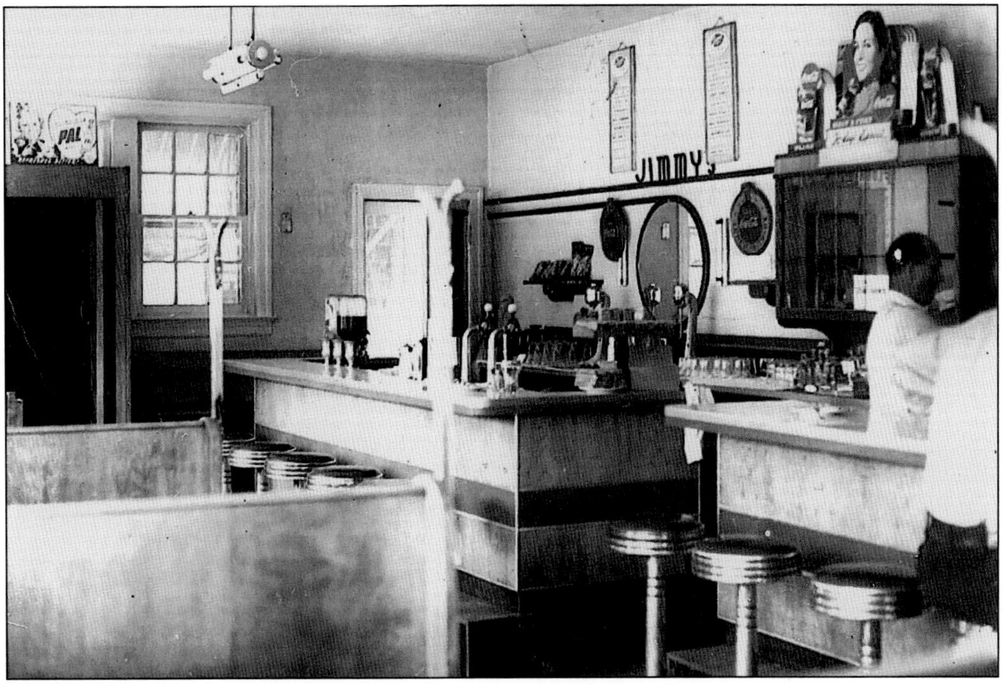

Jimmy's Restaurant, in downtown Florence, boasted the best hot dogs in town. Jimmy's also sold hot dogs at the town baseball games, picnics, and field days. Active from the 1920s to the 1950s, the business adjoined a poolroom at West 2nd and Foundry Streets. (Courtesy of Florence Historical Society.)

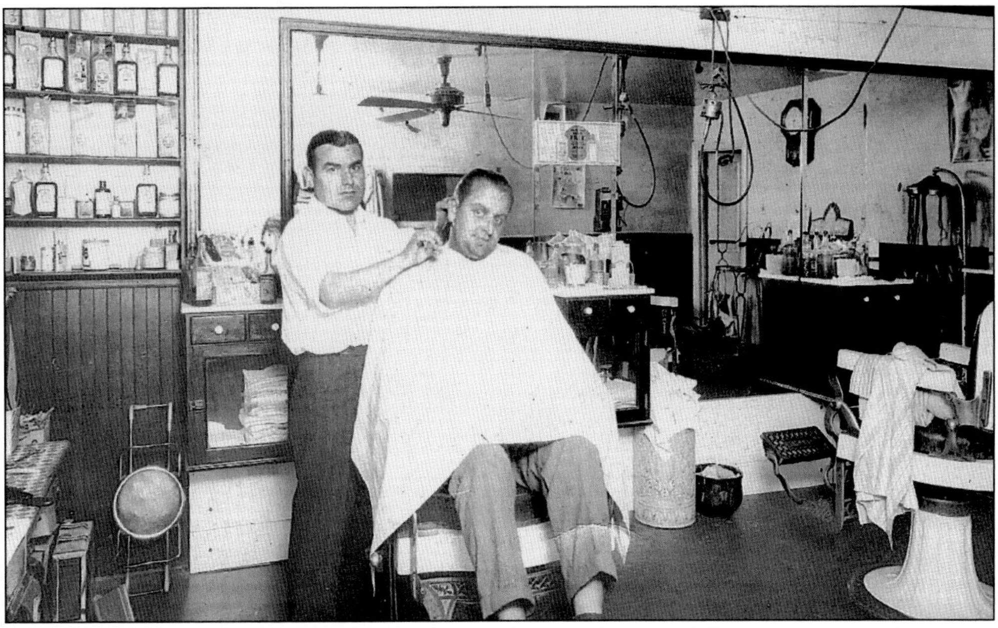

Tom Napoli is pictured in his barbershop at West Third and Zinc Streets in downtown Florence. Note the porcelain barber chairs, which are in great demand today. Stocked with a large assortment of hair tonics, this business was active for many years. (Courtesy of Florence Historical Society.)

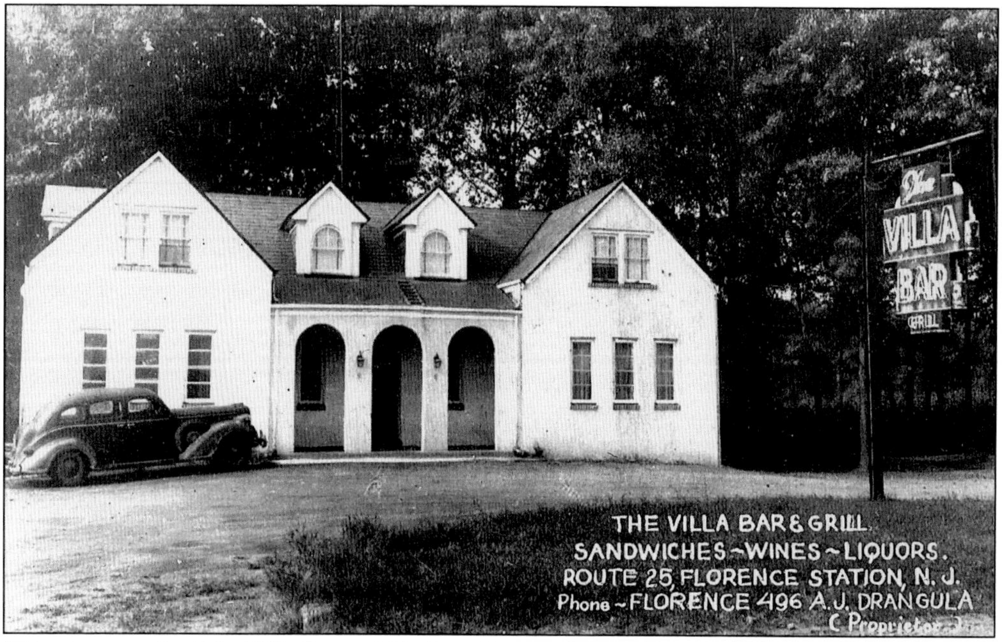

This photograph of the Villa Bar and Grill, on Route 25 (now Route 130), was taken as a Works Progress Administration project to invite tourism on the New Jersey highways during the post-Depression years. The automobile is of 1939 vintage, helping to date the picture. The building stood until 1999, when it was purchased by the New Jersey Turnpike Authority and demolished to enhance their road project. (Courtesy of Florence Historical Society.)

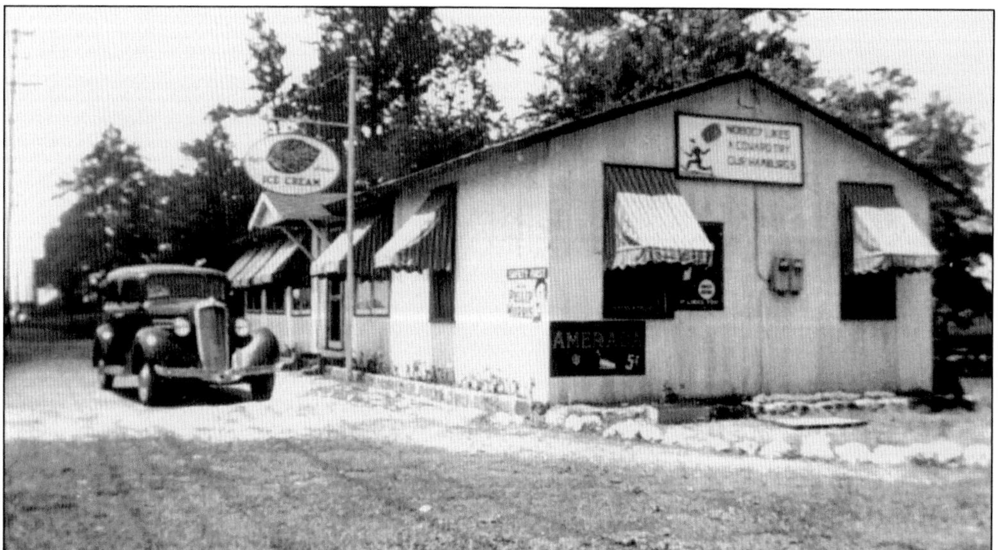

"Nobody Likes a Coward – Try Our Hamburgers" is the sign on this building known as Harkins' Luncheonette, located on the northeast corner of Cedar Lane and Route 25 (now Route 130). At one time the building was owned by a Mr. Wilson from Burlington. This picture was taken c. 1936. Note the telephone lines, somewhat modern compared to others at that time. (Courtesy of Florence Historical Society.)

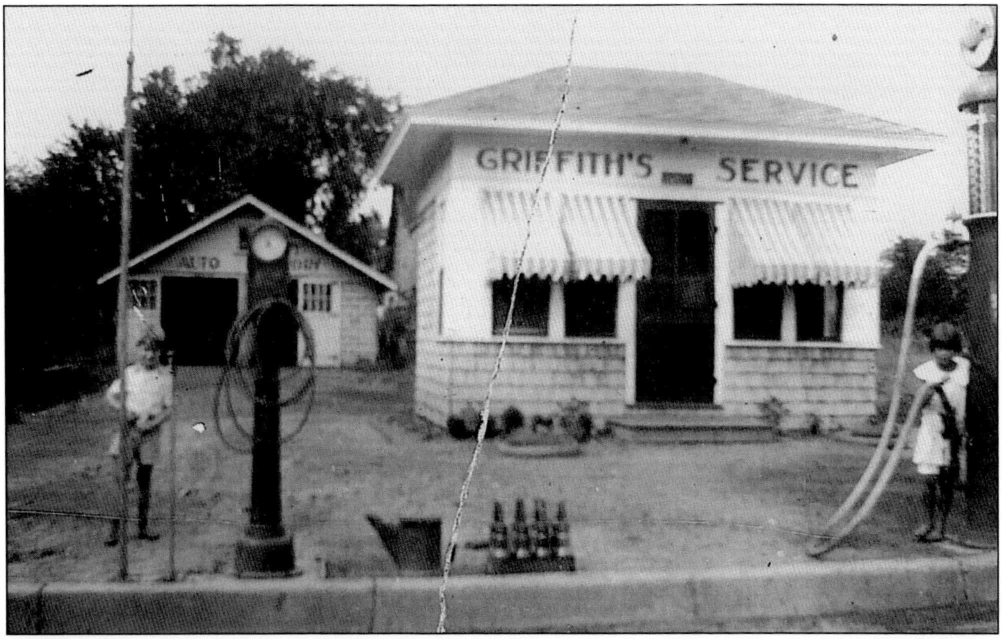

Griffith's Service Station, on East 3rd Street, is pictured *c.* 1930. Although the station has been replaced by a private home, the garage is still standing and mostly original inside. The Griffith family also had a coal and ice business in town. Note the spouted glass oil cans lined up on the curb and the large gas pump with the clear centerpiece. (Courtesy of Florence Historical Society.)

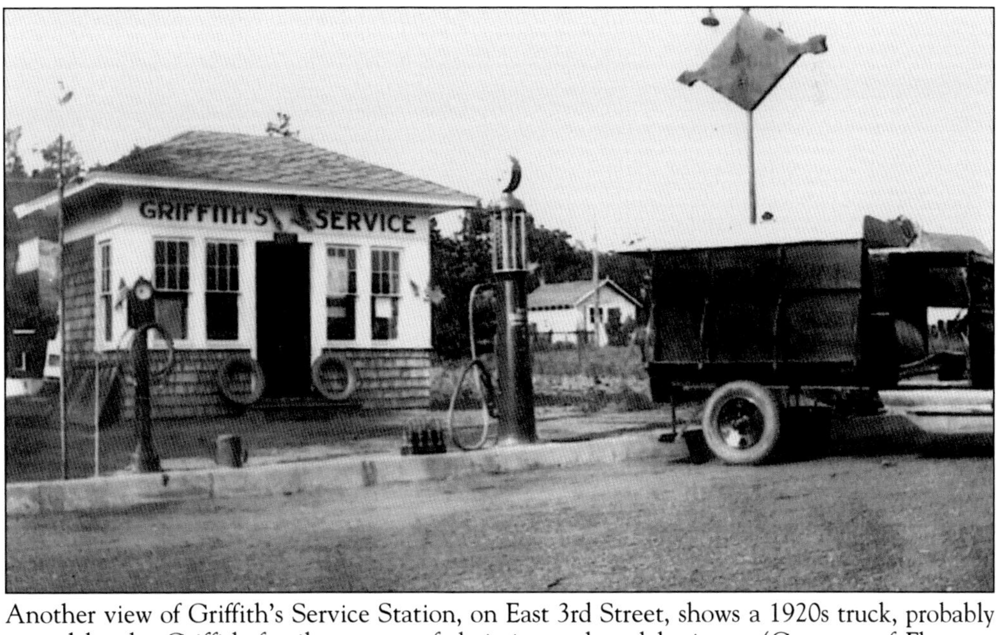

Another view of Griffith's Service Station, on East 3rd Street, shows a 1920s truck, probably owned by the Griffith family as part of their ice and coal business. (Courtesy of Florence Historical Society.)

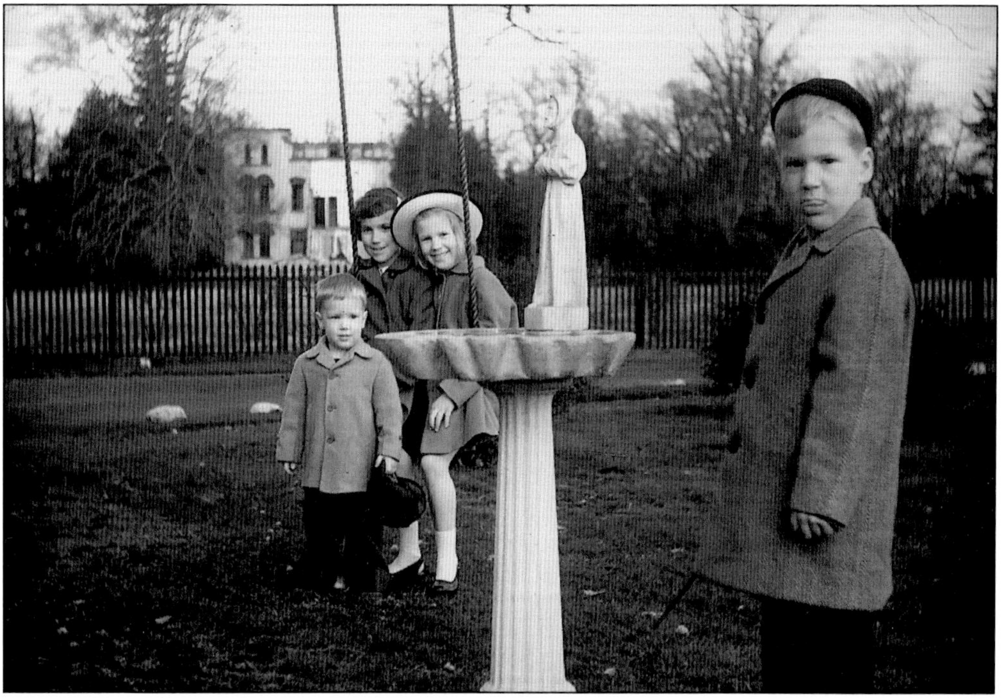

Four children play on the grounds of Iron House, adjacent to the Wood mansion on West Front Street, *c.* 1949. The fountain, cast at the Florence Iron Works, is now located in Mount Holly at a private residence. (Courtesy of Florence Historical Society.)

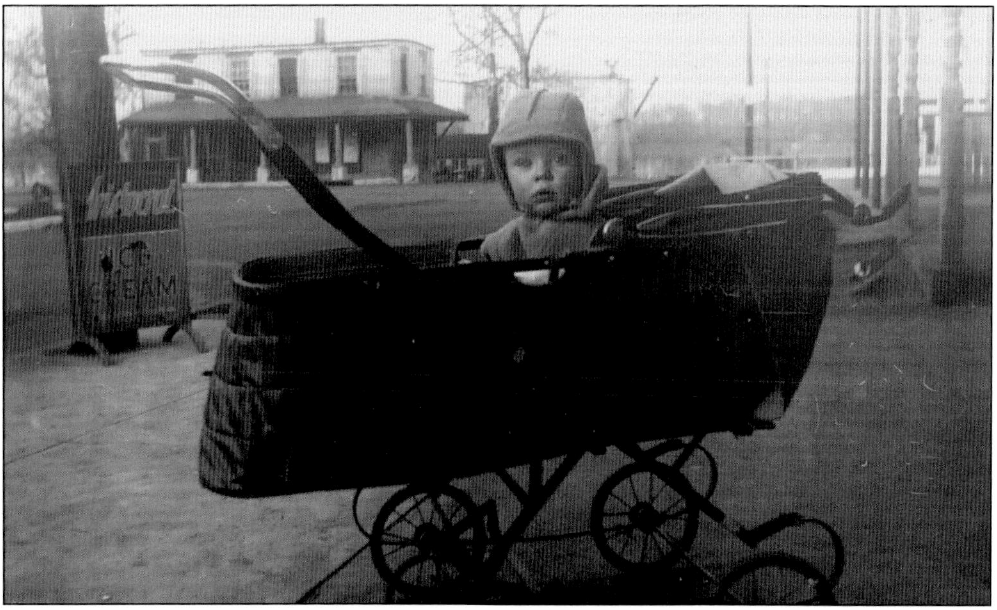

This baby sits near the southeast corner of Front and Broad Streets in a "modern" baby coach in 1941. The building on the river side of West Front Street, built in the 1870s, was once a waiting room and ticket office for steamboat patrons. Note the oil tank on the river behind the store, erected by McElven Fuel over vehement objections by the townspeople. (Courtesy of Florence Historical Society.)

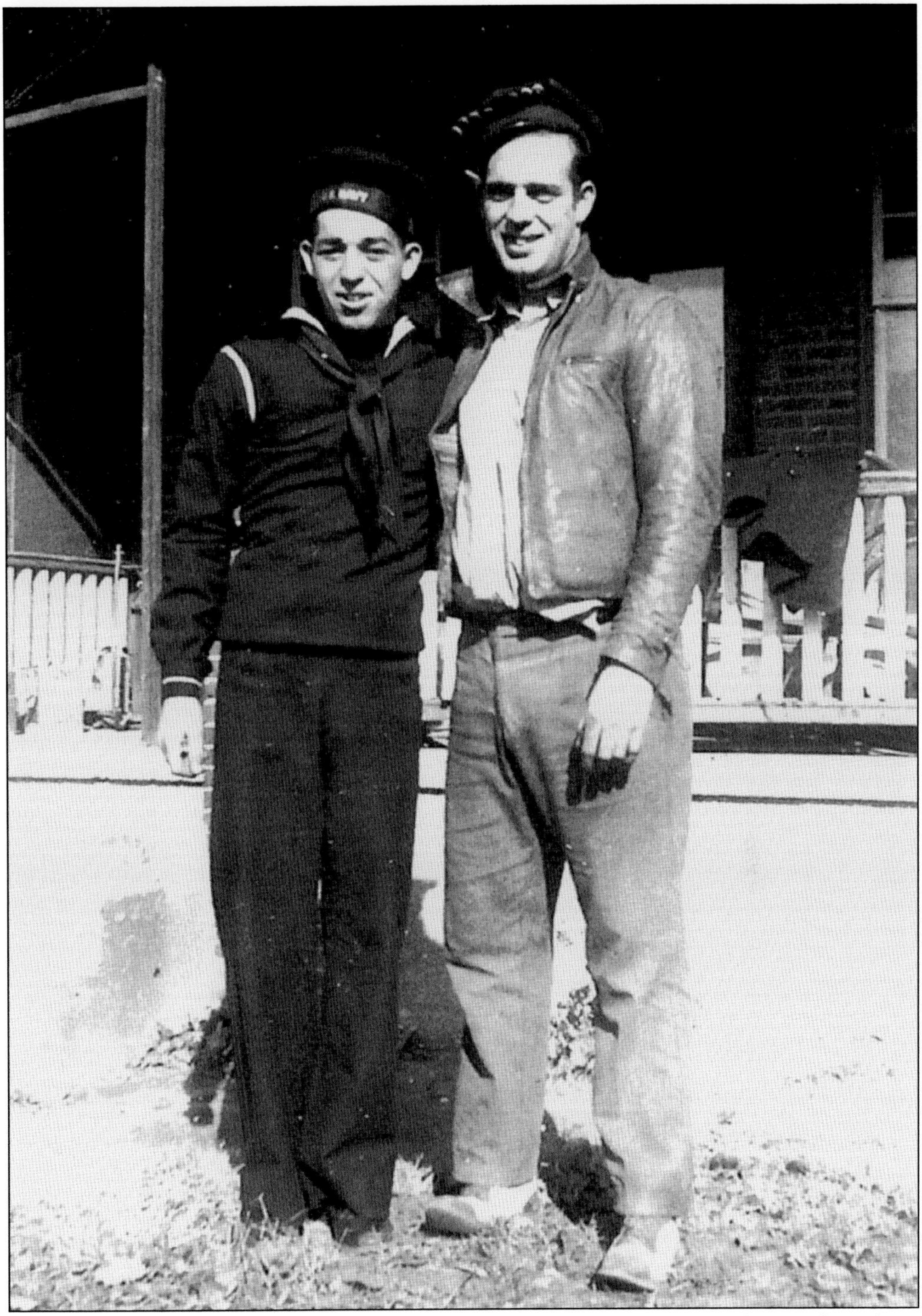

On leave from the navy in 1944, Harry Stiltz (left) stands with his brother Palmer Stiltz in front of their Woodlawn Avenue house. They were sons of Beatrice Mitchell and Palmer Stiltz, who were among the first four families to move into the new Woodlawn Avenue houses, which had both electricity and gaslights. (Courtesy of Jim and Hannah Roache.)

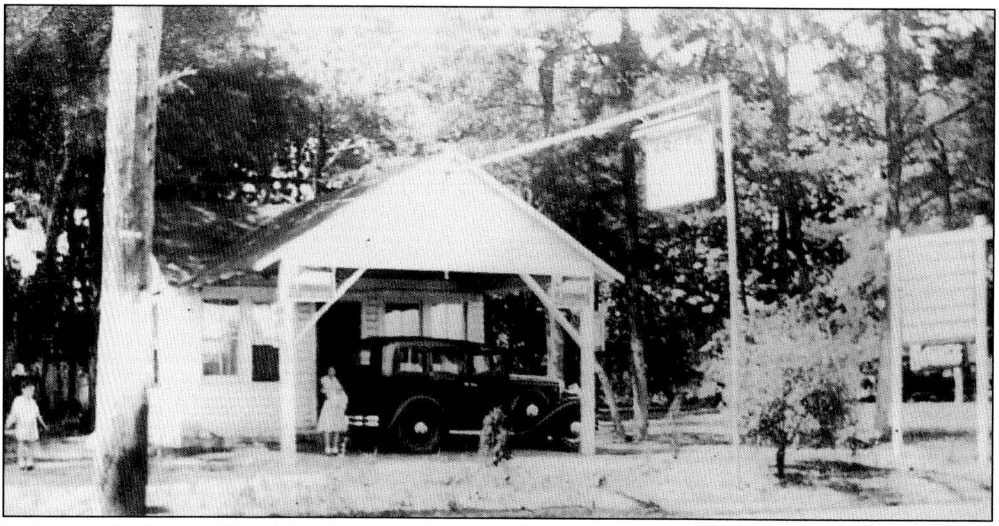

Taken in the late 1920s, this photograph shows the tourist cabin that stood on Route 25, the predecessor of the Villa Motel. The enterprise was later run by the Anthony Drangula family. (Courtesy of Don Cooper.)

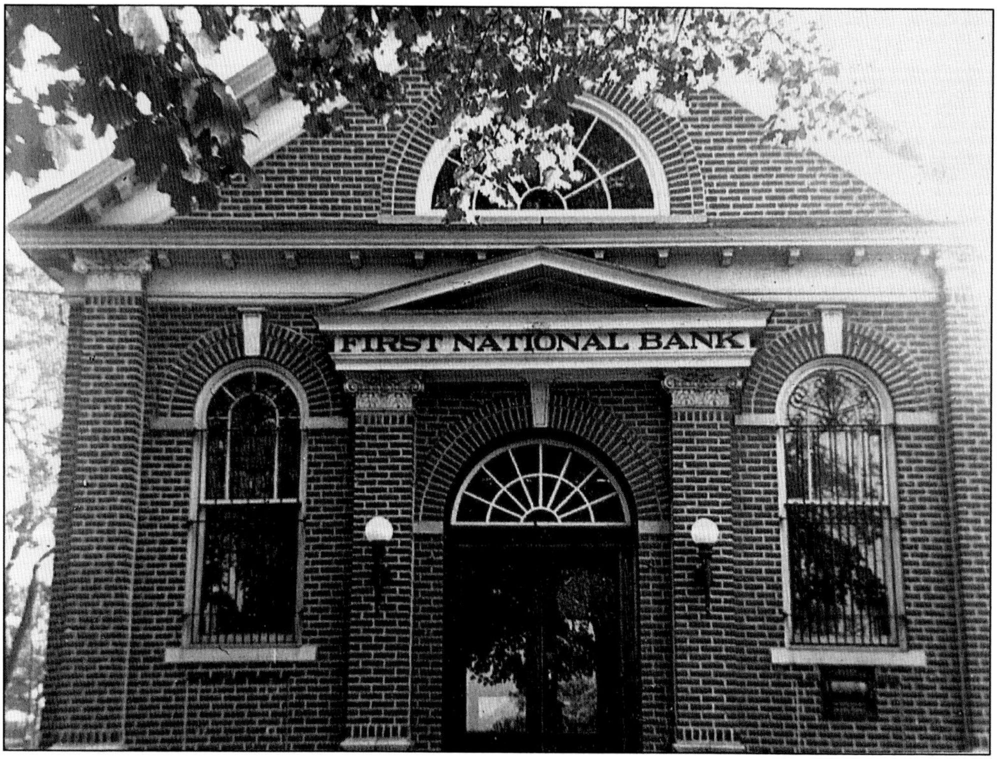

The First National Bank of Florence, *c.* 1951, has changed little since being built in the early 1930s. Established in 1916, the bank was originally housed in a building adjacent to the present one. An earlier photograph does not show the bars on the windows, probably the result of several daylight robberies after the early 1930s. Located in the second block of West Front Street, it has now been acquired and renamed Farmers and Mechanics Bank. (Courtesy of Florence Historical Society.)

Beatrice and Everett Mitchell, children of Harry and Lillie Harker Mitchell, pose for a studio portrait *c.* 1907–1909. Beatrice Mitchell married Palmer Stiltz and moved back to Florence in 1924 into a new home on Woodlawn Avenue. (Courtesy of Jim and Hannah Roache.)

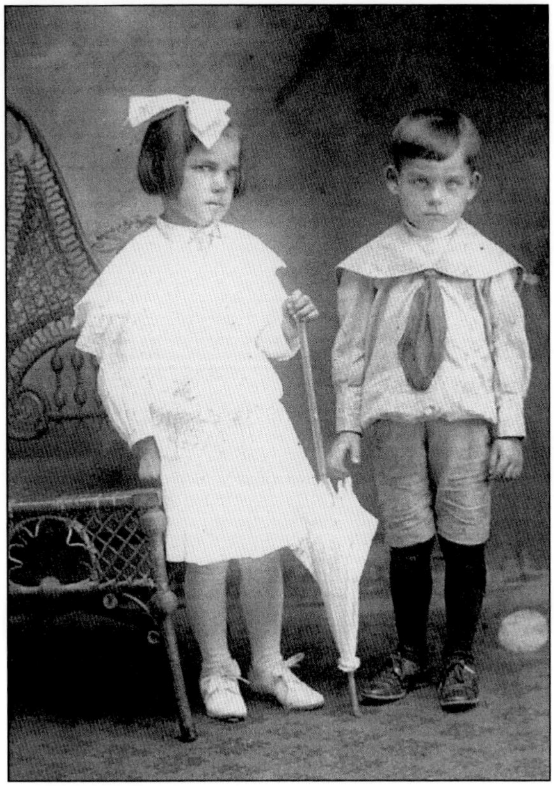

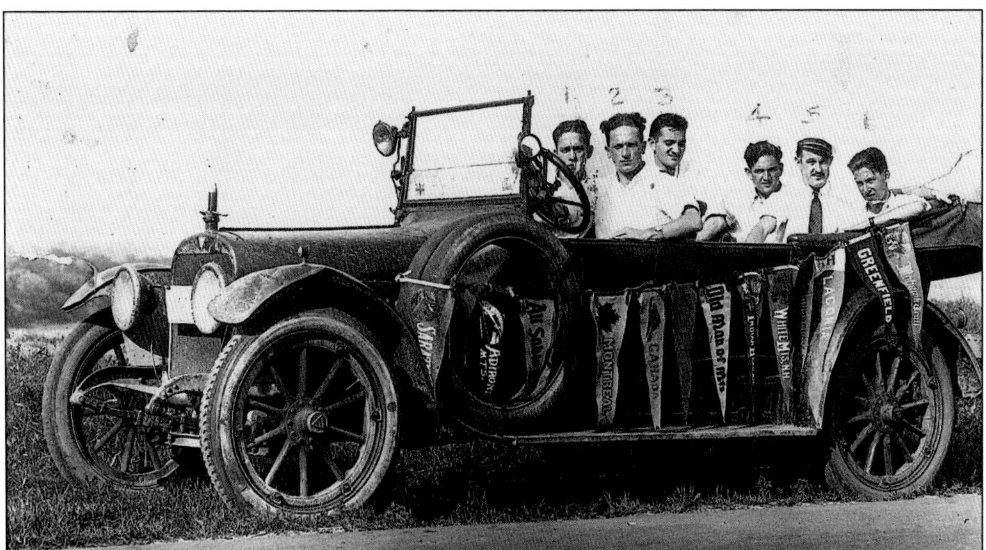

"Guest of Canada" on the car windshield tells where these tourists were bound *c.* 1920. From left to right are Paul Green, Donald Green, Paul Cunningham, Eletes Cunningham, George Weeast, and Lloyd Brown. (Courtesy of Florence Historical Society.)

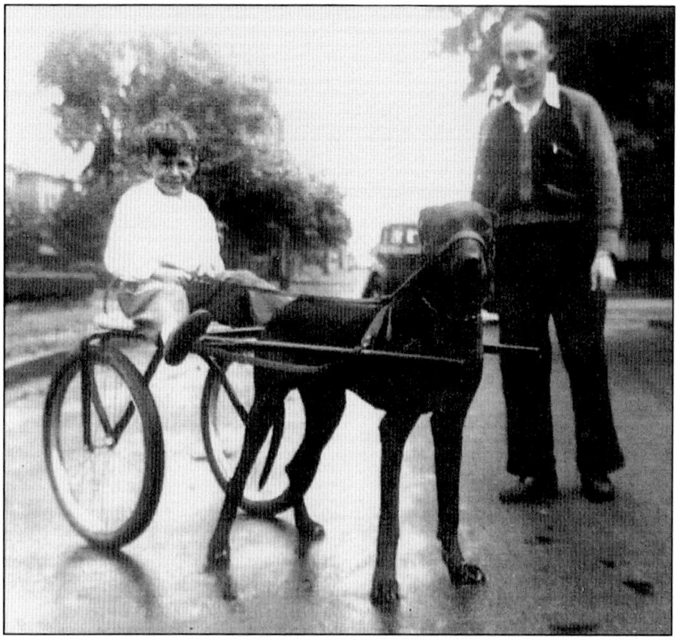

The Fourth of July historically has been a big celebration in Florence. Preparing for the parade in 1941 are 7-year-old Ed Panaro, his dog Duke, and his 26-year-old brother, Dan Panaro, who built the cart to enter the parade. The Panaro family moved to Florence from Pennsylvania in 1931 and raised a large family. The Panaros are still active in the community. (Courtesy of Ed Panaro.)

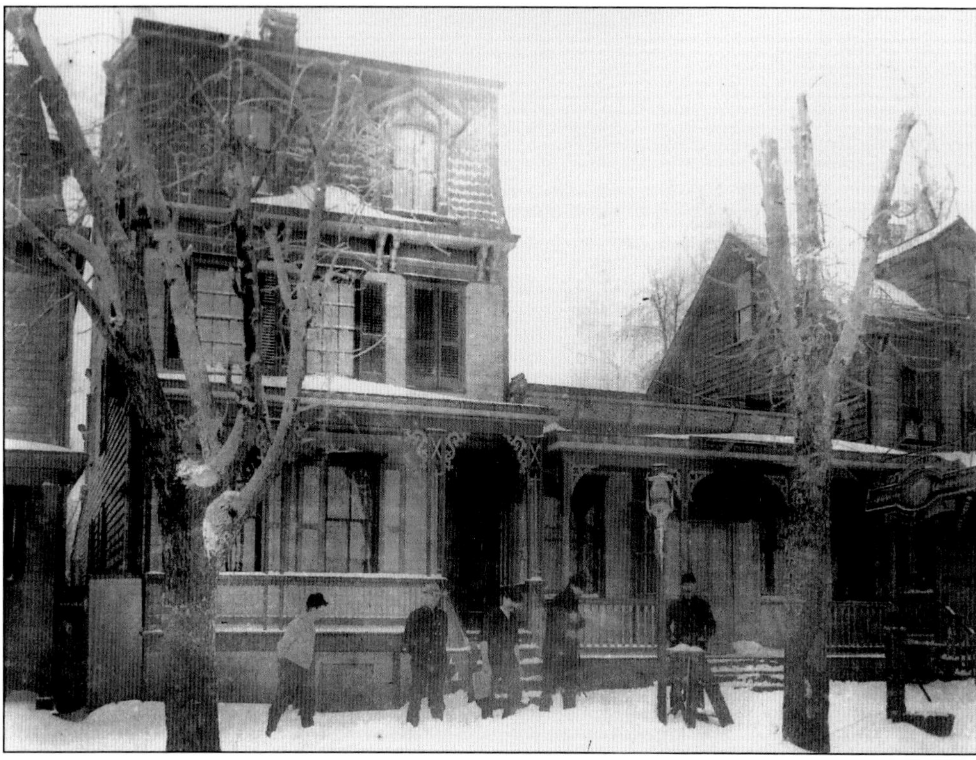

This snowball fight took place on West Front Street, west of the Parker House Hotel, in the early 1900s. These buildings are still standing, enriching the town's architectural landscape. The mansard-roofed building on the left dates to the Civil War period, and the dormered house on the right is probably older, although it does not appear on the 1859 map of the town. (Courtesy of Florence Historical Society.)

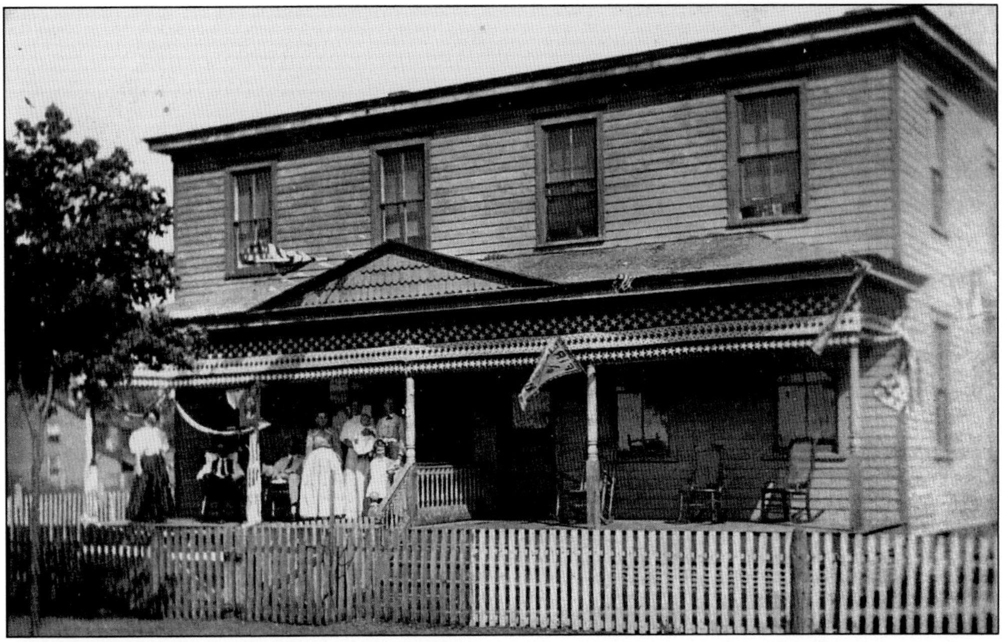

This double house, at 1002 West Front Street, is still standing, across from Griffin Pipe Products. Built in the early 1900s by R.D. Wood for rent to its workers, it appears to be decorated for a parade. Note the hitching post in front for horses. (Courtesy of Raymond Carugno.)

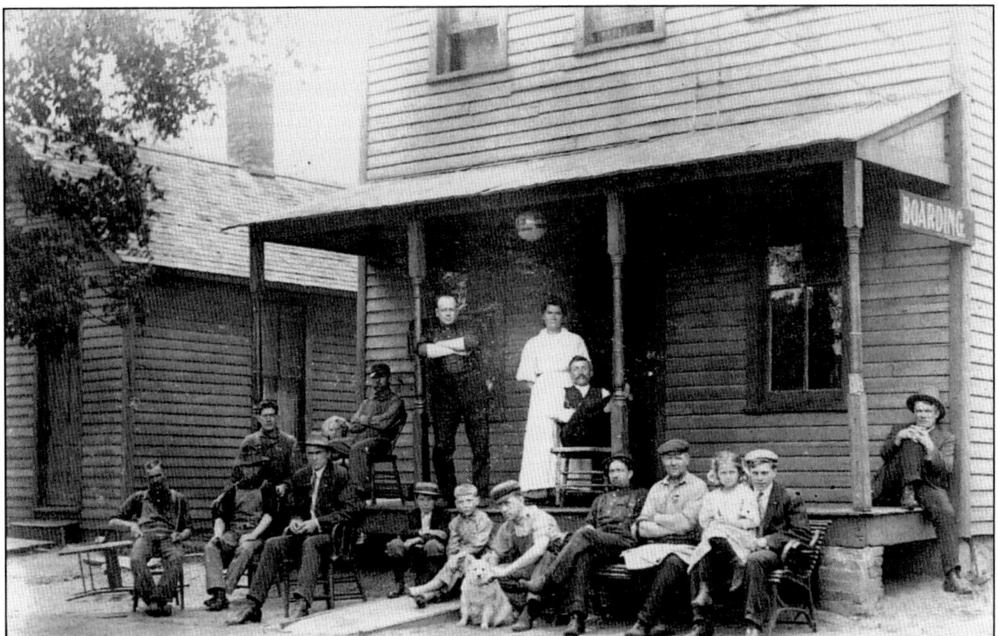

This boardinghouse has been confirmed as being a Florence home in the early 1900s. Many homes took in boarders who were immigrants coming to work in the Florence Iron Works. This group, seemingly comprised of several generations of one family and extended family members, probably lived in the house. (Courtesy of Florence Historical Society.)

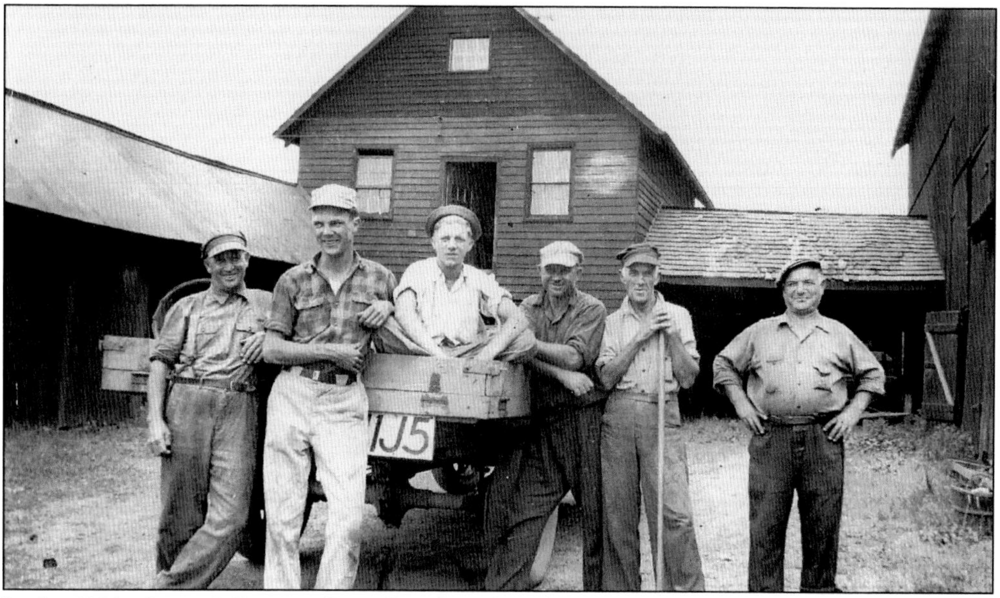

In the 1930s, Sutton's Farm on River Road produced great quantities of vegetables and fruits for the local and city markets. From left to right are Bob Danley (Harry Danley's father), Robert Sutton, Jesse Hannum, Oscar Sory, Harvey Campbell, and Tony ? of Philadelphia. This farm is no longer in existence. (Courtesy of Florence Historical Society.)

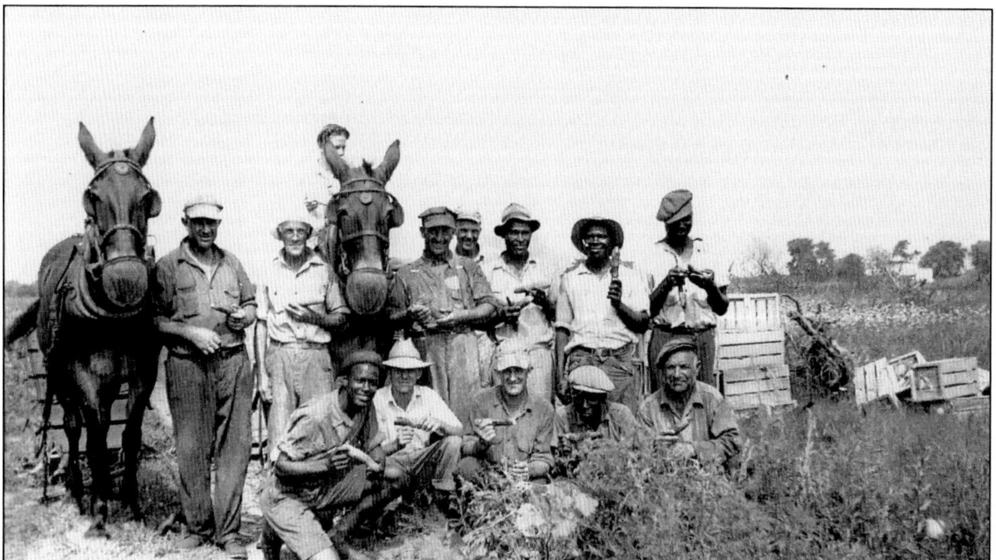

Farming was an important part of early Florence. Shown is Robert Sutton (front row, second from the left) on his farm, on River Road in adjacent Burlington Township. The Jamaican pickers helped harvest corn, tomatoes, and fruit trees for the city markets. This picture is dated c. the 1930s. (Courtesy of Florence Historical Society.)

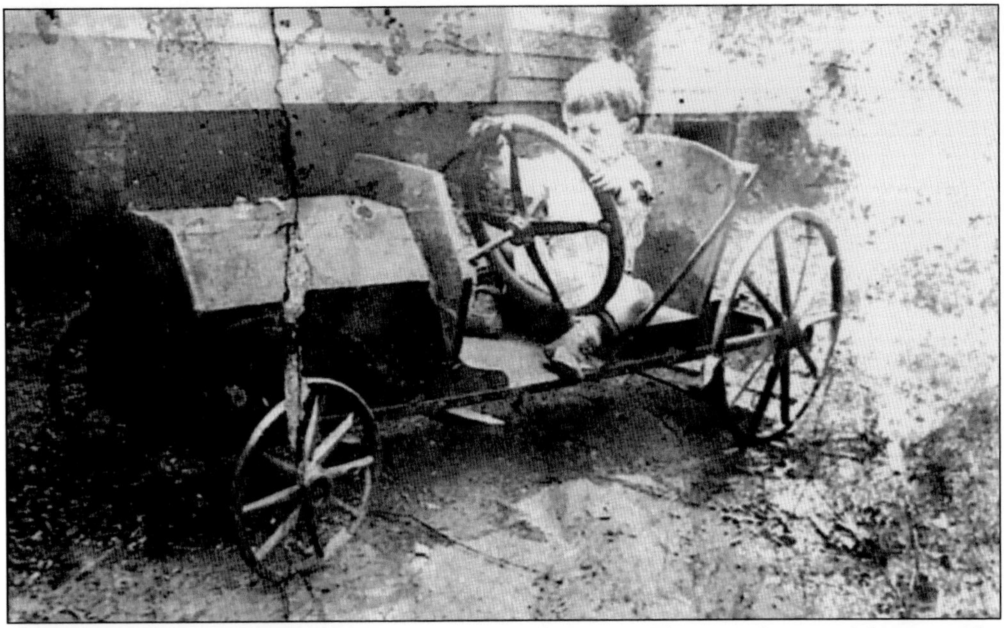

Wayne Campbell tries out his "first" car *c.* 1920 in downtown Florence. As no pedals are visible, he is most likely waiting for a push in the side yard. His driving ability came in handy later, when he drove the bus for the Ray Anthony Orchestra during the 1940s and 1950s. (Courtesy of Florence Historical Society.)

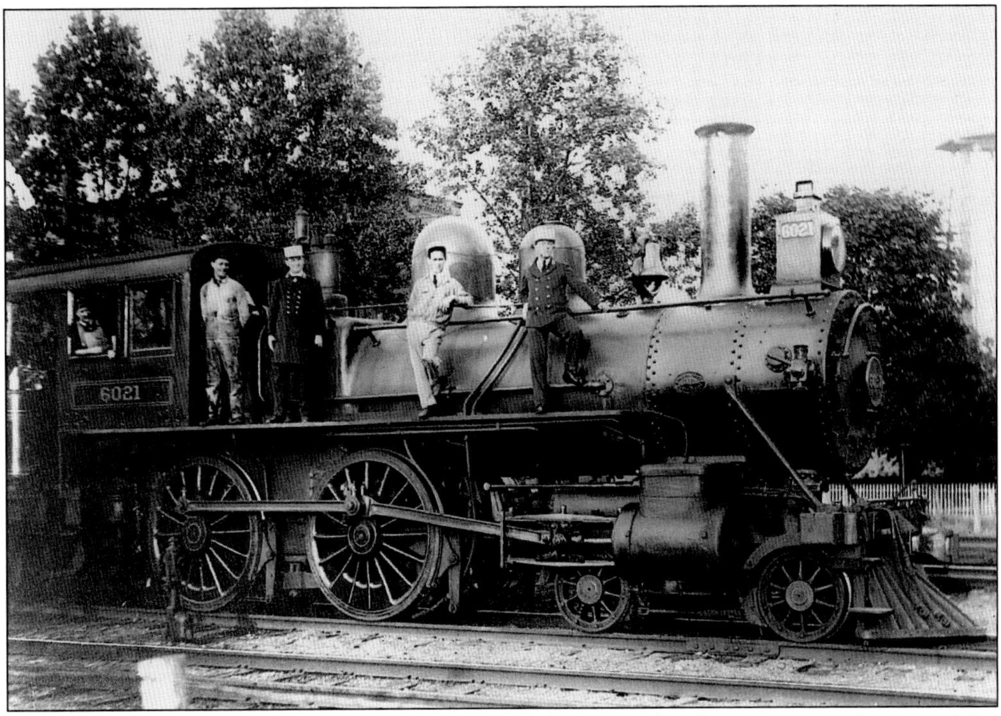

Some Florence men pose at their job on the Pennsylvania Railroad train in a nearby town. The sound of the train whistle from this steam engine is missed by many in the area who remember hearing it during the night outside of town. (Courtesy of Florence Historical Society.)

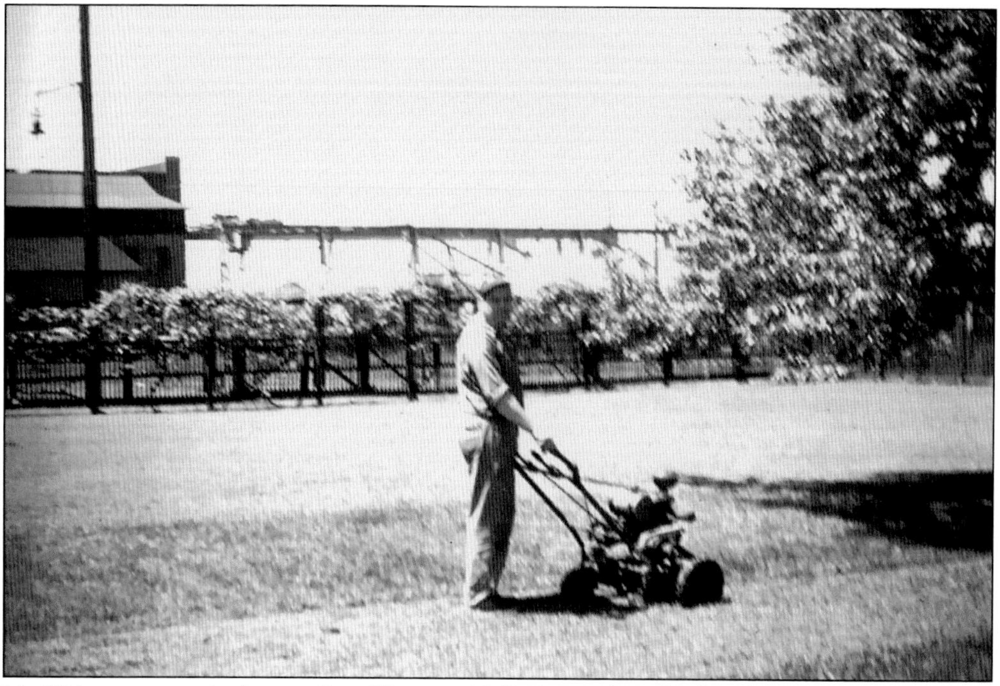

Mr. Ridgway mows the lawn at Iron House in 1949. Located on the foundry mansion grounds, on West Front Street, the house was the residence of Douglas J. Peake, Florence Pipe Foundry and Machine Company superintendent. Part of the company is shown in the background. (Courtesy of Florence Historical Society.)

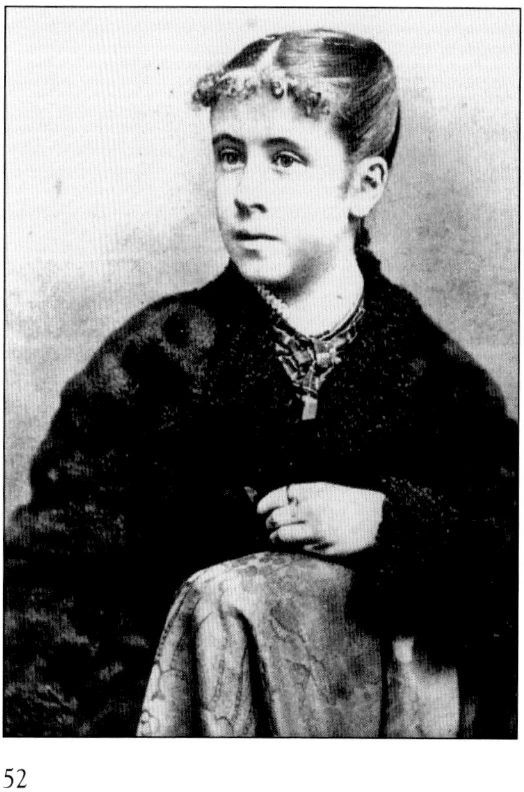

The Lower family was established early in Florence Station. Hannah Lower was born in 1864 and was 13 years old when this photograph was taken *c.* 1877. She later married Joseph Parker, and together, they raised nine children. Her father-in-law, John S. Parker, rode with the 1st New Jersey Cavalry at Gettysburg. (Courtesy of Albert L. King.)

Dolores King and Donald Lambert were married in 1953 at the Florence United Methodist Church. The maid of honor is Dolores's sister, Joan, and the best man is George Berry. (Courtesy of Joan King Shafer.)

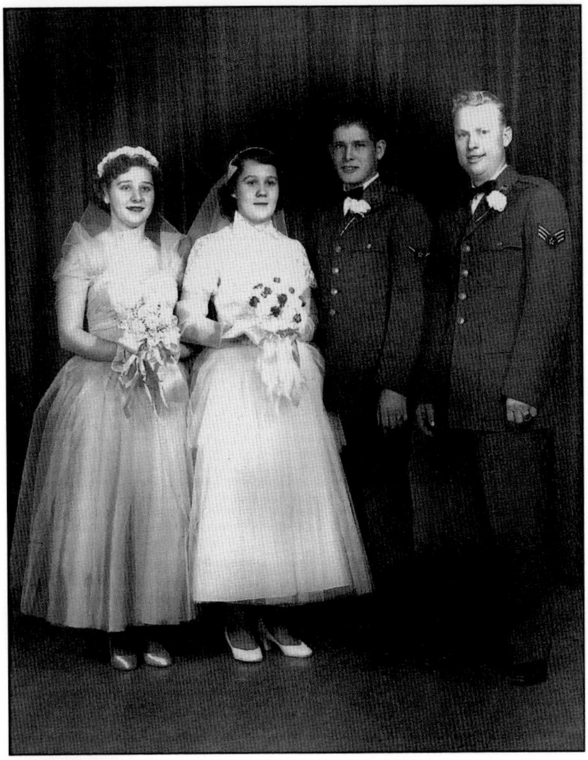

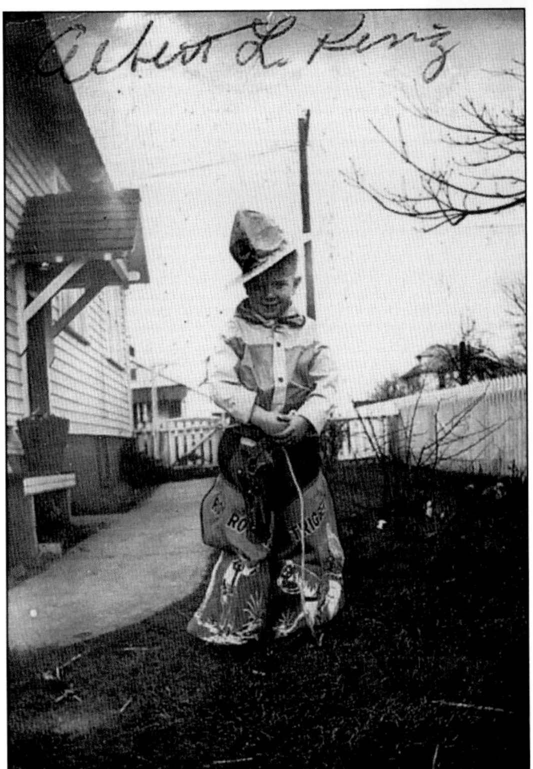

In the 1940s, cowboy films were the most popular at the movies, and most young boys had this kind of outfit, including Albert L. King. This shot was taken in the side yard of his home, at 214 West 4th Street. (Courtesy of Florence Historical Society.)

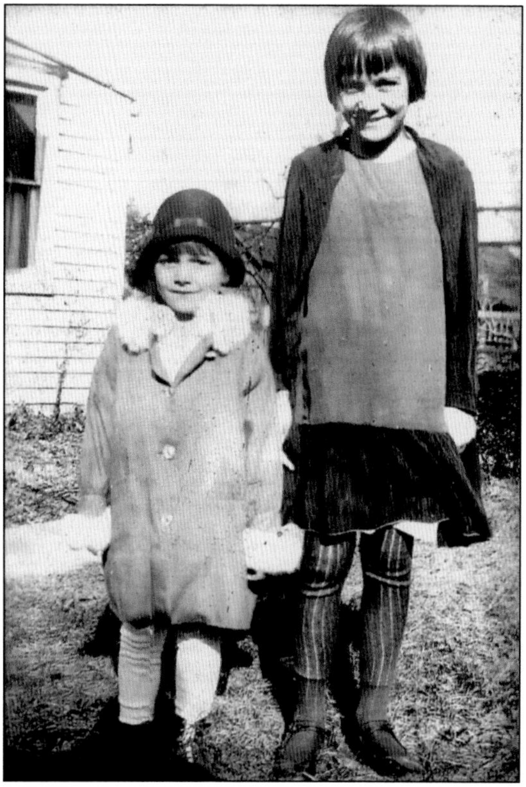

The depression years were difficult for Florence residents, but the large Panaro family kept warm, as shown in 1929. Sisters Lois and Helen Panaro are photographed in front of their home in Florence Station. (Courtesy of Helen Panaro Henderson.)

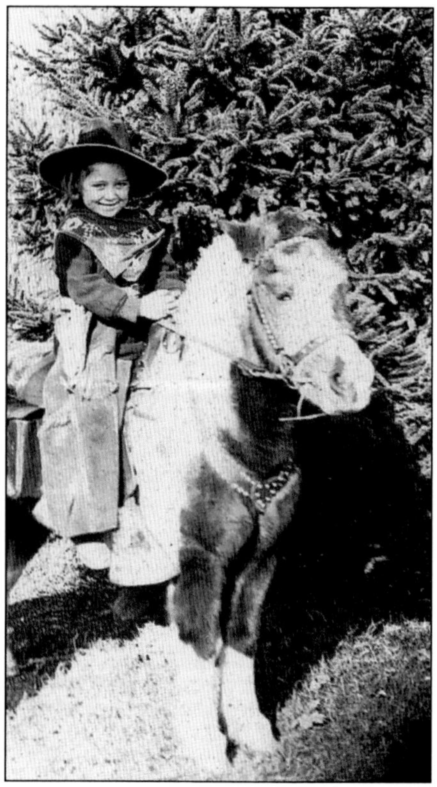

Not to be outdone by her brother, Joan King had her picture taken in the early 1940s on a pony. The Dale Evans outfit was appropriate. (Courtesy of Joan Shafer.)

Joseph "Whitey" Crammer and Alberta "Bert" Ireland stand in back of her parents' home, on East Front Street, *c.* 1940. The large double house was later demolished. Today, a brick apartment house, built by Anthony "Reds" Getz, occupies the site. (Courtesy of Florence Historical Society.)

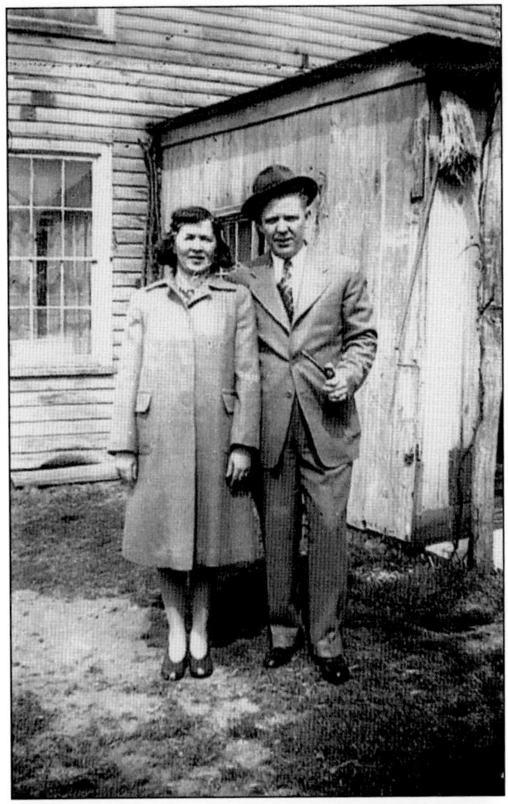

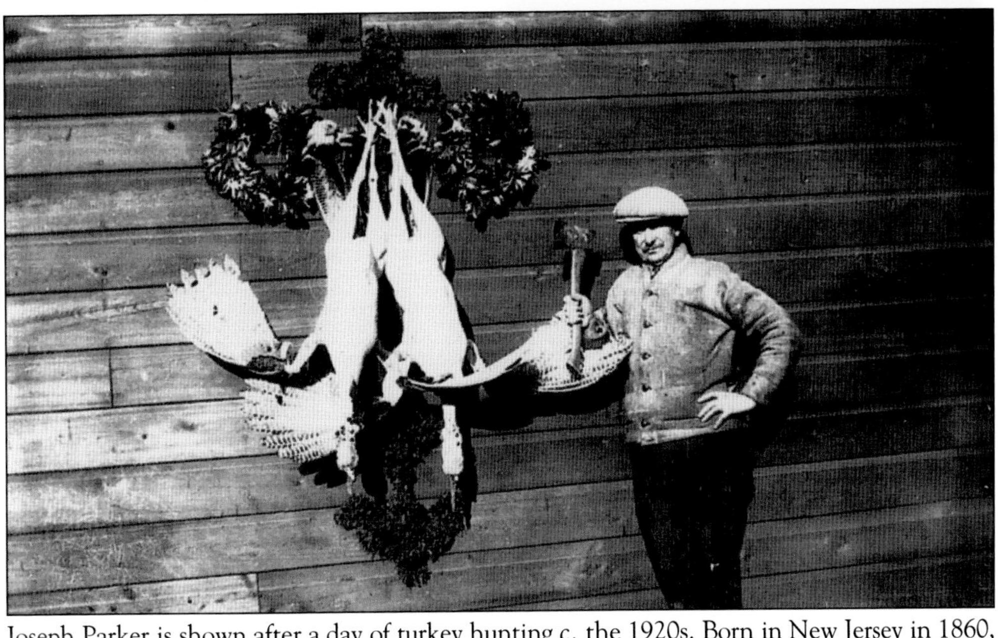

Joseph Parker is shown after a day of turkey hunting *c.* the 1920s. Born in New Jersey in 1860, he married Hannah Lower in 1881 and died in 1931. His family came from Monmouth County, and his father, John S. Parker, fought with the cavalry at Gettysburg in the Civil War. (Courtesy of Albert L. King.)

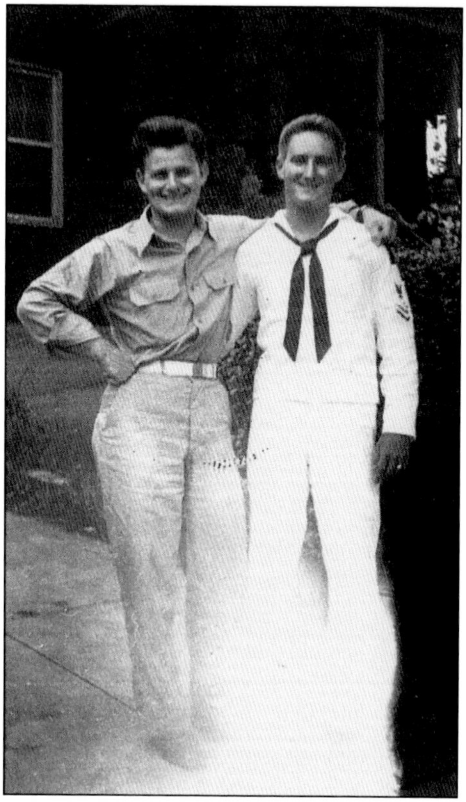

The Tapper brothers served during World War II. Nelson Tapper (left) was in the U.S. Army and James Tapper was in the U.S. Coast Guard. (Courtesy of Mary Tapper.)

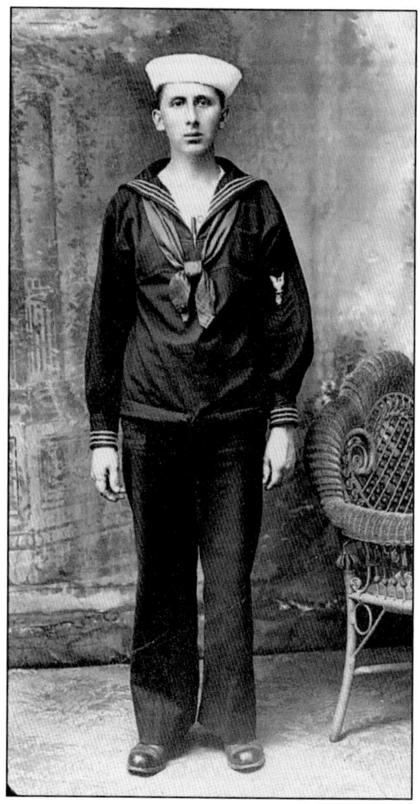

Herman Parker, uncle of Alice Ireland, poses in his World War I navy uniform for a studio portrait. Born in 1895, he died in 1949. (Courtesy of Albert L. King)

Three

CHURCHES

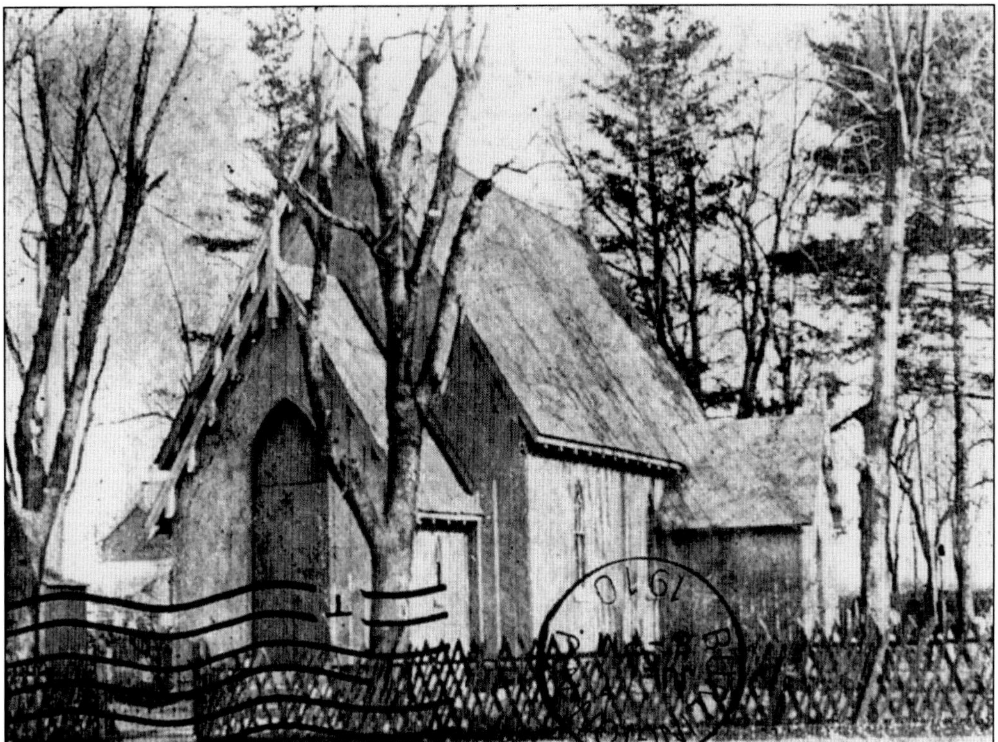

St. Stephens Protestant Episcopal Church, erected in 1860, is shown in the first block of West Second Street. The property was donated by James Spencer. The cemetery adjacent is the resting place of several Civil War veterans. (Courtesy of Florence Historical Society.)

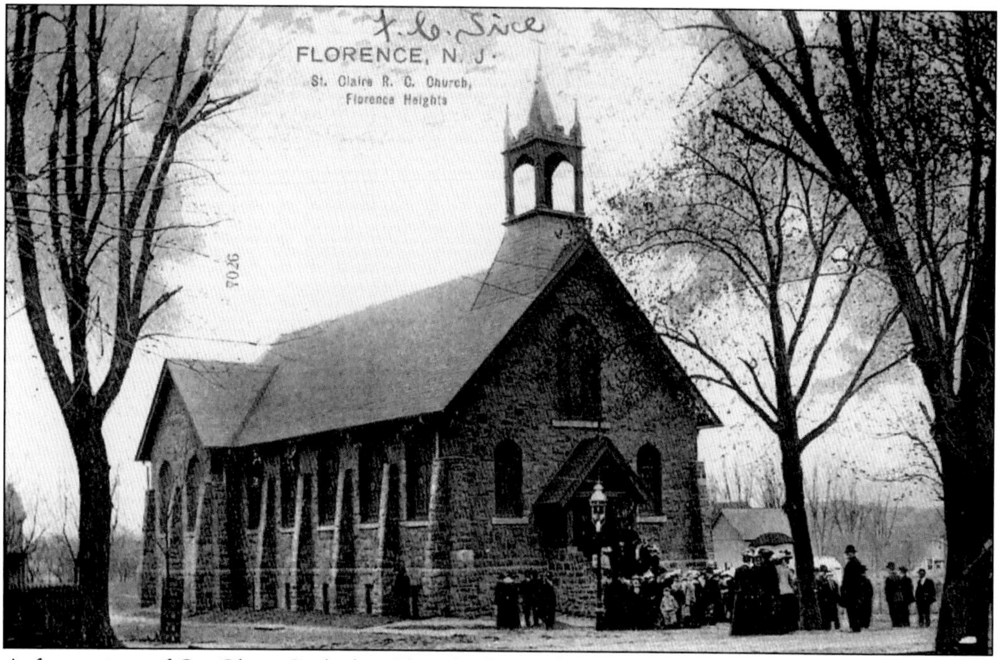

A front view of St. Clare Catholic Church shows the long dark dresses commonly worn by women in 1907. The building stands at the southwest corner of Front and Walnut Streets, and the only noticeable change today is the absence of the gaslight and trolley tracks in front. (Courtesy of Florence Historical Society.)

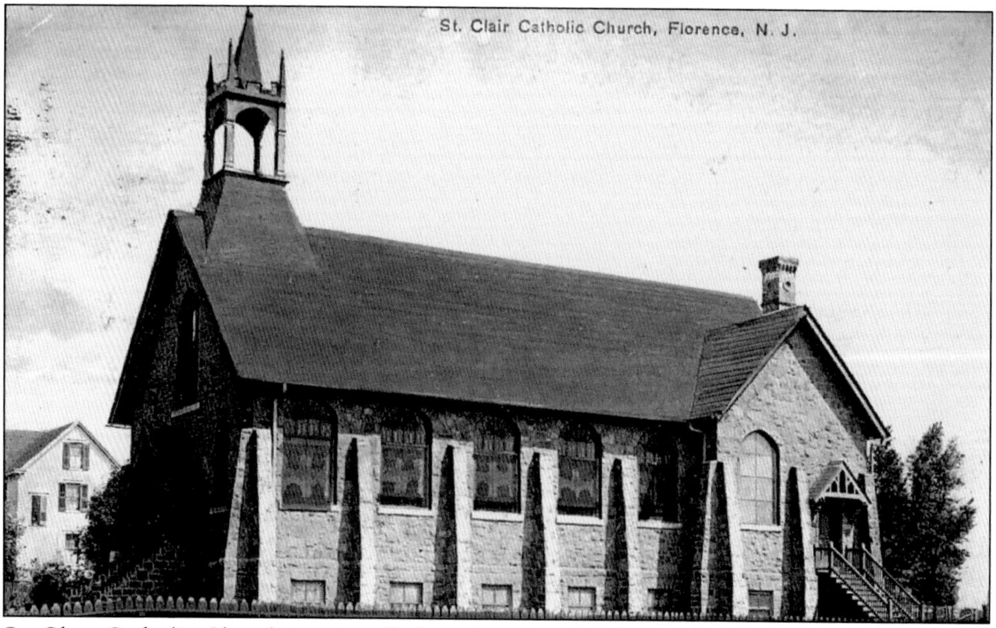

St. Clare Catholic Church is misspelled on this postcard. Erected in 1904 entirely by church members, this building still stands, largely unchanged, except for the long-gone picket fence. The postcards of this period were photographed in America and sent to Germany for hand coloring before resale. William McCune Jr. mailed this card to Amanda Davidson in 1909. (Courtesy of Florence Historical Society.)

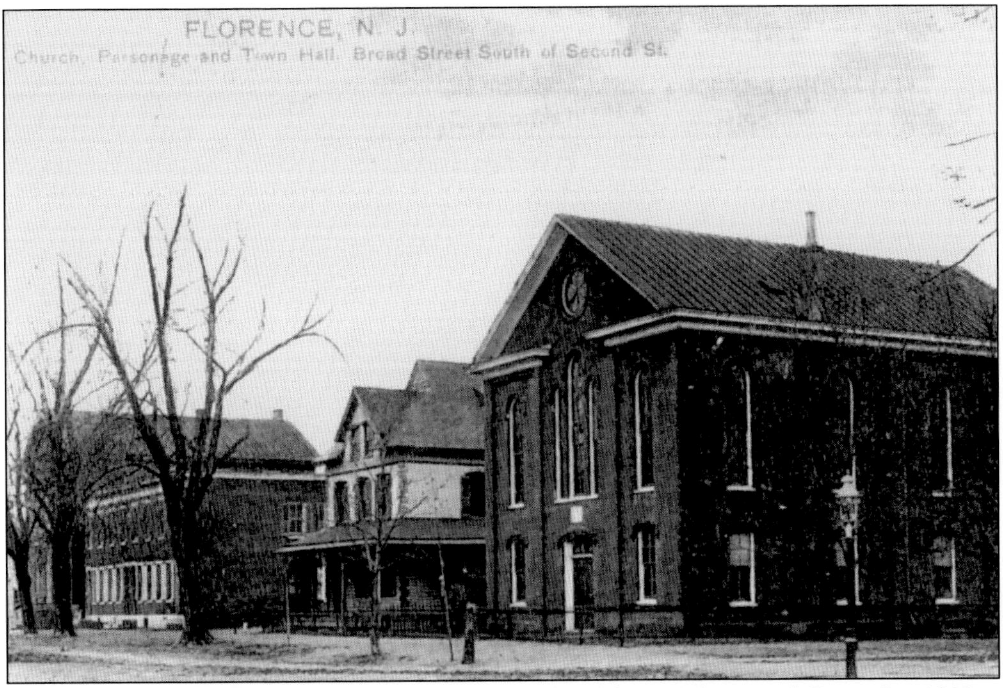

The Florence Methodist Church is shown on the right of this 1905 postcard. Erected in 1882 at the southwest corner of Broad and Second Streets, the church is an excellent example of Greek Revival architecture. To the left stands the parsonage, torn down in the early 1950s to make way for parking. (Courtesy of Florence Historical Society.)

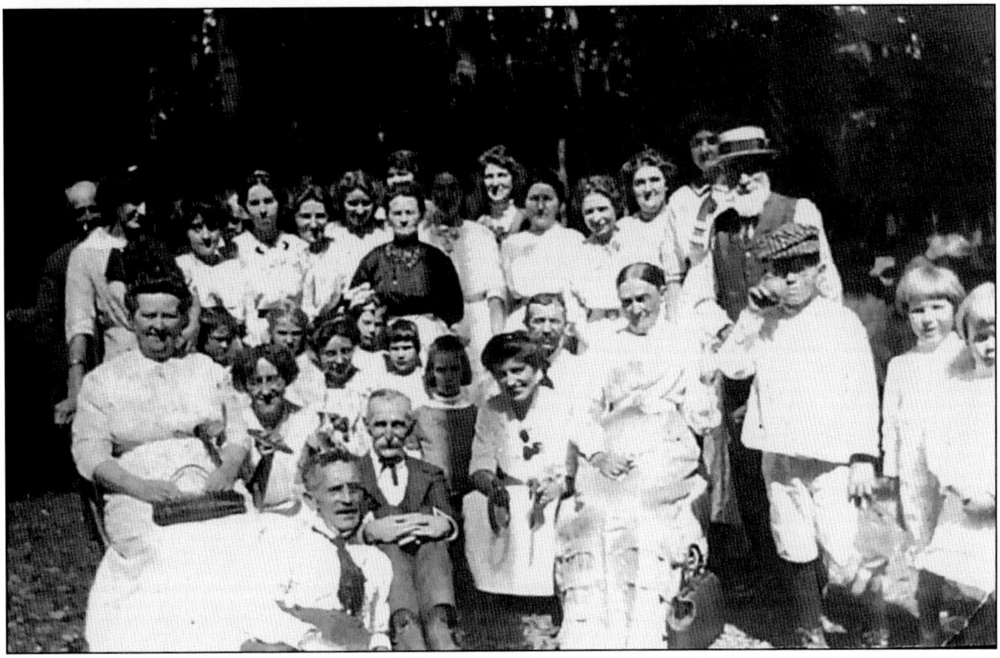

A Methodist church picnic is shown *c.* 1905. Many picnics were held in Lloyd's Grove, which was located where the old Fourth Street School now stands. (Courtesy of Virginia Elliott Speed.)

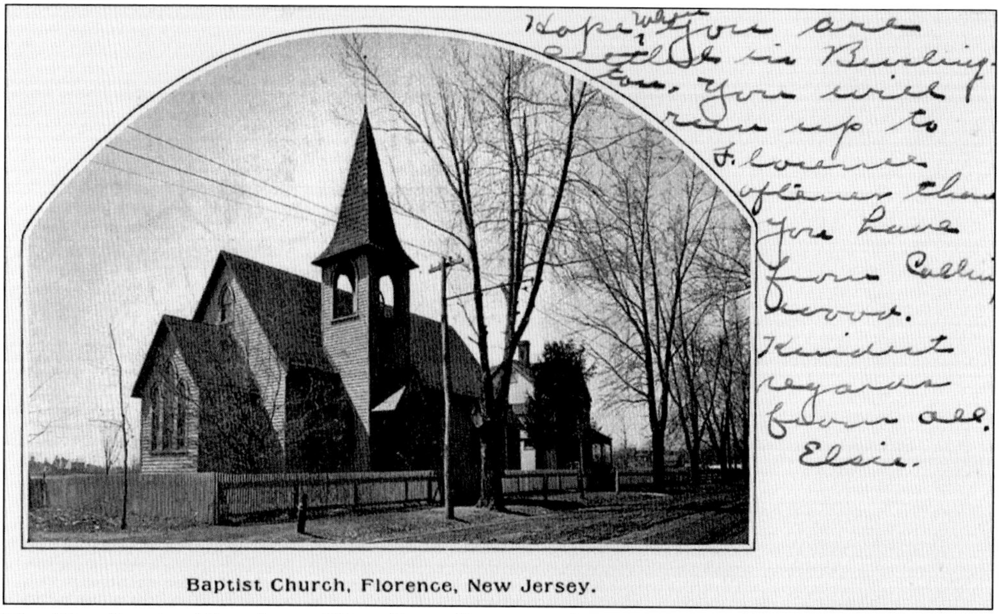

The First Baptist Church, on West Front Street, is shown in an early postcard dated 1903. Although the picket fence is gone, the building remains unchanged, as does the parsonage to the right. Erected in 1879, the property was donated by R.D. Wood for this Gothic structure. (Courtesy of Florence Historical Society.)

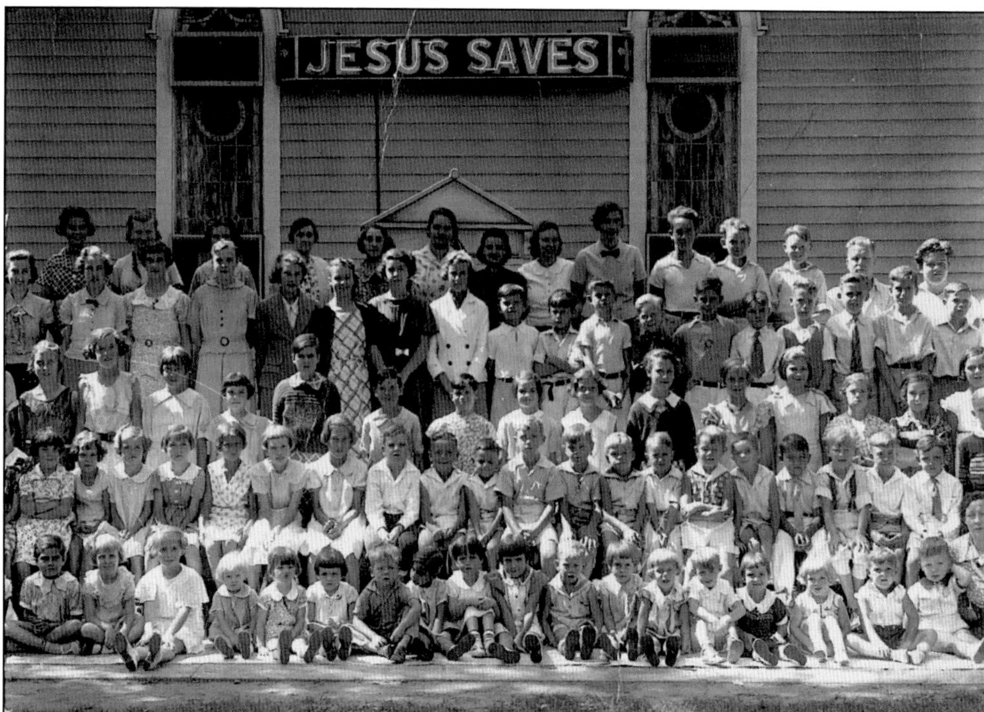

What appears to be the full membership of the Baptist Church is shown on West Front Street in the 1930s. This church was organized in 1875, and the building shown was erected in 1879 on property donated by R.D. Wood. (Courtesy of Florence Historical Society.)

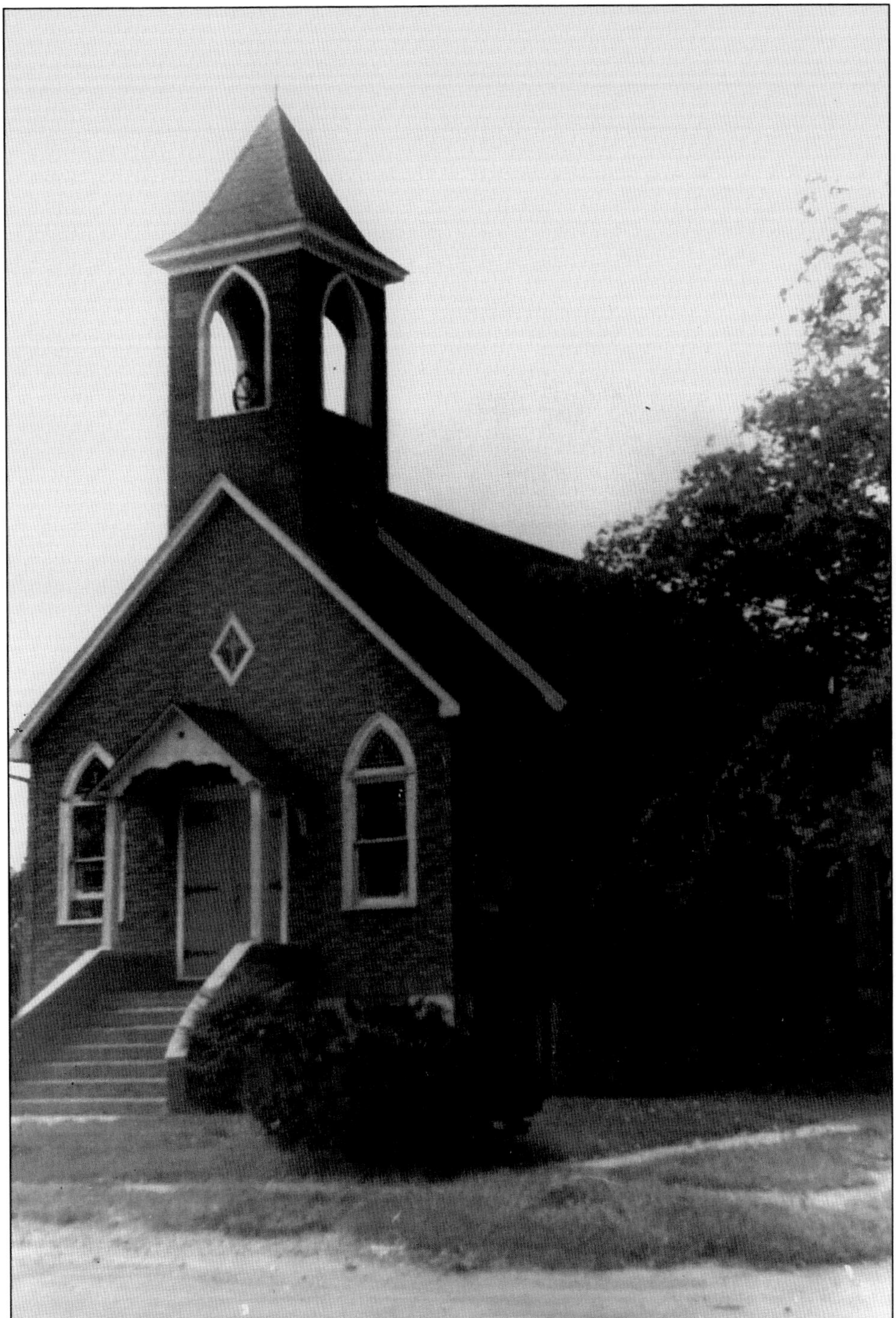

St. Paul Baptist Church is shown in a recent photograph. Built on land purchased from R.D. Wood, it is located at 5th and Eyre Streets. The building is largely unchanged, except for some fire damage that resulted in the door and steps, as well as the arched roof over the door, being removed. (Courtesy of Florence Historical Society.)

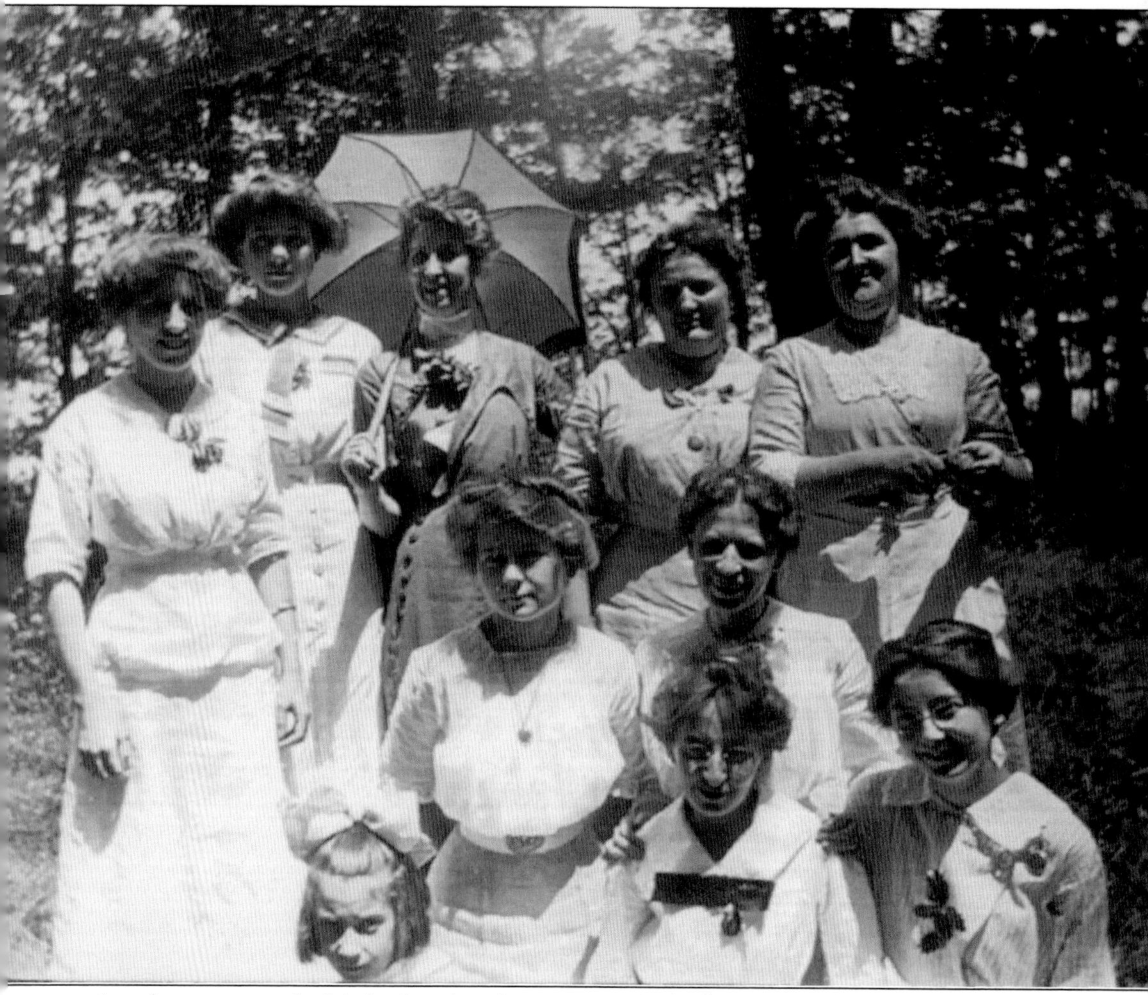

Another group at the Methodist church picnic in 1905 offers an excellent example of the upswept hairdo of the day and the Victorian jewelry and parasol. (Courtesy of Virginia Elliott Speed.)

Four

Business and Industry

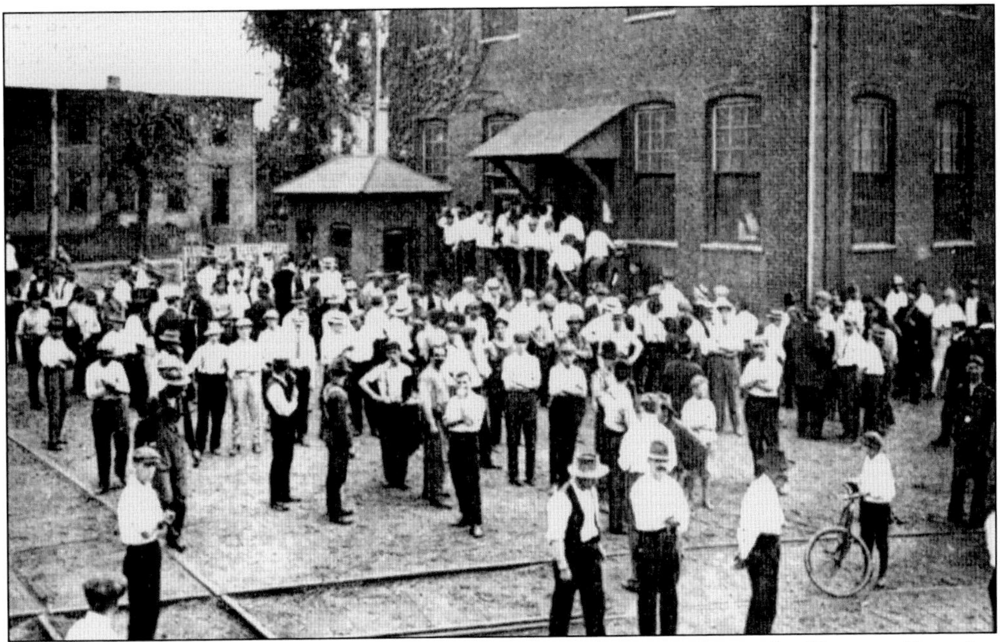

This postcard, printed by the Florence Foundry Store, shows payday at the Florence Foundry, when workmen dressed up in white shirts to pick up their wages on West Front Street in the early 1900s. (Courtesy of Florence Historical Society.)

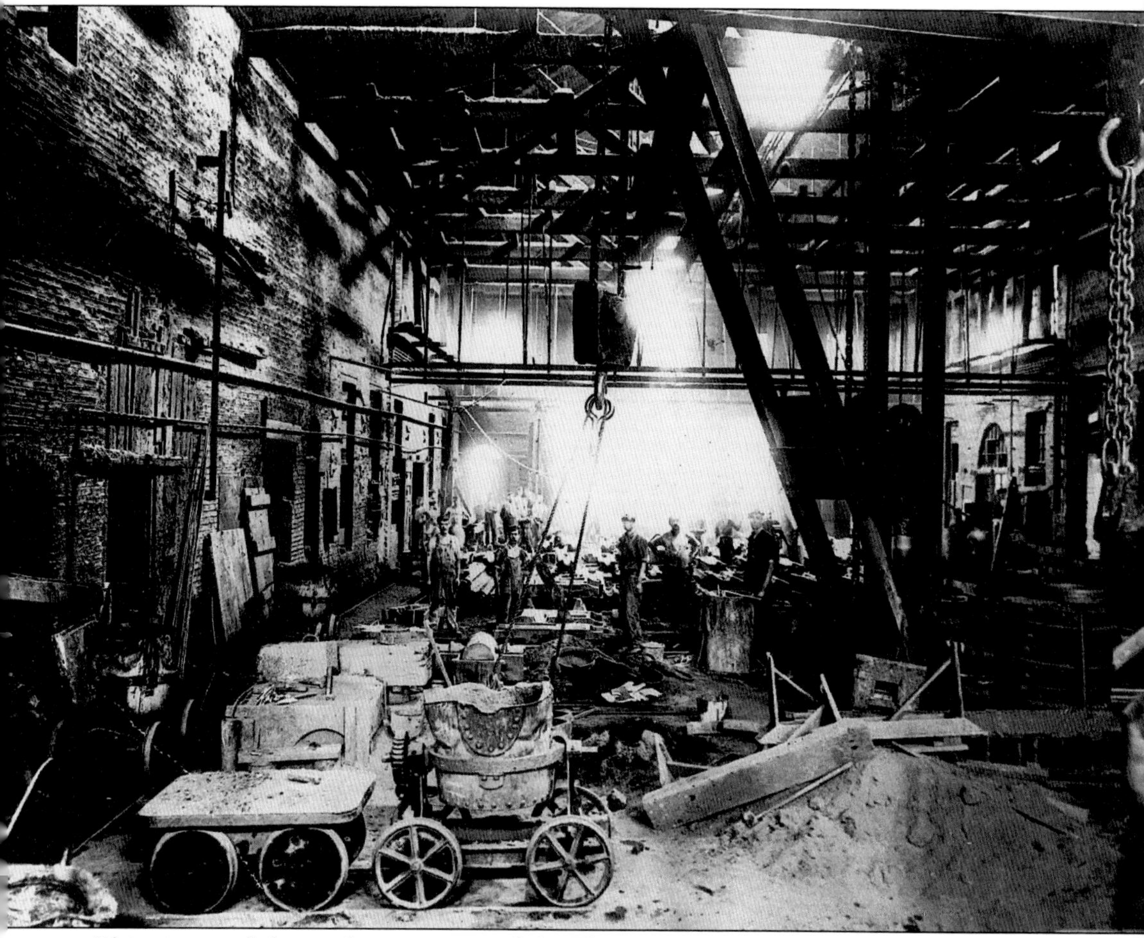

This picture of the sandspun section of the Florence Pipe Foundry and Machine Company shows a typical workday within the brick walls in the early 1900s. (Courtesy of Florence Historical Society.)

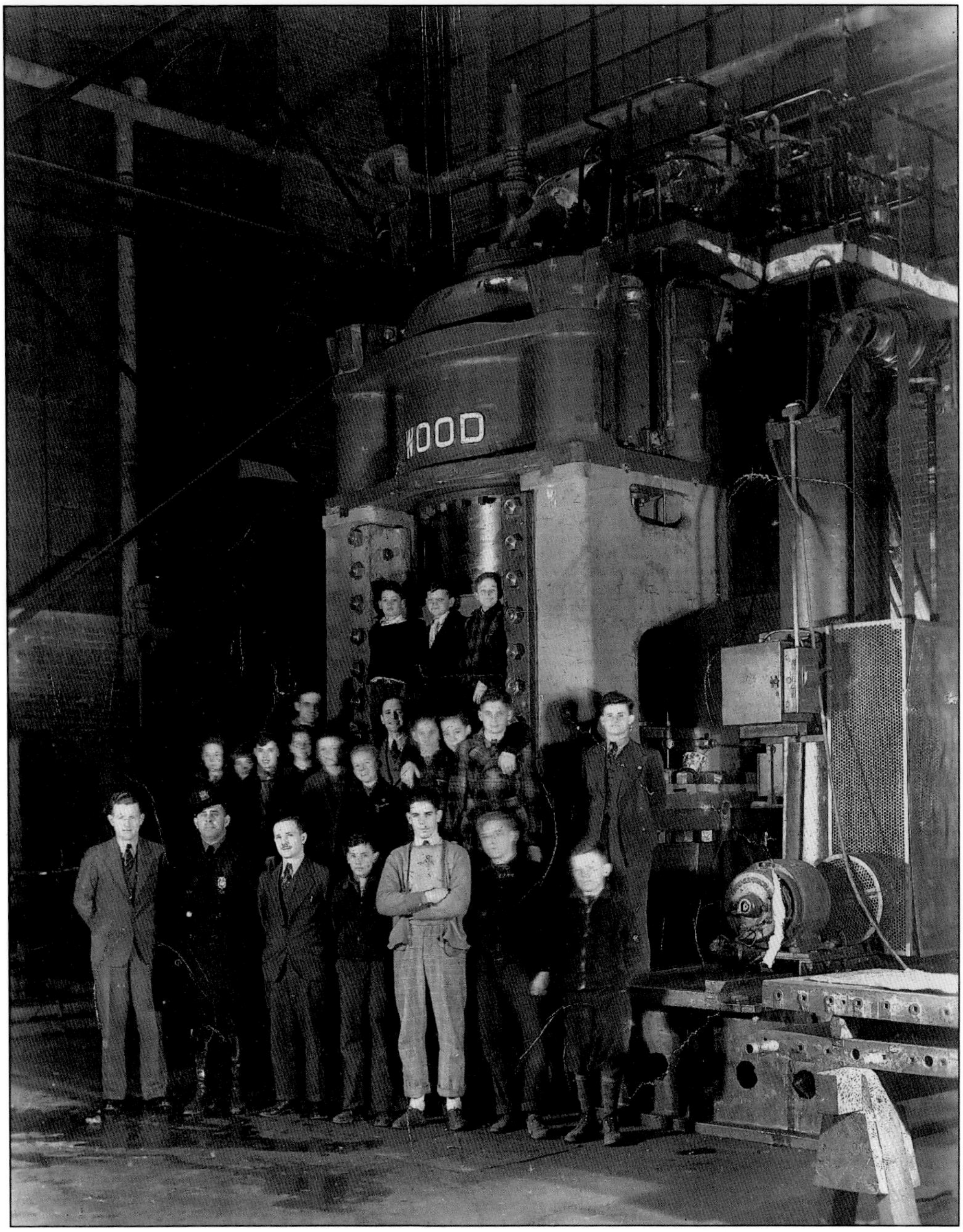

This group standing in front of an R.D. Wood turbine in the early 1930s appears to a Boy Scout troop touring the Florence Pipe Foundry and Machine Company. With the group is Arthur Foulks (left) of the police department. (Courtesy of Florence Historical Society.)

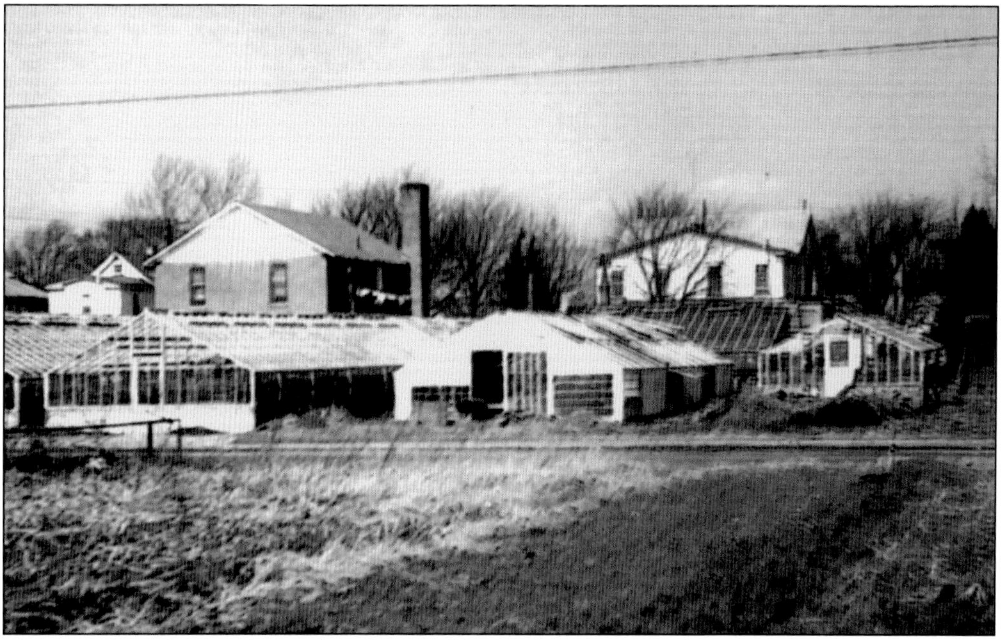

Florence Greenhouses, located in the 200 block of West 4th and Summer Streets, was owned and operated by the Panaro family from 1931 to the early 1960s. This picture was taken in the early 1950s from the south side of 4th Street. (Courtesy of Helen Panaro Henderson)

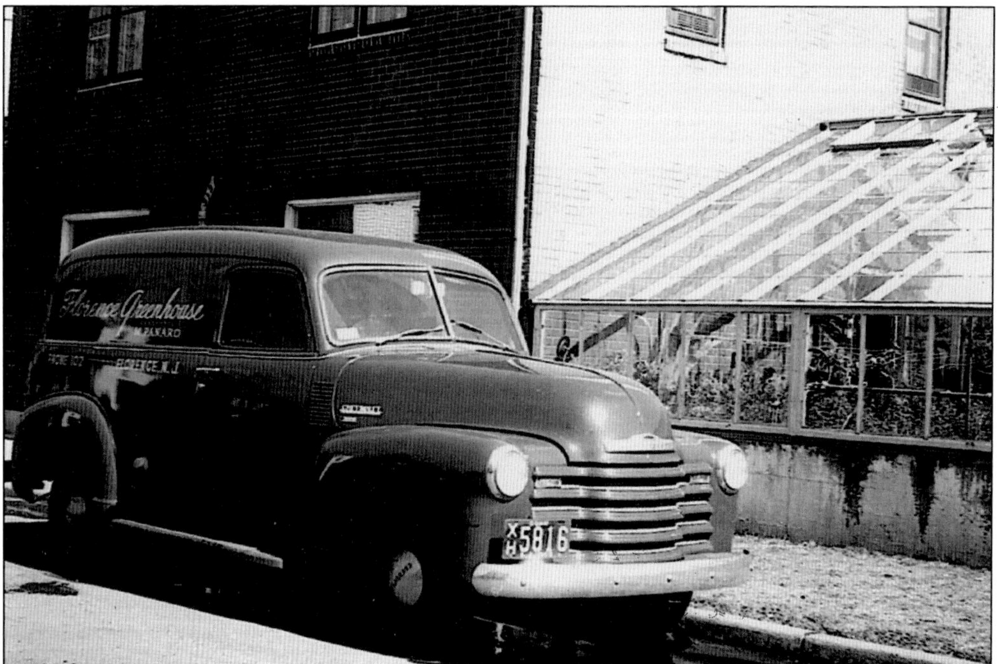

The Florence Greenhouse truck is parked on Summer Street in front of the showroom in the early 1950s. The large building to the left is now Joey's Deli and Catering; the greenhouses are gone. (Courtesy of Helen Panaro Henderson.)

Helen Panaro is pictured in 1941 inside the Florence Greenhouse in a profusion of chrysanthemums. The greenhouse was open seven days a week, day and night, with free delivery, run by the Michael Panaro family, including eight children. (Courtesy of Helen Panaro Henderson.)

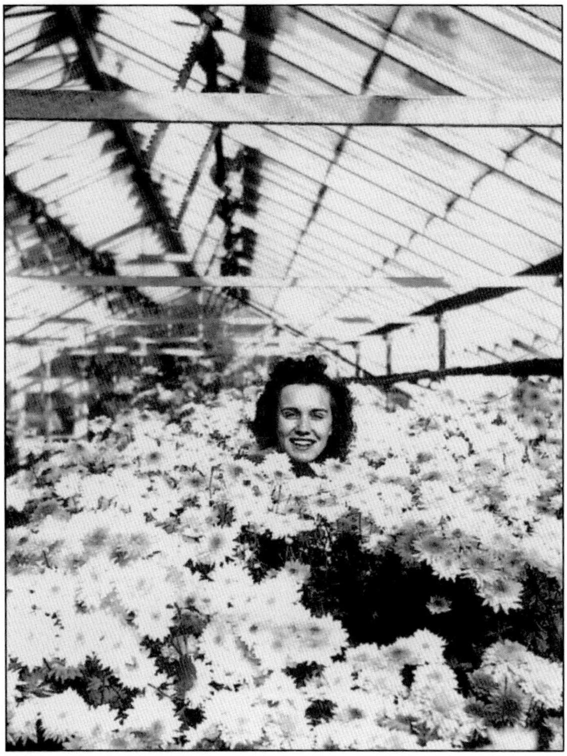

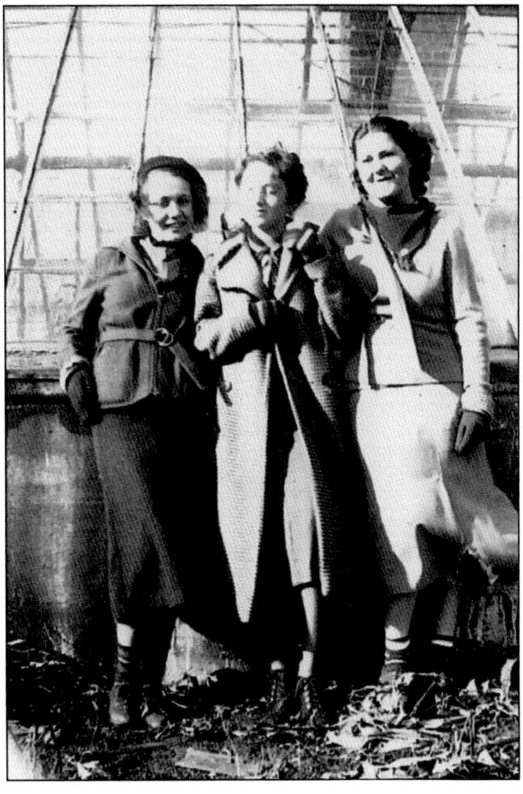

Dressed for the weather in front of the Florence Greenhouse in April 1938, from left to right, are Helen Panaro, Corinne Romano, and Mary Murphy. Panaro's father, Michael Panaro, was known as the "plant and tree doctor" of the area. (Courtesy of Helen Panaro Henderson.)

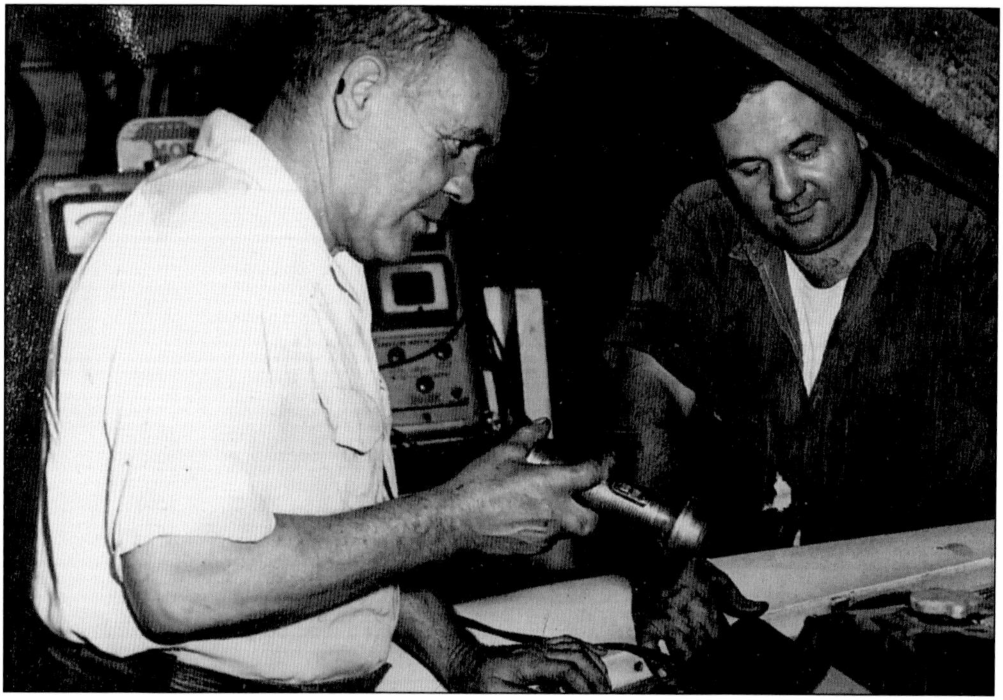

Sam Carlani (left) and his son Joe Carlani are shown working on an automobile at their garage on West 2nd Street in the 1940s. The garage was run by the Carlani family for some 50 years. (Courtesy of Florence Historical Society.)

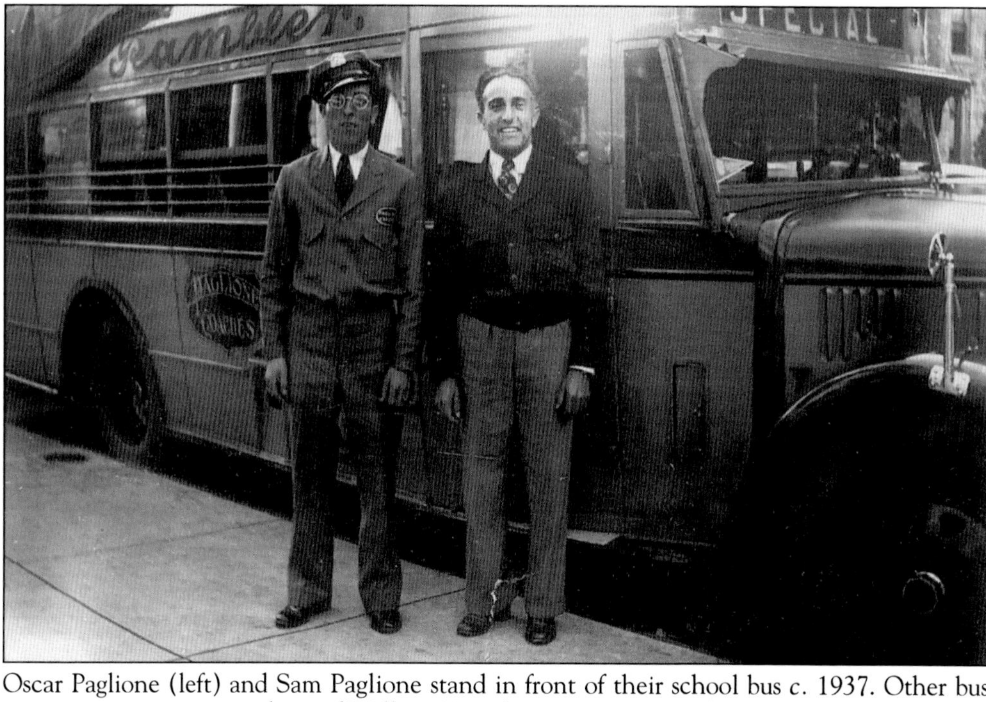

Oscar Paglione (left) and Sam Paglione stand in front of their school bus c. 1937. Other bus companies in town were those of William Hamilton, Mr. Carty, and Frank Peacock. (Courtesy of Florence Historical Society.)

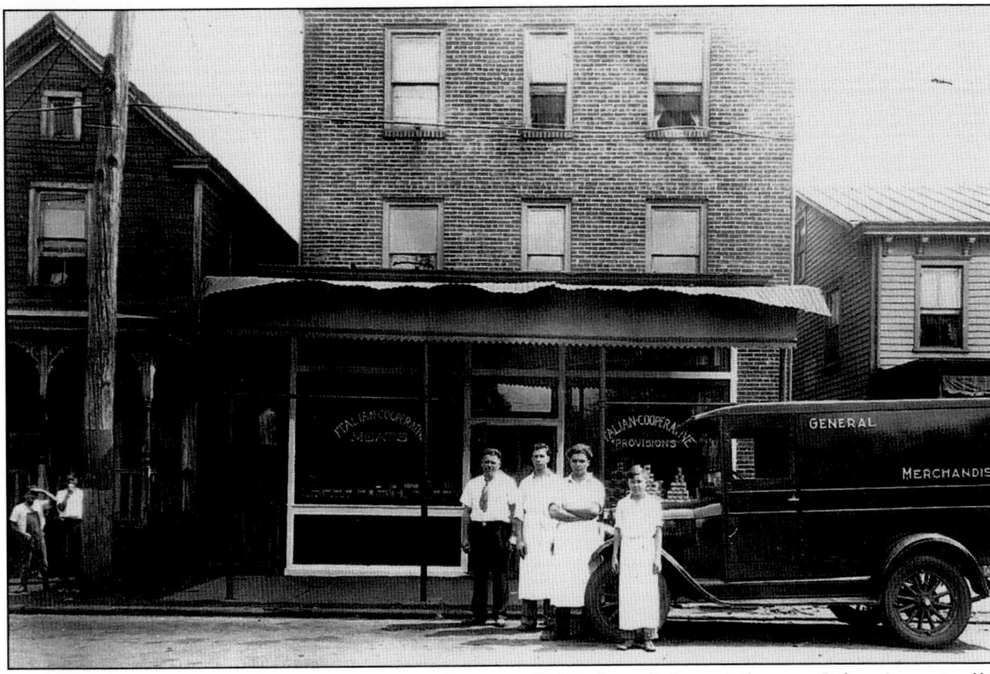

Standing outside the Italian Cooperative Store c. 1935, from left to right, are John Agostinelli, William Legnaioli, Primo Cesaretti, and Alex Cohets. Also shown is the store's modern panel truck, used for home deliveries. (Courtesy of John Williams and Mary Tapper.)

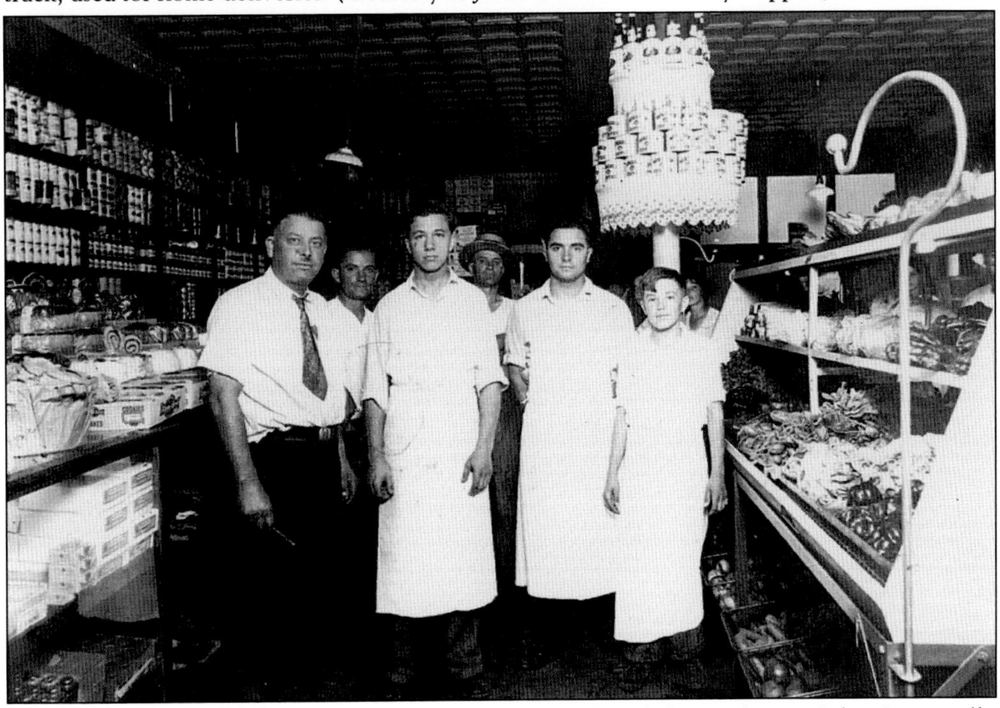

Standing inside the Italian Cooperative Store c. 1935, from left to right, are John Agostinelli, Nick Frappolli, William Legnaioli, P. Della Croce, Primo Cesaretti, and Alex Cohets. The store was located at 218 Foundry Street. (Courtesy of John Williams and Mary Tapper.)

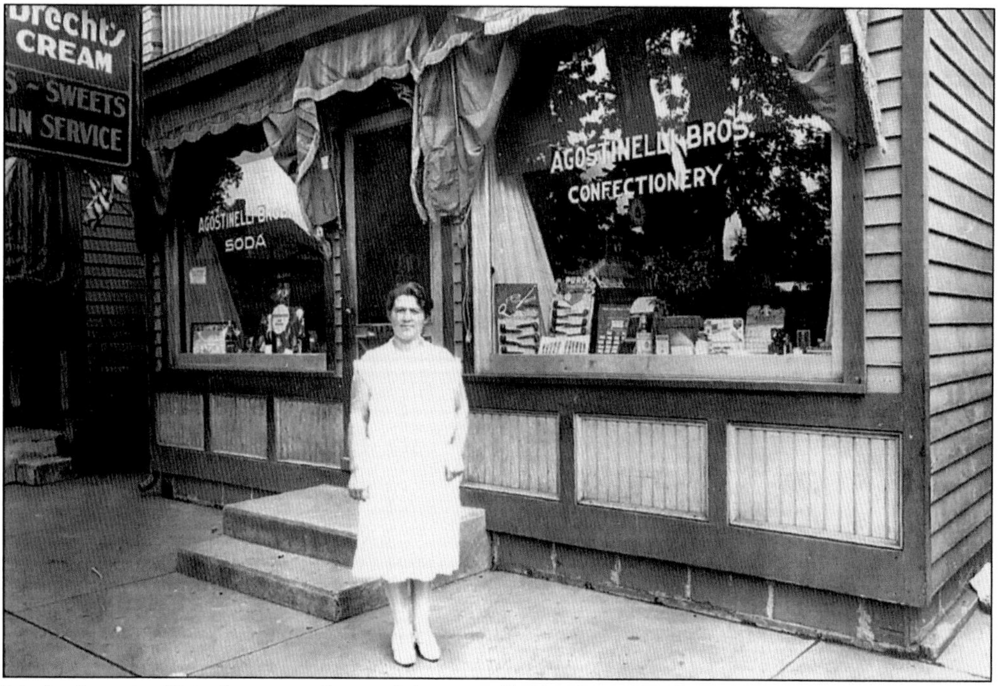

Linda Agostinelli is shown in front of Agostinelli Brothers Confectionery, on Foundry Street, *c.* 1930–1935. In November 1936, this ice-cream store became Agostinelli's Green Star Inn. (Courtesy of Mary Tapper.)

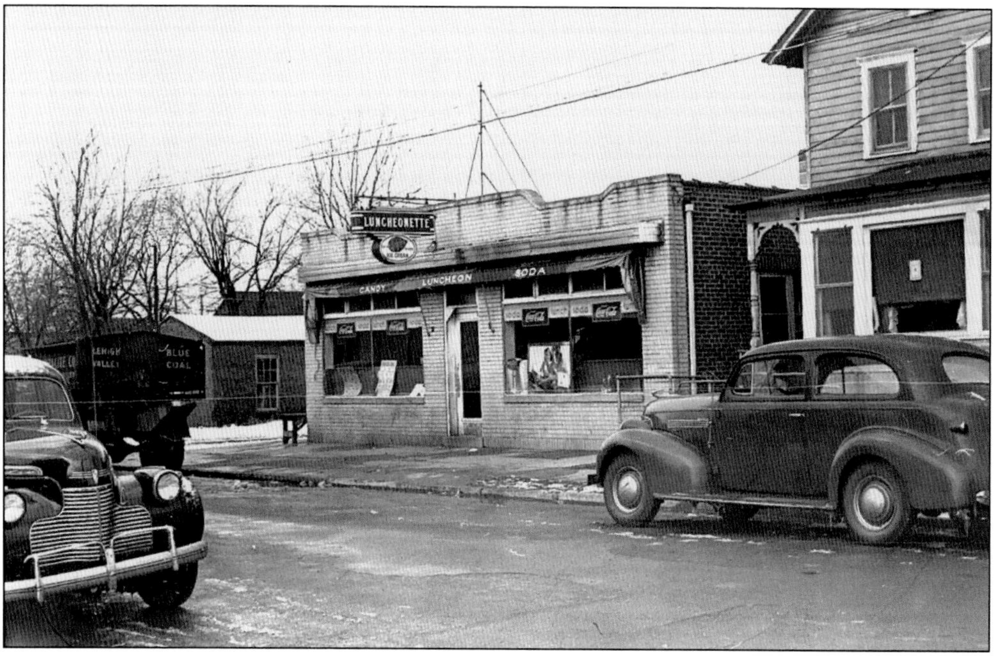

The inside of Jimmy Dinucci's Luncheonette is shown *c.* 1937. Adults would enter the luncheonette to buy hot dogs here for their waiting children to avoid exposing them to the poolroom adjoining this business, at West 2nd Street and Foundry Street. (Courtesy of Florence Historical Society.)

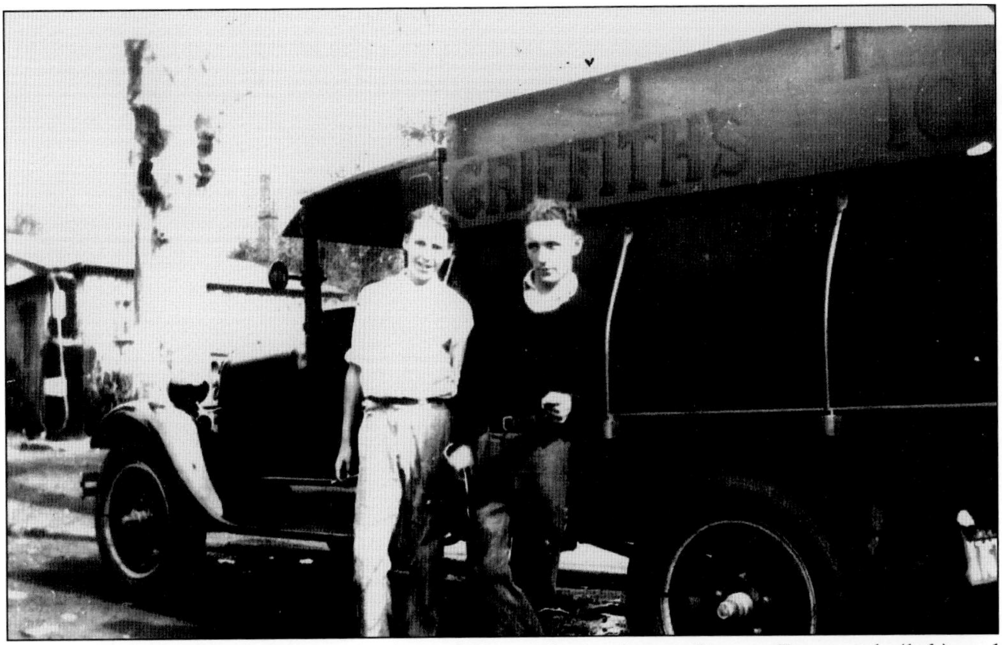

Griffith's Ice truck is shown in the late 1920s, with employees Francis Fitzpatrick (left) and William Cooper. The icehouse was on the alley between East 2nd and East 3rd Streets. (Courtesy of Donald Cooper.)

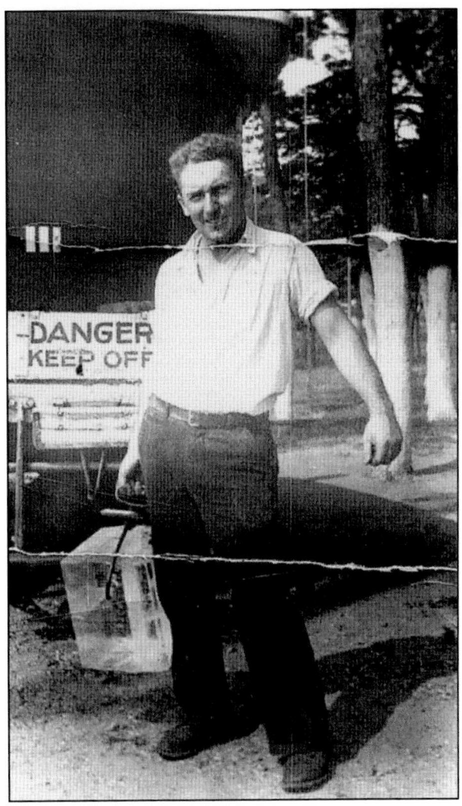

Joe Pasqualine is shown delivering ice from the back of Cooper's Ice truck in the late 1920s or early 1930s. This sight has not been seen in Florence since the 1930s, and the ice tongs are now a desirable item at antique stores. (Courtesy of Donald Cooper.)

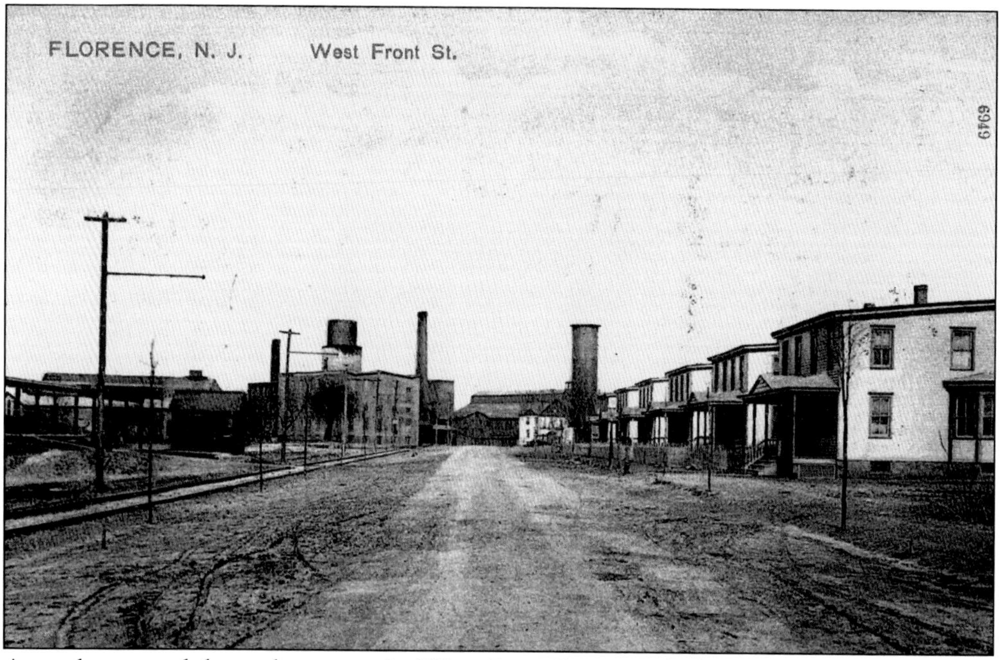

An early postcard shows the east end of West Front Street, with the foundry on the left, some early foundry houses on the right, and the trolley tracks on the left side of the street. These homes still stand, but the standpipe on the right has been demolished to make room for a city park. (Courtesy of Florence Historical Society.)

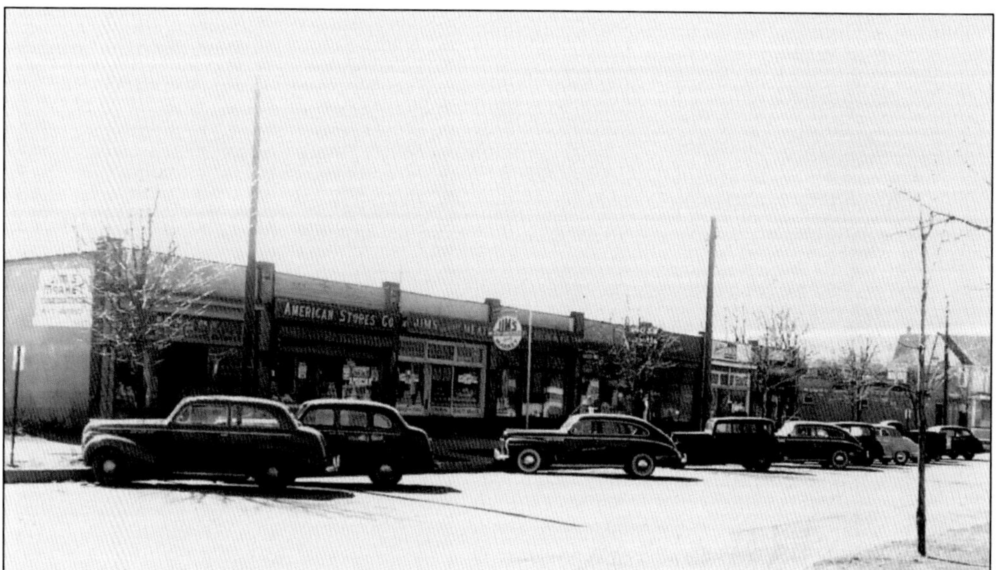

The row of stores in the 300 block of West Front Street is pictured in the early 1940s. Constructed by Israel Galanter of Burlington, it housed a post office, two grocery stores, a drugstore, a news shop, a 5 & 10, a bakery, and a meat market in 1937. (Courtesy of Florence Historical Society.)

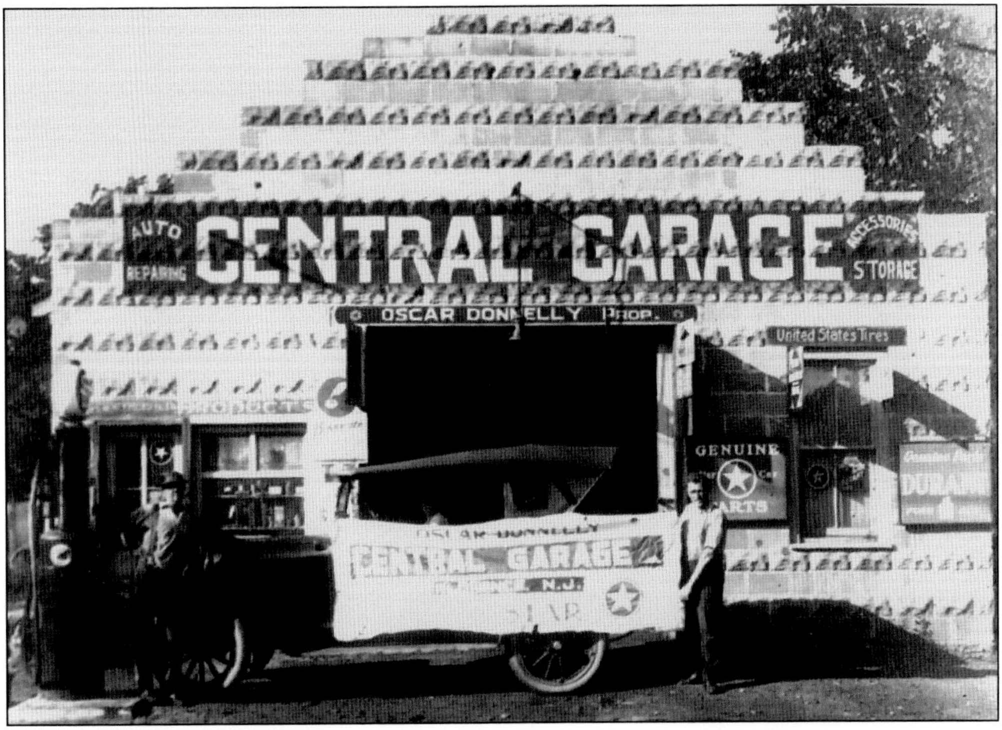

Central Garage, in the 300 block of West 2nd Street, was operated by Oscar Donnelly (left). This photograph also shows Ben Olden and a car, which dates the photograph to the early 1920s. Donnelly also sold the Durant Star automobile. (Courtesy of Don Cooper.)

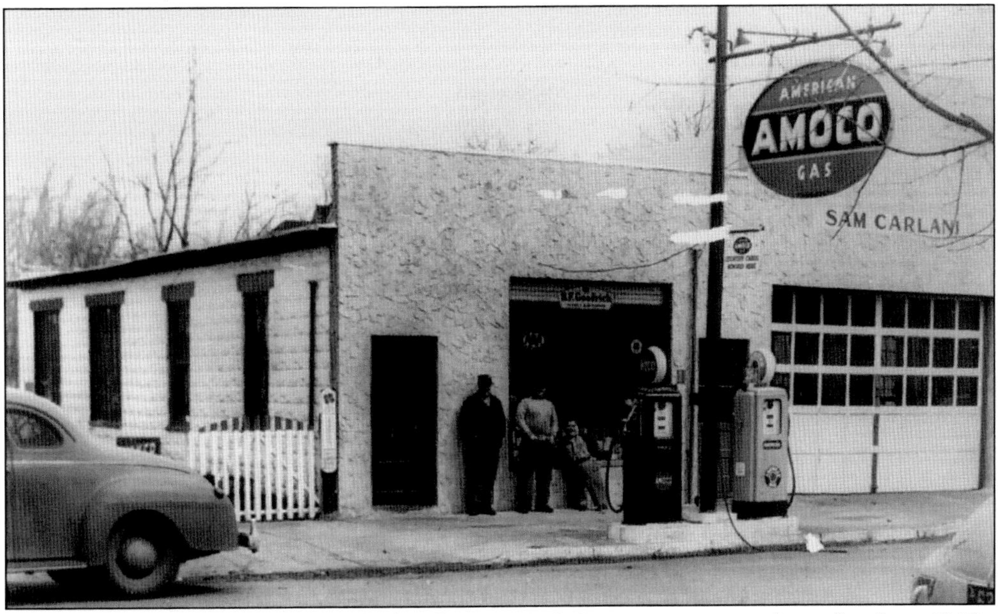

Carlani's Garage, in the 300 block of West 2nd Street, is pictured in the late 1940s. Standing in front, from left to right, are Sam Carlani, Joe Carlani, and Sam Picotti. This garage was formerly Central Garage. Today, it is in operation under new management. (Courtesy of Florence Historical Society.)

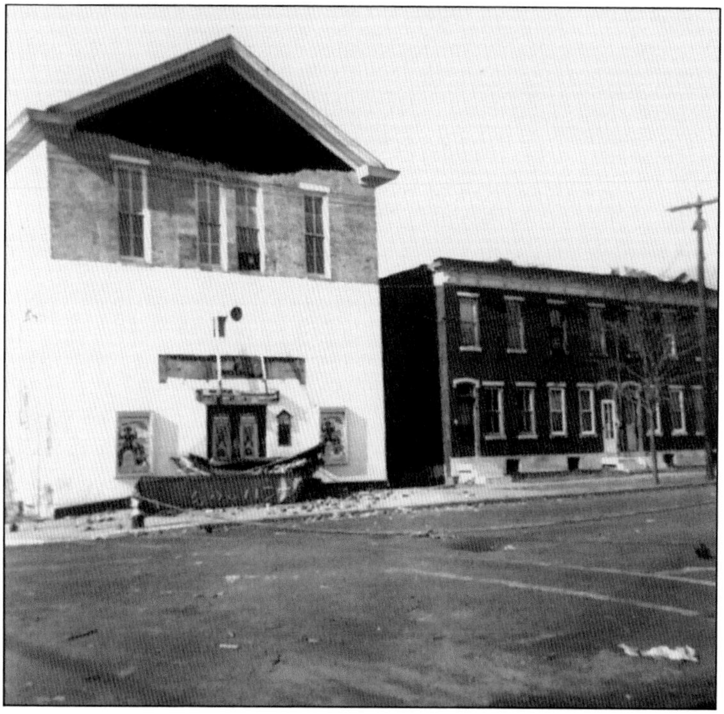

The Florence movie house was originally Redmens Hall, located at the northwest corner of West 3rd and Broad Streets. Originally three stories tall, it was renovated in 1936 to accommodate a dressmaking company from New York City. It is shown in 1951 after a hurricane tore down part of the building's facade. (Courtesy of Florence Historical Society.)

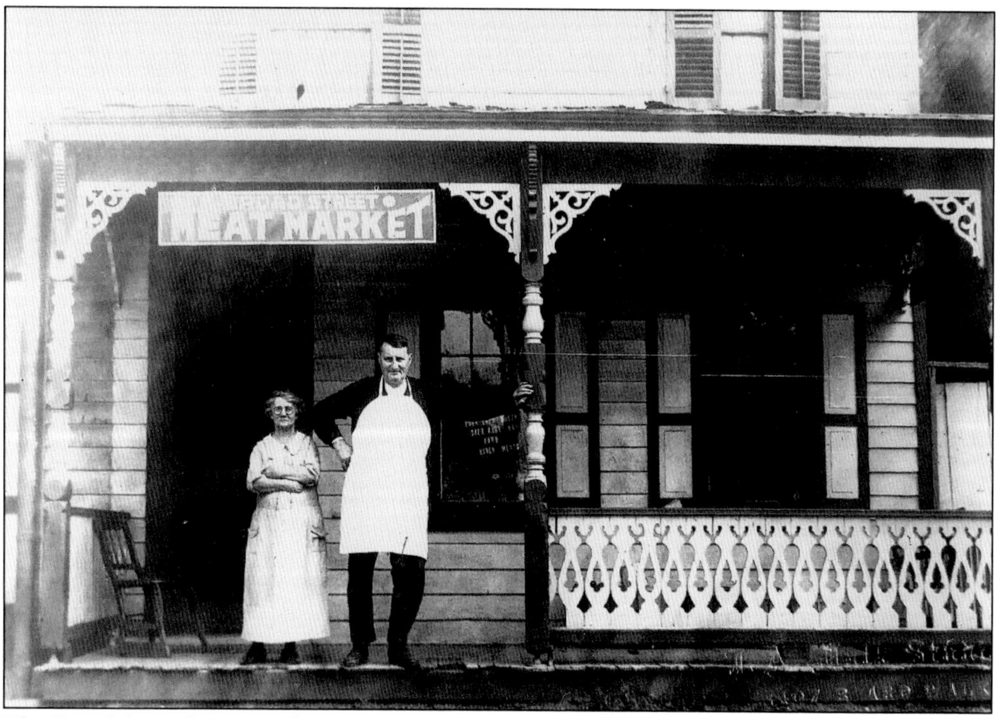

The Broad Street Meat Market is pictured in the early 1900s with the proprietors on the porch. This building, which burned down in the 1940s, was located on the southeast side of the first block of Broad Street, where Peoples Bank now stands. (Courtesy of Florence Historical Society.)

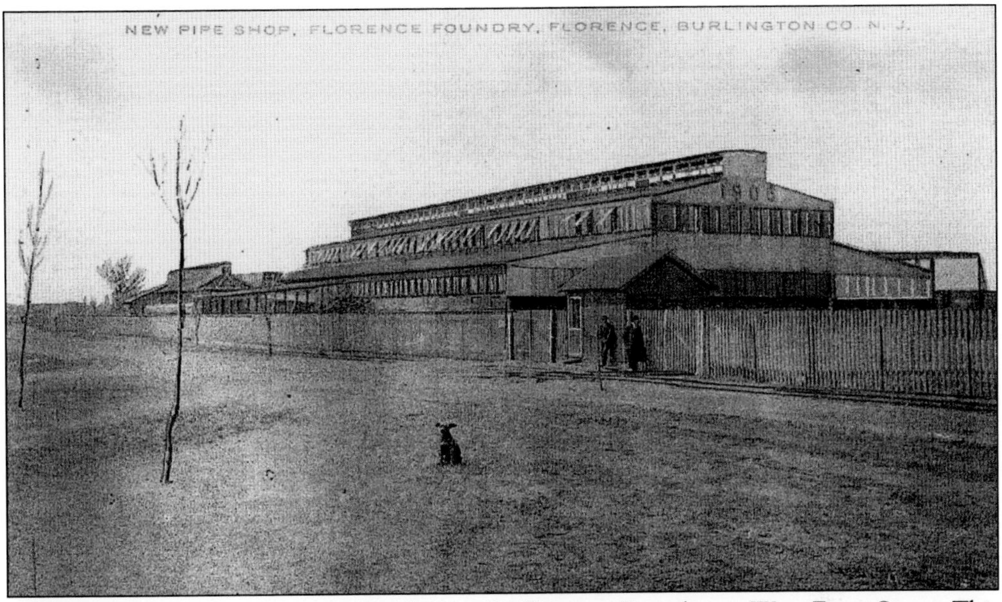

A 1906 postcard shows the new pipe shop at the Florence Foundry on West Front Street. This building still stands, but the picket fence has been replaced by chain link. The young saplings are now large sycamore trees. (Courtesy of George Miller.)

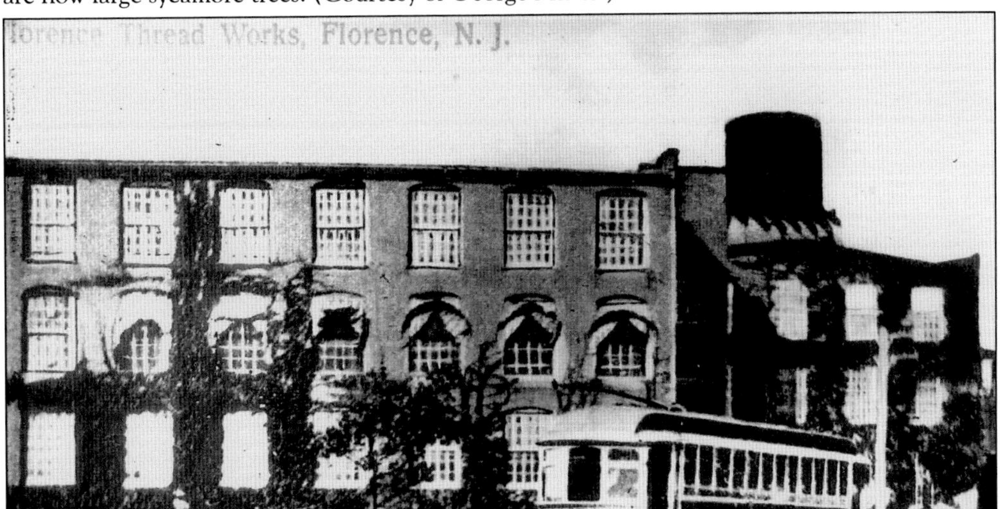

The Florence Thread Company, incorporated in 1894, was located on the north side of West Front Street, just around the bend and across from the standpipe, on the grounds of the Florence Iron Works. It employed 250 people and moved to Riverside in 1931. The Thacher and Sturtevant families were prominent in the operation of this business. (Courtesy of Florence Historical Society.)

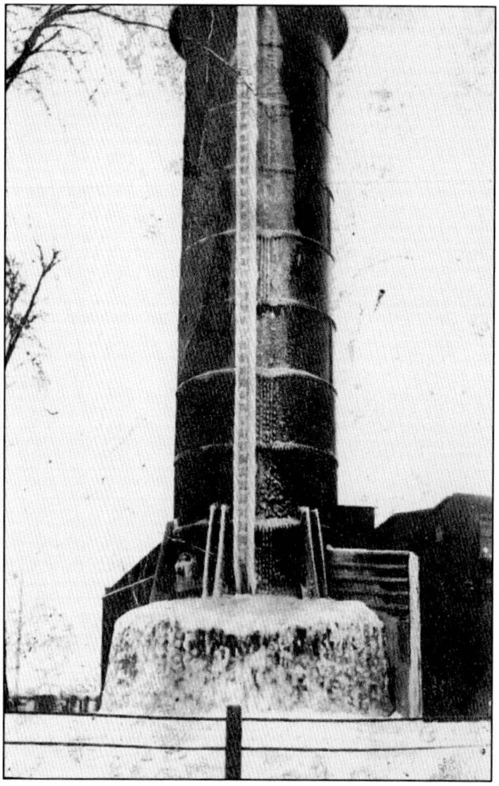

This standpipe was located at the corner of West Front and Union Streets. Boys would climb the pipe in the summer, throw a rope over the top, and then swim in the water to cool off. It was demolished to make way for a city park. (Courtesy of Florence Historical Society.)

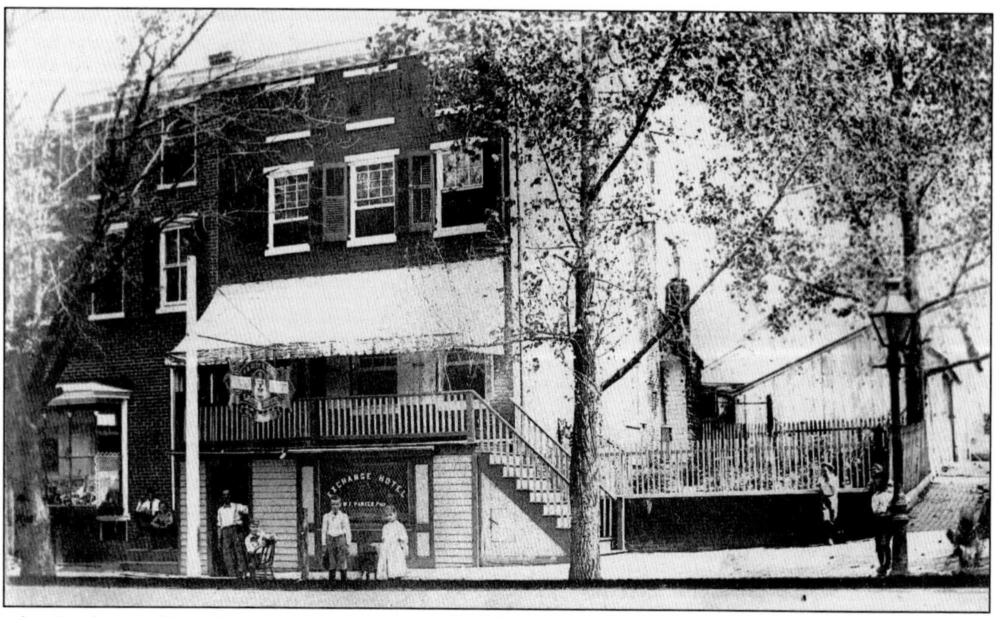

The Exchange Hotel, in the first block of Broad Street, is shown in the early 1900s. The hotel was managed by William F. Parker, who later opened the Parker House Hotel. The building still stands on the southeast side of the street, north of 2nd Street. The fence is gone and the vacant lot on the right is the site of many impromptu ball games. (Courtesy of Florence Historical Society.)

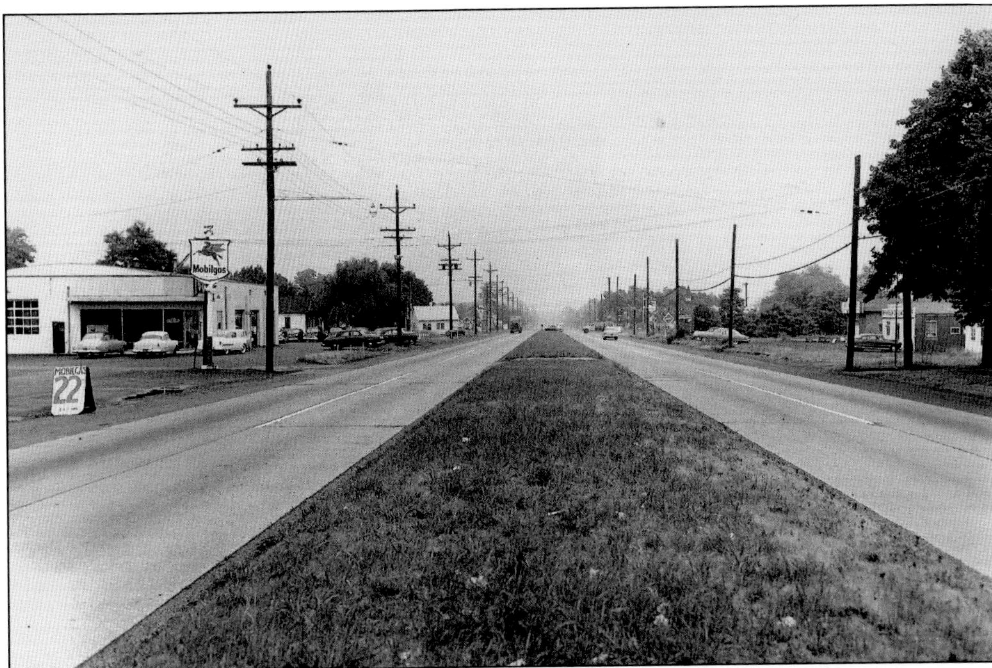

This *c.* 1955 view of Route 130 in Florence Station faces north. Wilson Chevrolet on the left. The building and showroom are largely unchanged in the business's current incarnation as Brandow Chevrolet. (Courtesy of Florence Historical Society.)

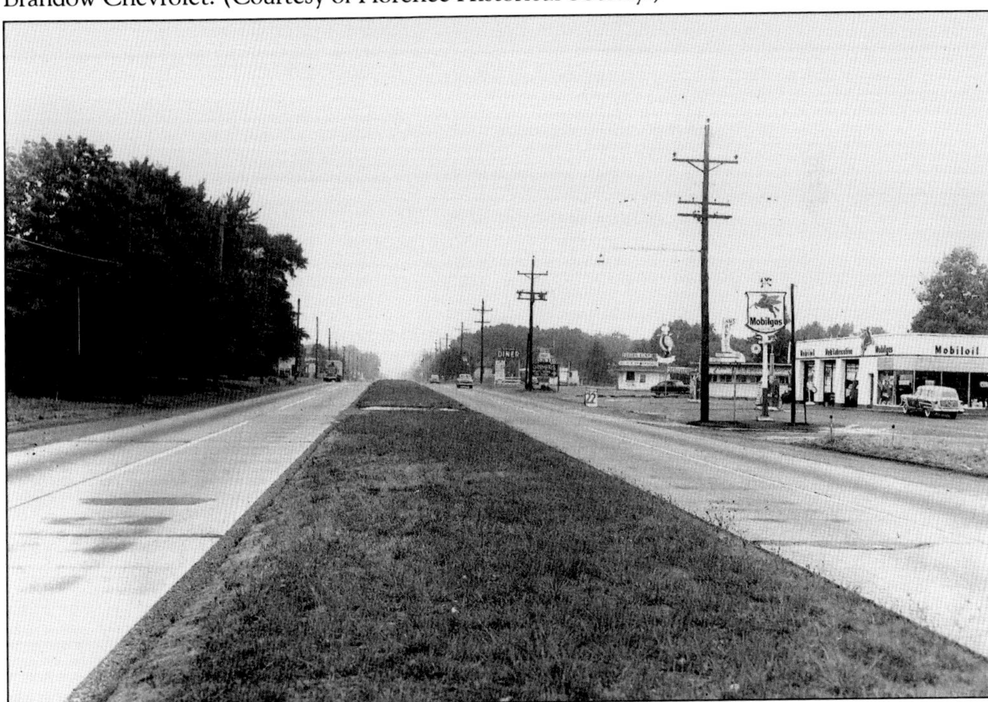

This *c.* 1955 view of Route 130 in Florence Station faces south, just past Wilson Chevrolet. Beside the Mobil station are Ben's BarBQue, now Mario and Frank's, and farther down, Florence Diner, now gone. (Courtesy of Florence Historical Society.)

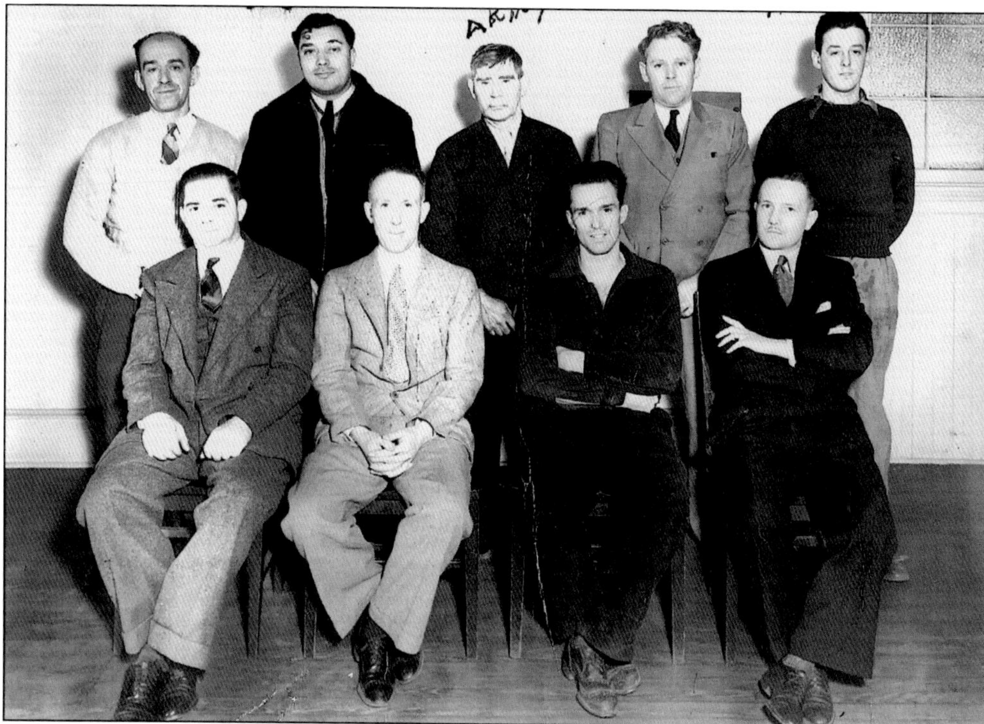

The Florence Pipe Foundry and Machine Company gave plant suggestion awards to these employees in 1941. From left to right are the following: (front row) Fred Danner, John MacKay, Craig Bodine, and Charles M. Stadvec; (back row) Elton Wilson, John Durham, Albert A. King Sr., E. Ridgway, and Frank Sweeney. (Courtesy of Albert L. King)

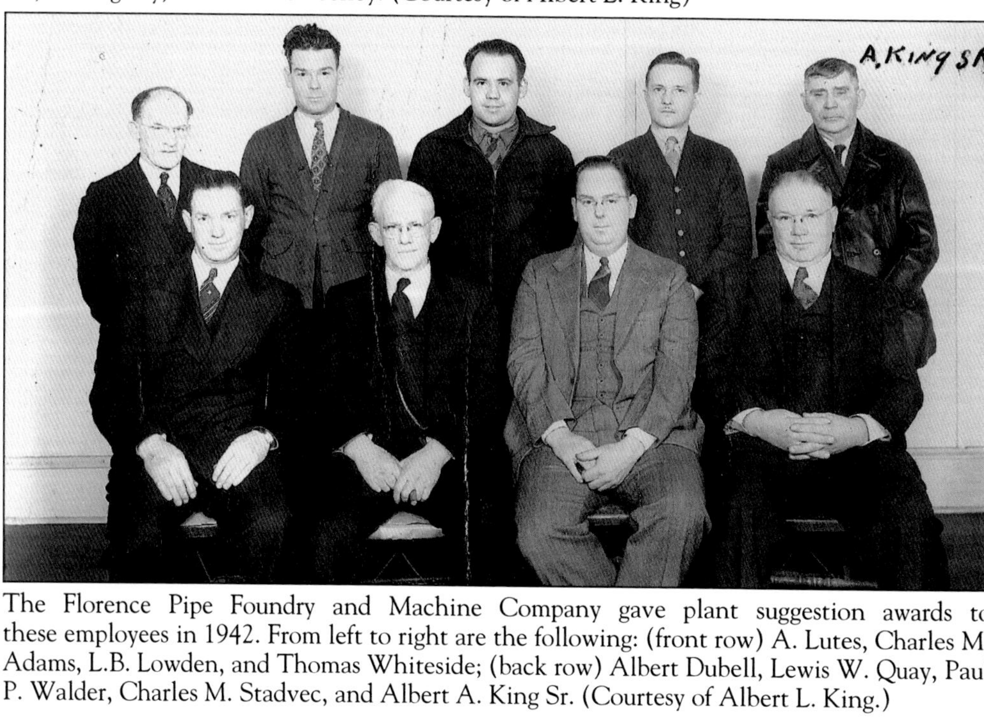

The Florence Pipe Foundry and Machine Company gave plant suggestion awards to these employees in 1942. From left to right are the following: (front row) A. Lutes, Charles M. Adams, L.B. Lowden, and Thomas Whiteside; (back row) Albert Dubell, Lewis W. Quay, Paul P. Walder, Charles M. Stadvec, and Albert A. King Sr. (Courtesy of Albert L. King.)

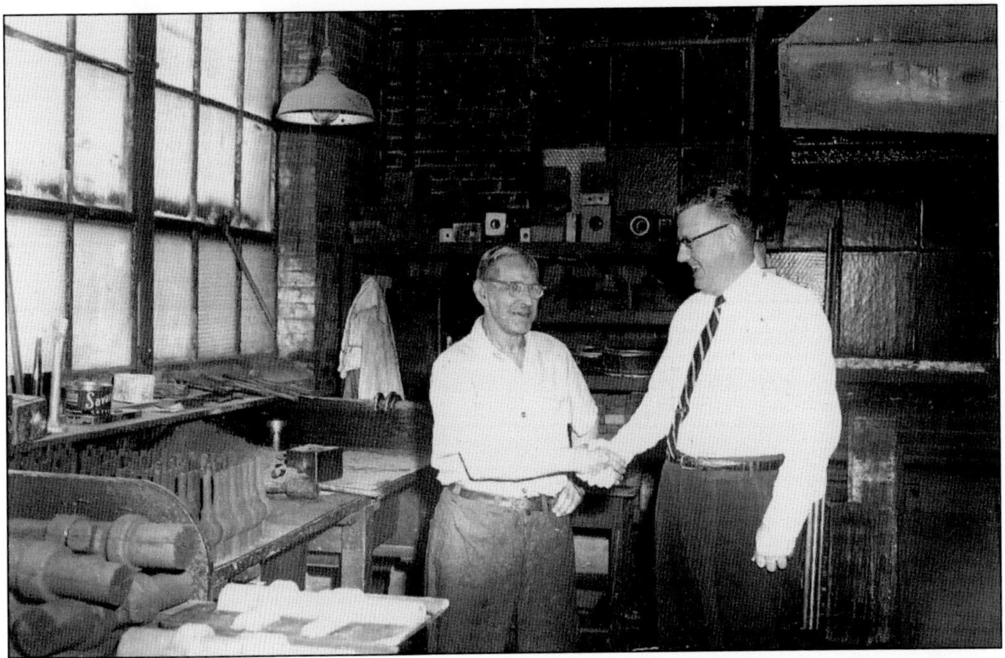

On his retirement day, John B. Bishop (left) is congratulated by plant foreman Warren Brown. Bishop worked at the brass foundry of the Florence Pipe Foundry and Machine Company for 63 years before retiring in June 1951. (Courtesy of Florence Historical Society.)

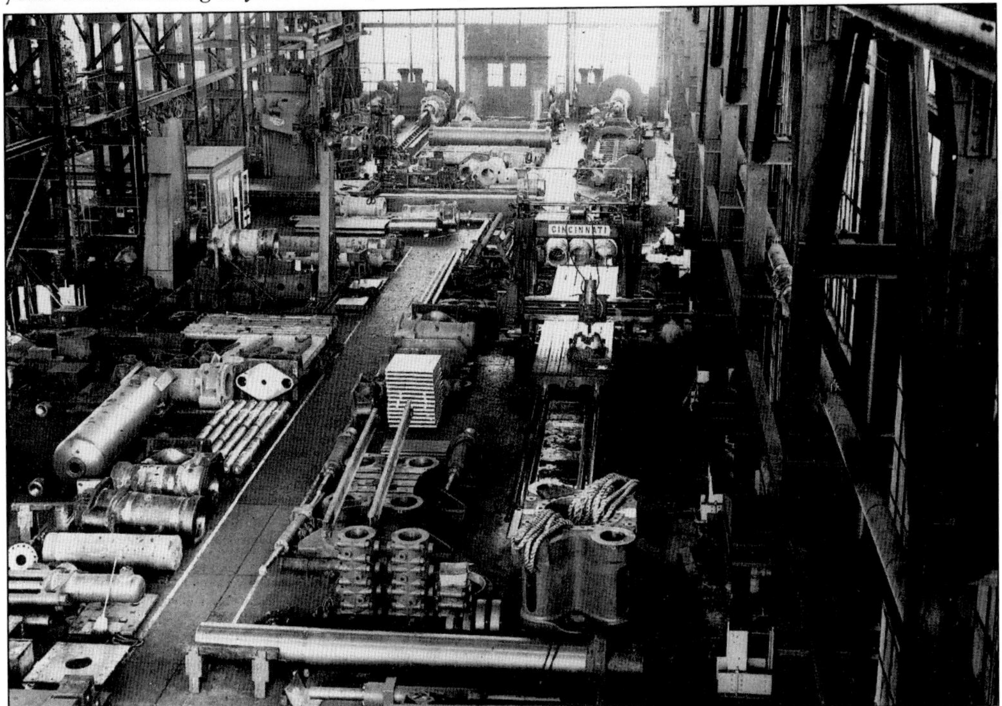

An overhead shot gives an idea of what was produced at the sandspun section of Florence Pipe Foundry and Machine Company. This photograph was taken in the mid-1930s. (Courtesy of Florence Historical Society.)

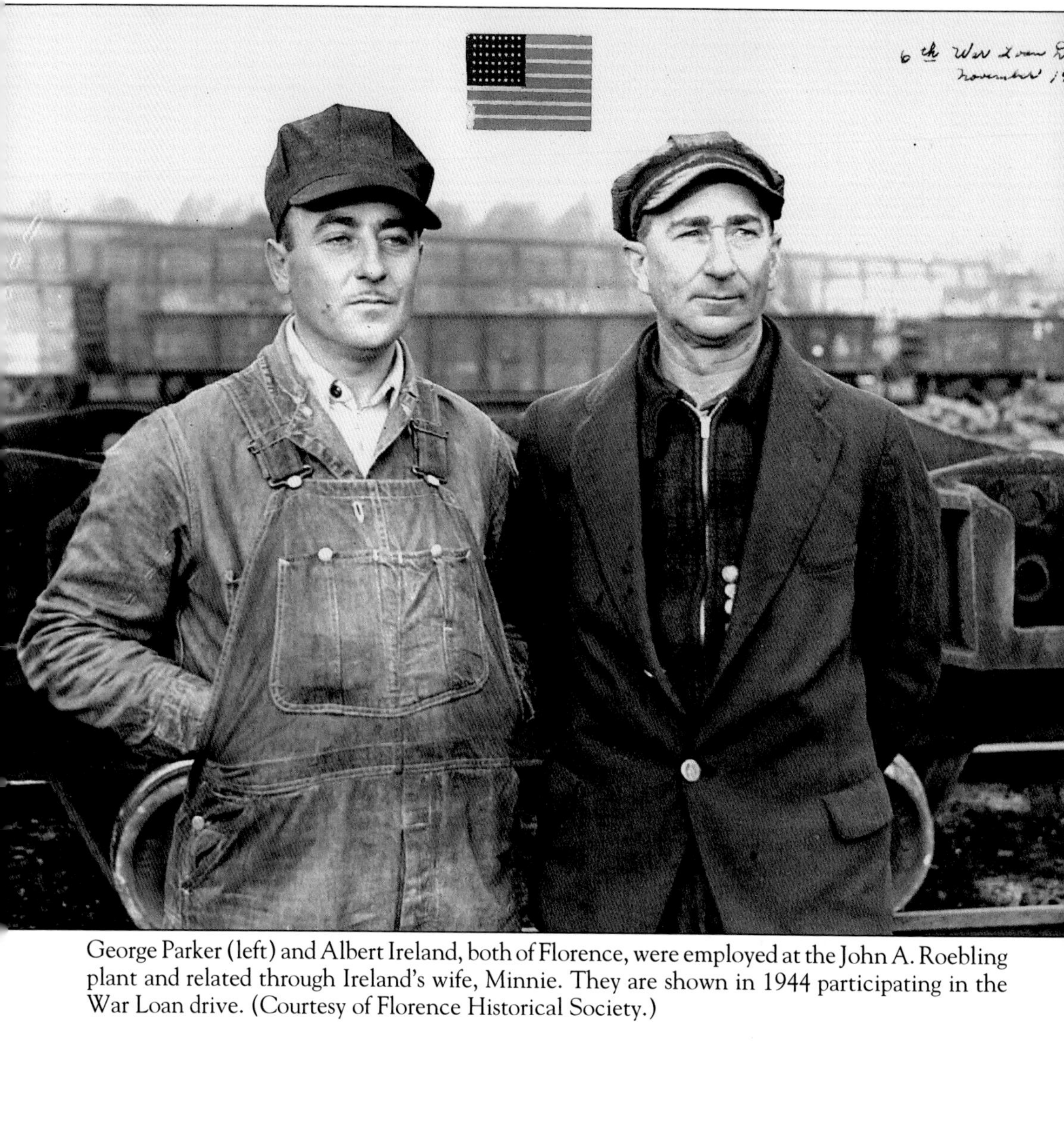

George Parker (left) and Albert Ireland, both of Florence, were employed at the John A. Roebling plant and related through Ireland's wife, Minnie. They are shown in 1944 participating in the War Loan drive. (Courtesy of Florence Historical Society.)

William F. Thacher was a prominent citizen of Florence. A volunteer in the 16th Pennsylvania Cavalry during the Civil War, he was struck by a minie ball and underwent amputation of his arm as a result. He served as superintendent of the Florence Thread Company beginning in 1874 and was manager of the Florence Iron Works for 34 years until his death in 1908. (Courtesy of Florence Historical Society.)

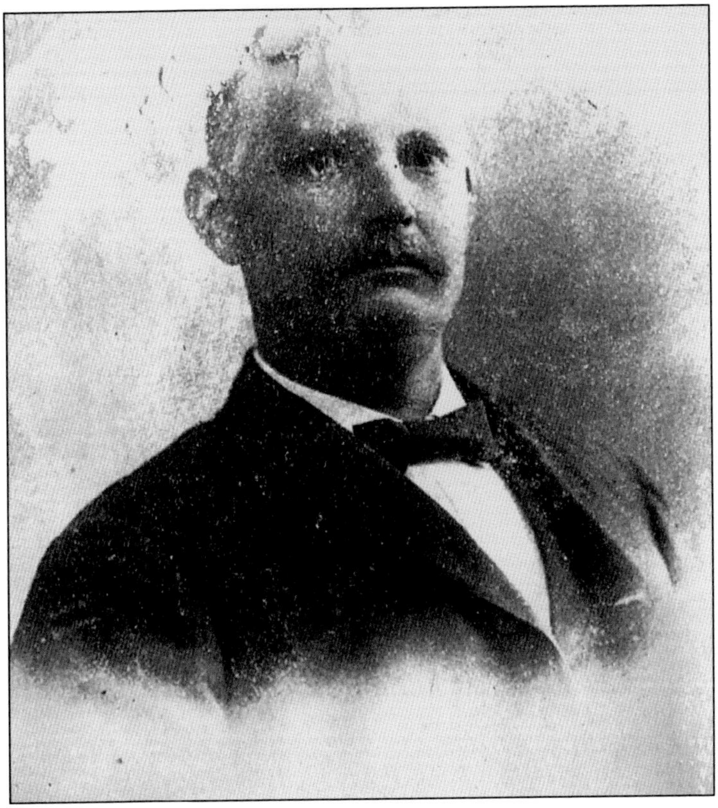

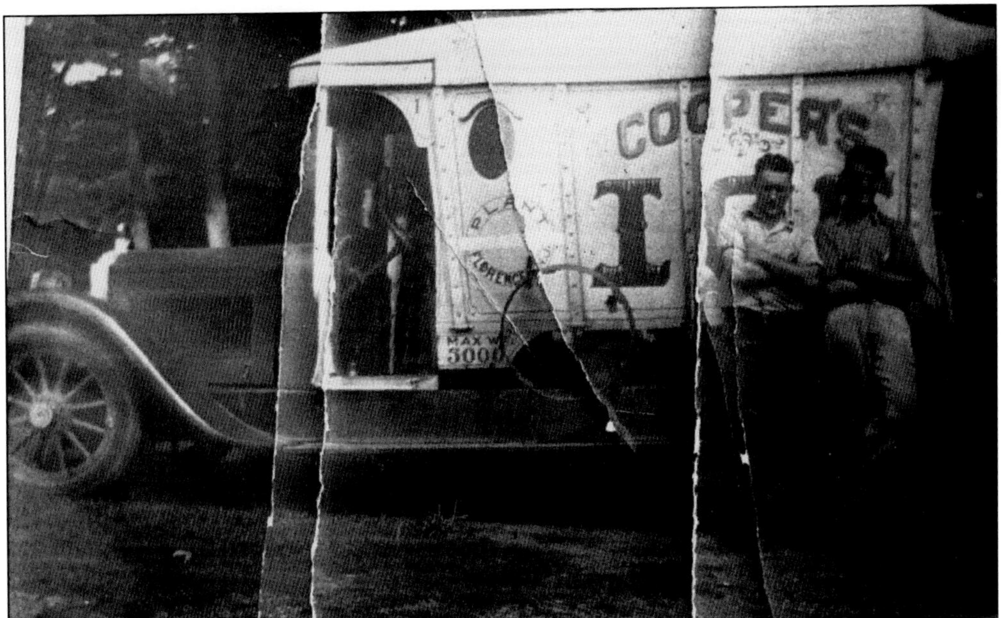

Another familiar ice truck in 1925 was the Cooper's Ice truck. Shown are Joe Pasqualine (left) and William Cooper. (Courtesy of Don Cooper.)

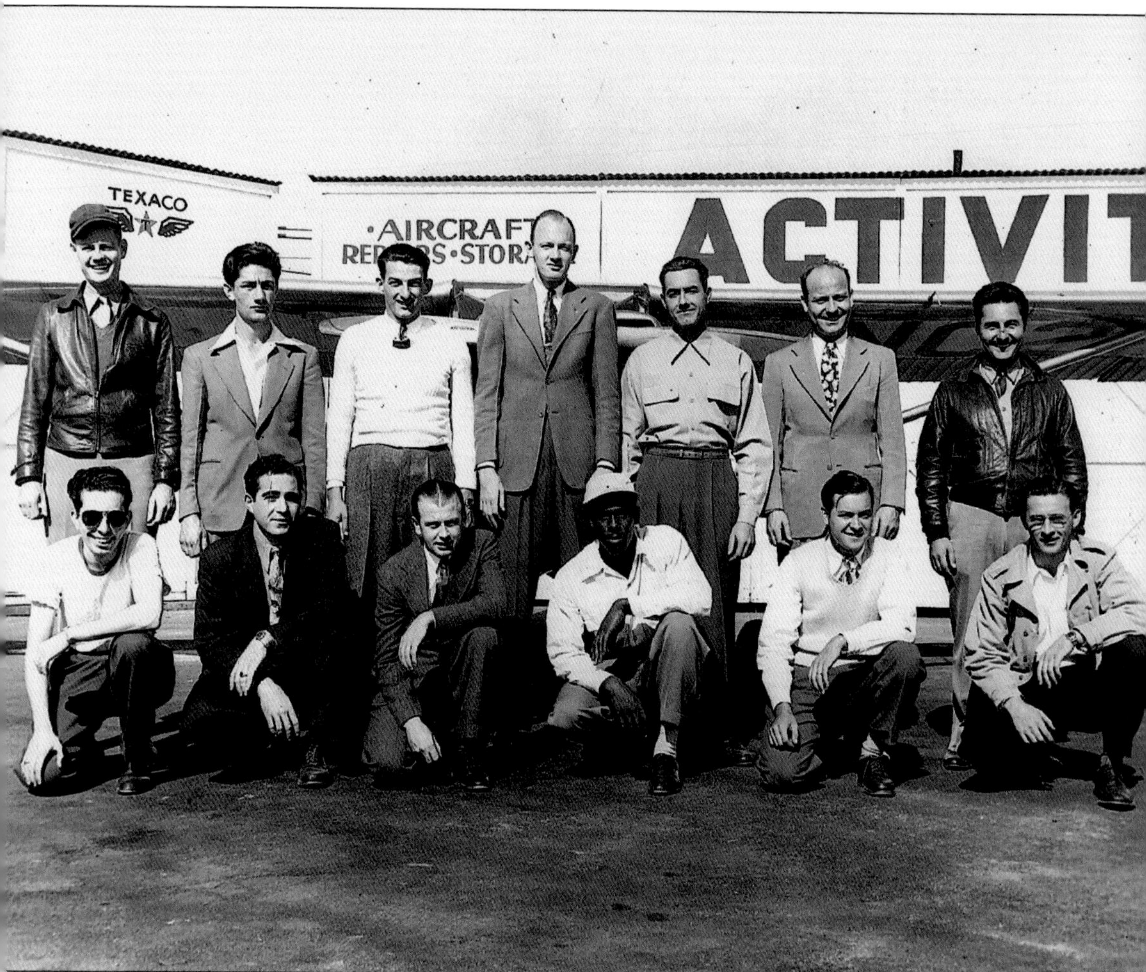

A group gathers at the Florence Airport, located on Olive Street and running south to the railroad track. In this July 1947 photograph, from left to right, are the following: (front row) Alex Simonka, William Capritti, Frank Walters, unidentified, Alvin Panaro, and ? Monahan; (back row) t are unidentified, Tony Angelini, Frank Rainier, Robert Wilkie, Bob Ekelburg, William Parker, and unidentified. (Courtesy of Alvin Panaro.)

Five

Monuments and Celebrations

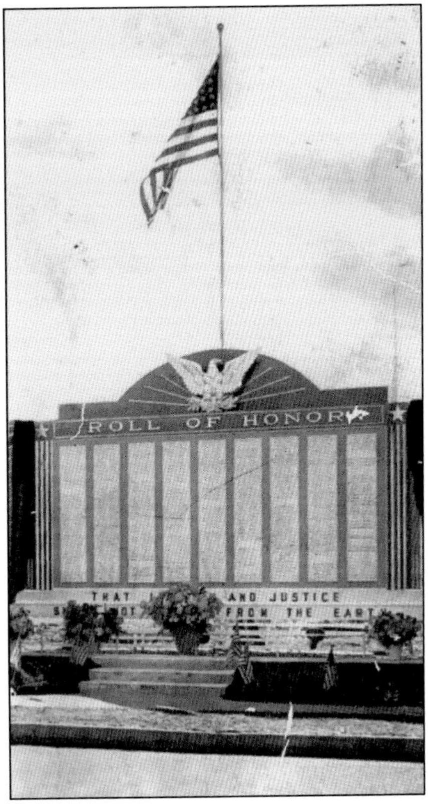

The Roll of Honor was erected on the first block of West Front Street on November 25, 1943, to memorialize Florence residents who served in World War II. The monument was blown down during a windstorm in the 1950s, and the lot next to the shoemaker shop of Attilio Addari stood vacant for years. (Original woodblock courtesy of Harry and Eleanor Sullivan; print courtesy of Evelyn Talpas.)

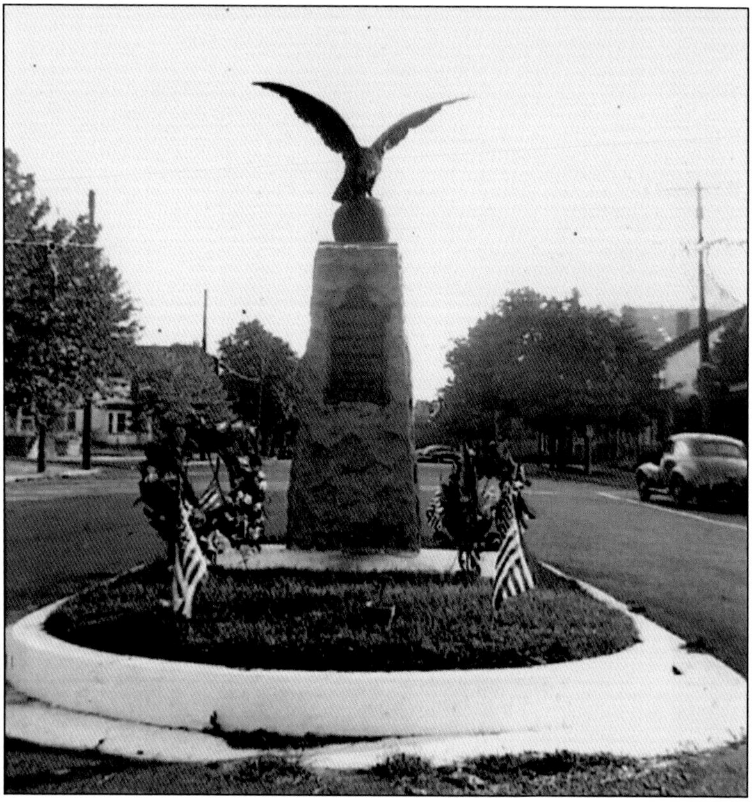

The Golden Eagle monument, erected on October 1, 1927, memorialized those from Florence who served in World War I. Located at the intersection of Front and Broad Streets, the monument was damaged in 2002, repaired, and reset in the same spot. This view date from c. 1947. (Courtesy of Florence Historical Society.)

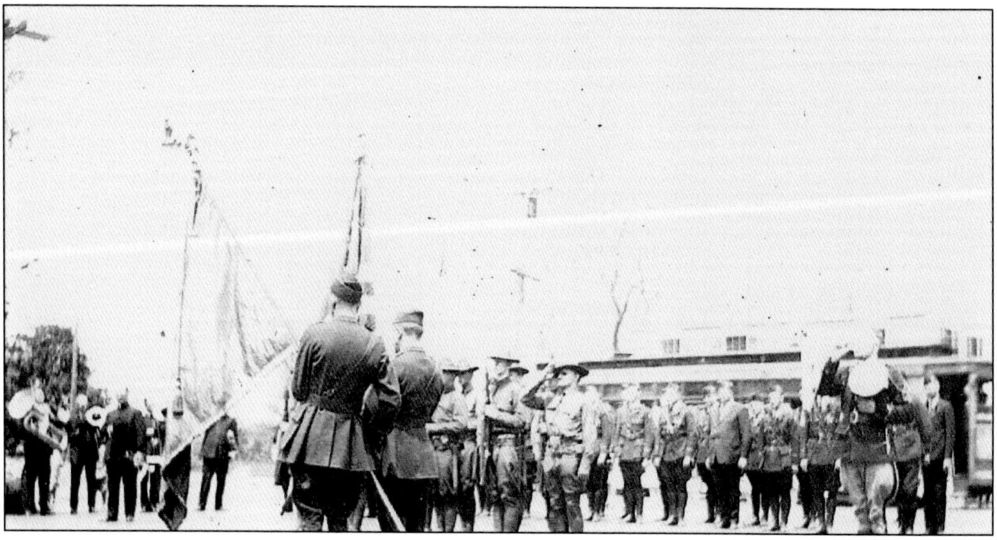

Armistice Day in 1918 was celebrated in Florence with a parade, for which soldiers assembled soldiers at the intersection of Front and Broad Streets. The banner flies near the Acme store, now long gone. This was also a trolley stop, as seen in the background along the river (Courtesy of Florence Historical Society.)

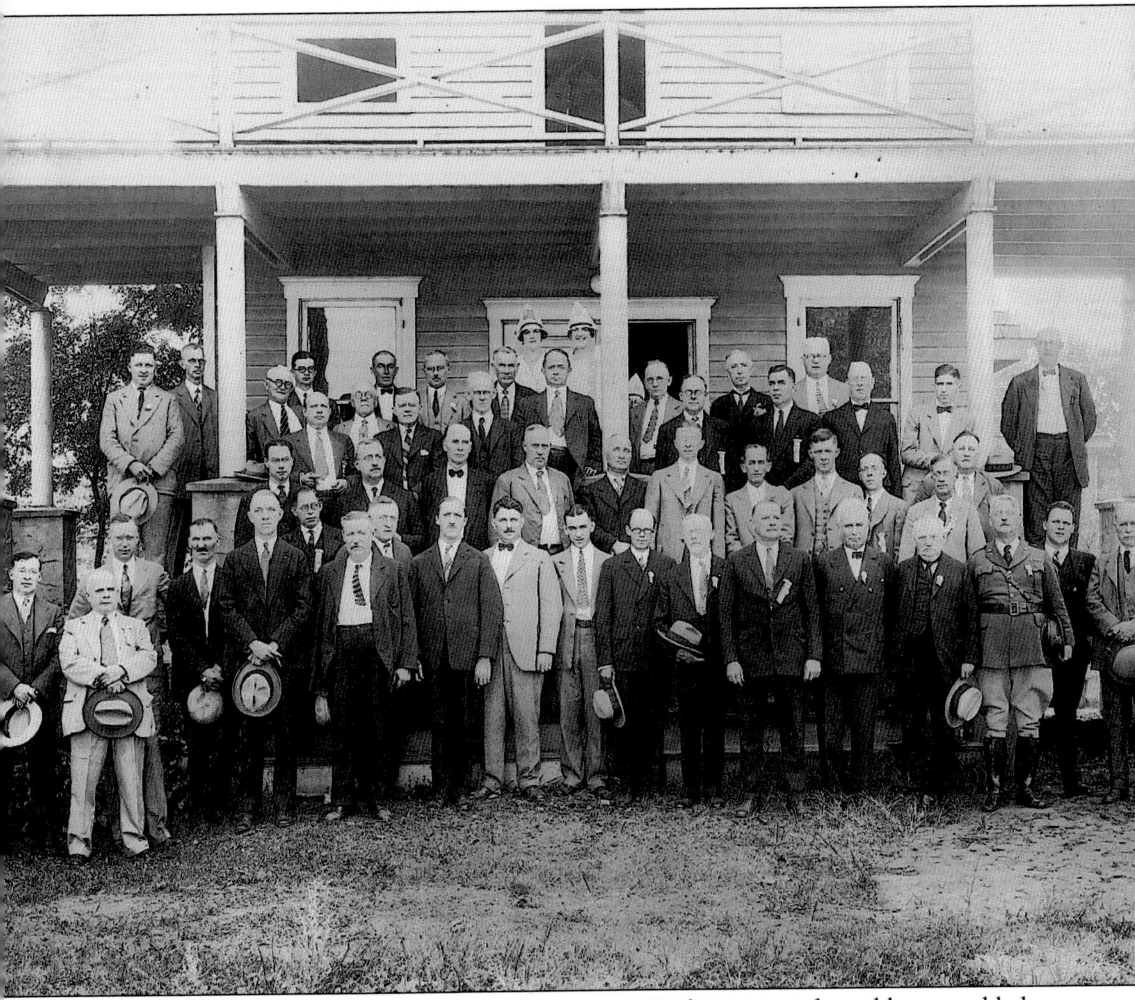

In celebration of the Golden Eagle monument in 1927, this group of notables assembled at the Mohican Boat Club on Riverview Avenue. From left to right are the following: (first row) Robert Peacock, Dr. David Baird, Robert Cox, Alfred Earley, Harry Ziegler, Harry Bishop, Stuart McFarland, Fred Lippincott, Lloyd Wright, Brevoort Smith, Alfonza Adams, William Heisler Jr., Curwen Fisher, Charles R. Stout, U. S. Rep. Isaac Bacharach, Gov. Edward Stokes, Col. Landon of Bordentown Military Institute, Herbert Blizzard, Newton Morton, and William Bishop; (second row) Howard Stackhouse, Joseph Thomas, Dr. Marcus Newcomb, A. Engle Haines, William A. Reeves, Edward Kashner, Charles Green, George Michalis, Fred Schaible, William Gummere, and Roscoe C. Shinn; (third row) Pettit Joy, John Tilton, Henry Worrell, William Murphy, Percy Baker, Joseph Kingdon, Jesse Foulks, Dr. Harold Longdorf, Spencer Hazard, Charles M.N. Adams, Charles Joyce, Judge William Slaughter, Edward Troth, Clarence Jones, M. Matlack, Howard Kenney, George Strick, George Wilmer, Judge Frank Hendrickson, and John Rainier; (fourth row) Susie Gilbert, Sara Foulks McCabe, and Mrs. Charles M.N. Adams. (Courtesy of Florence Historical Society.)

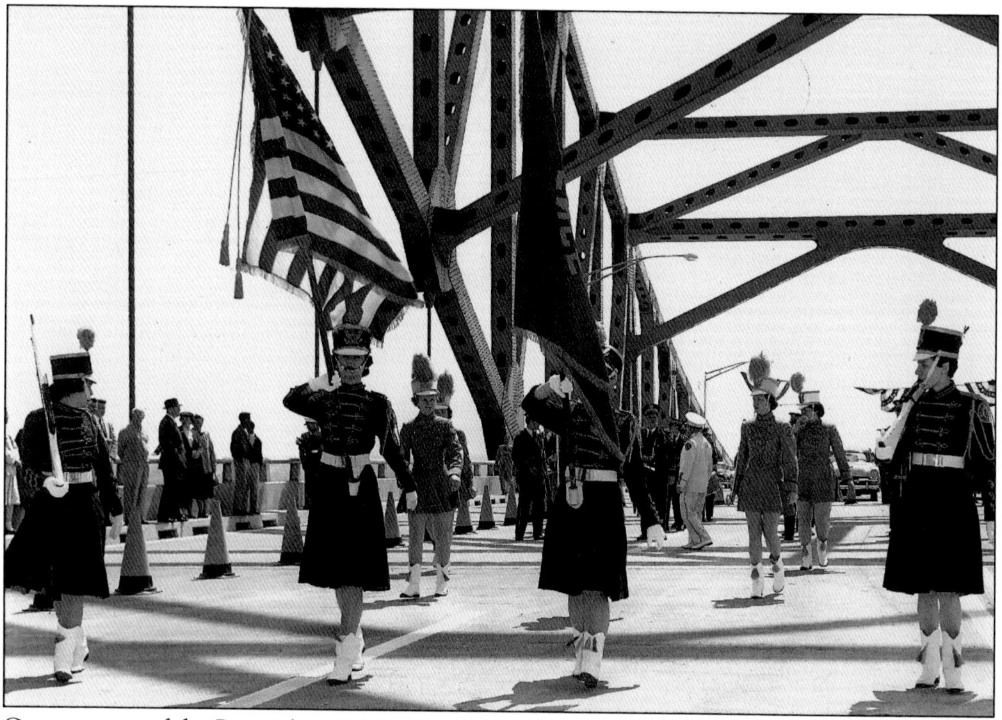

Construction of the Pennsylvania Turnpike Bridge at Florence in the early 1950s was cause for celebration. This picture shows the Florence High School color guard and band. (Courtesy of Florence Historical Society.)

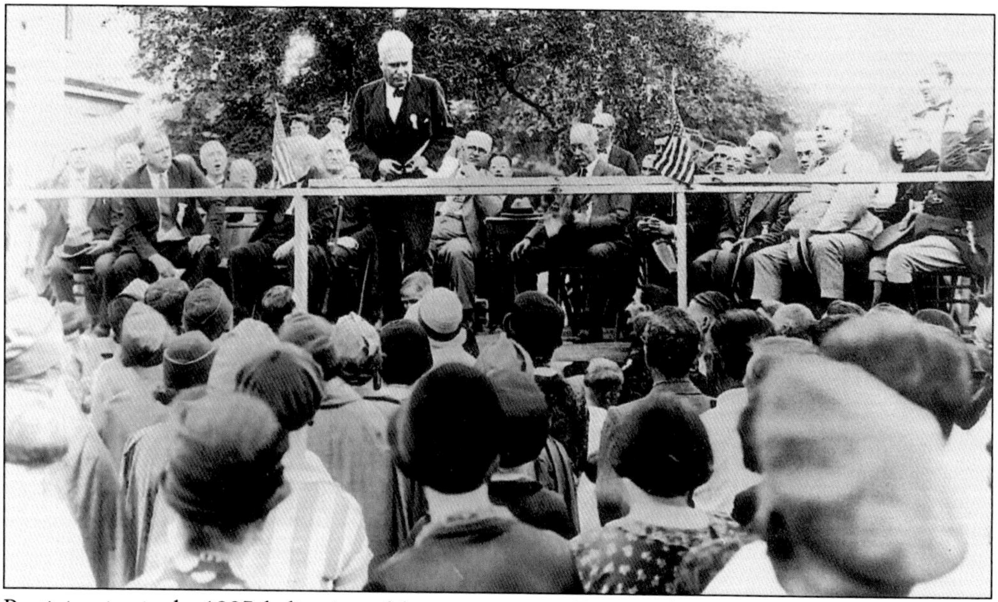

Participating in the 1927 dedication of the monument at Front and Broad Streets are the following notables: Charles Stout, freeholder (second from the left); M. Matlack, freeholder; William Reeves, county clerk; Gov. Edward Stokes (standing); Pete Joy, congressman; Newton Morton; Jack Rainier; Fred Schaible, township committeeman; Col. Landon of Bordentown Military Institute; and Pettit Joy. (Courtesy of Gary Bykowsky.)

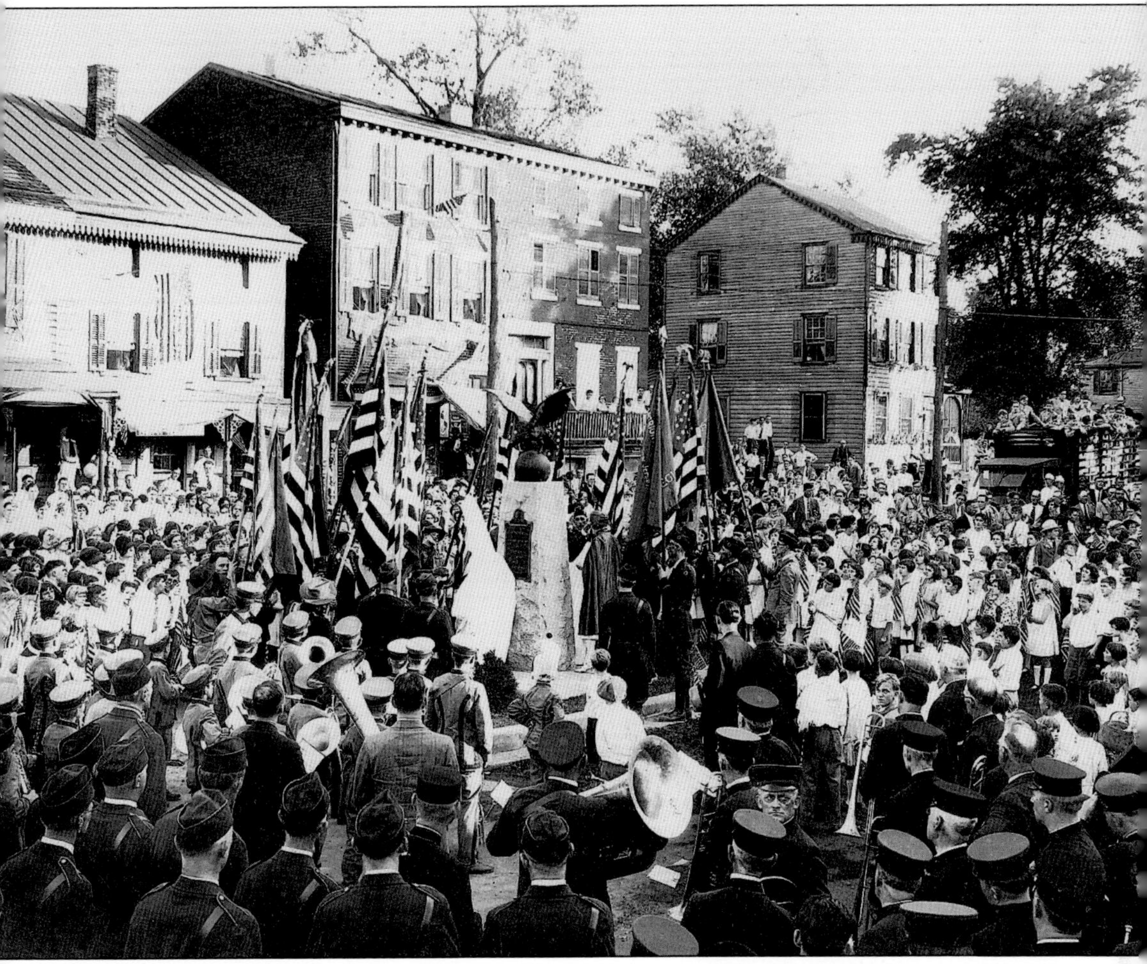

This overhead shot of the 1927 dedication of the Golden Eagle monument gives an idea of the large crowd assembled, including boys piled on the truck (upper right). The three-story apartment buildings in the center still stand, as does the clapboard building to the right. (Courtesy of Florence Historical Society.)

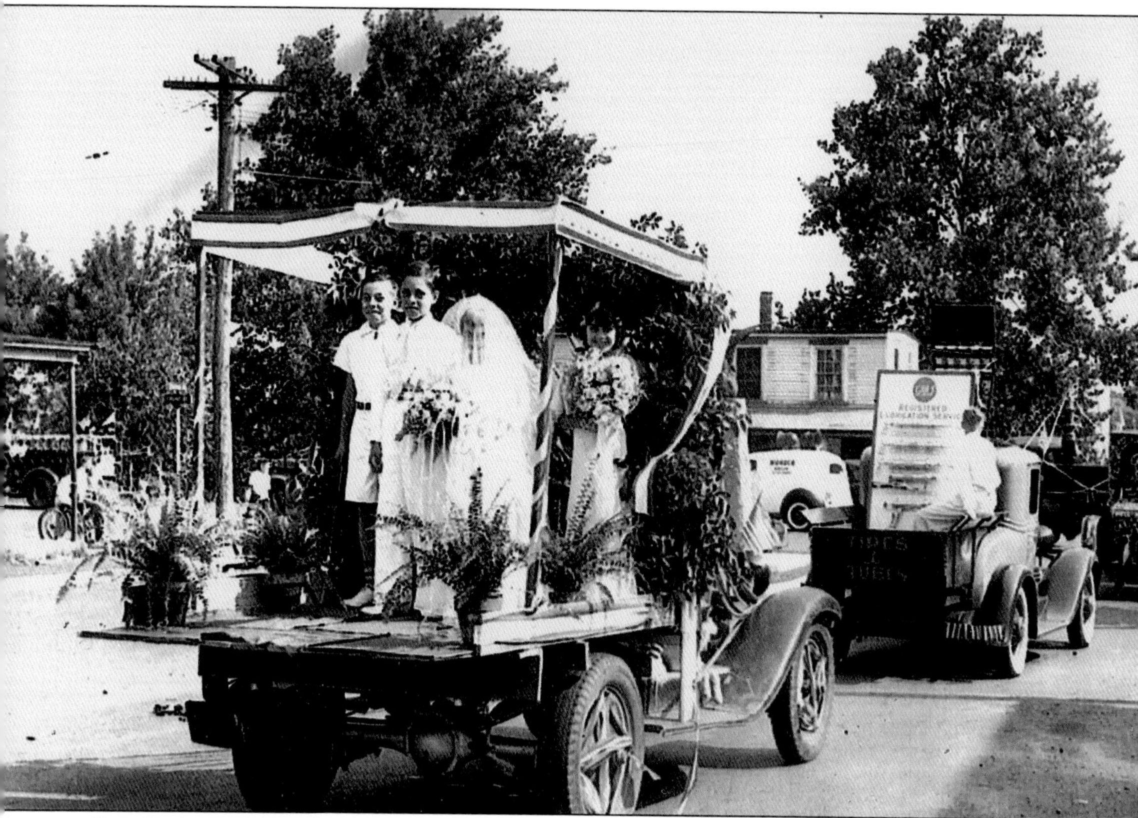

Parades in town are always popular, and this Fourth of July event in 1939 captures the Florence Greenhouse float. The groom is Charles Ercol of Beverly, the bride is Betty Jean Panaro of Florence, the best man is David Panaro of Florence, and the maid of honor is Marjorie Ercol of Beverly. The float is proceeding to the corner of Front and Broad Streets, and turning west on Front Street. (Courtesy of Ed Panaro.)

Six

The Police, Fire Company, and Beach Patrol

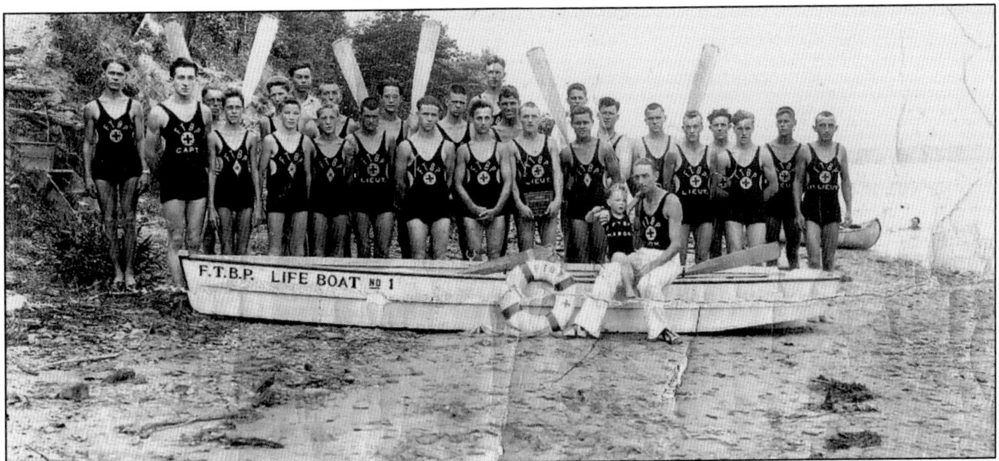

The Florence Township Beach Patrol was organized in 1929 by August Glass. Pictured are the members in 1934. The diamond-shaped emblem denotes a junior member under 17 years of age. From left to right are the following: (first row) August Glass (commander) and his son, Richard Glass (mascot); (second row) Floyd Gravener, Ralph Hamilton, William Petitt, John Roe, Albert "Nudge" Hamilton, Benjamin Brown, Thomas Dickinson, James Galbally, Joseph Hamilton, Joseph Kilchesty, Louis Ames, Robert Myatt, and Robert Hamilton; (third row) Wilbur Sayers, Edward Burkhardt, George Hamilton, Francis Fitzpatrick, Fredrick Heydorn, Joseph Pasqualine, Robert Walsh, Anthony Kilchesty, Edward Miller, and Radcliff Patterson; (fourth row) Edson Hopkins, Norman Sayers, and William "Jim" Sitzler. Members not shown are Arnold Sayers and Russell Gravener. (Courtesy of Mary Tapper.)

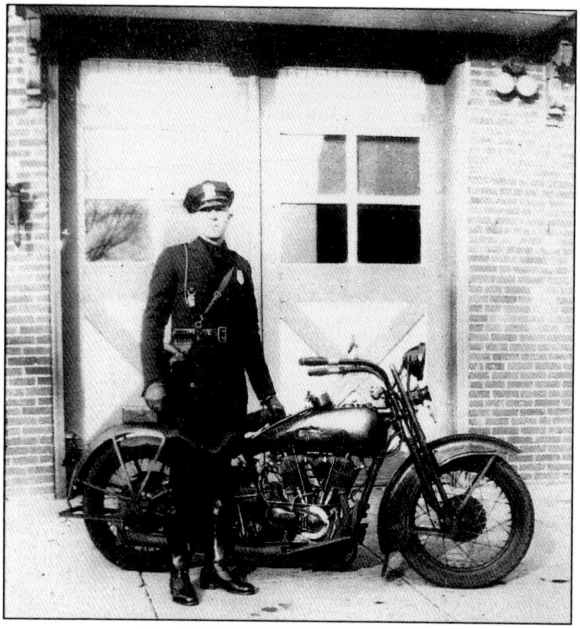

Police Chief August Glass poses with his Indian motorcycle in 1938. The picture was taken in front of the firehouse on West 2nd Street, which also served as the police station and town jail in the 1930s. (Courtesy of Richard Glass.)

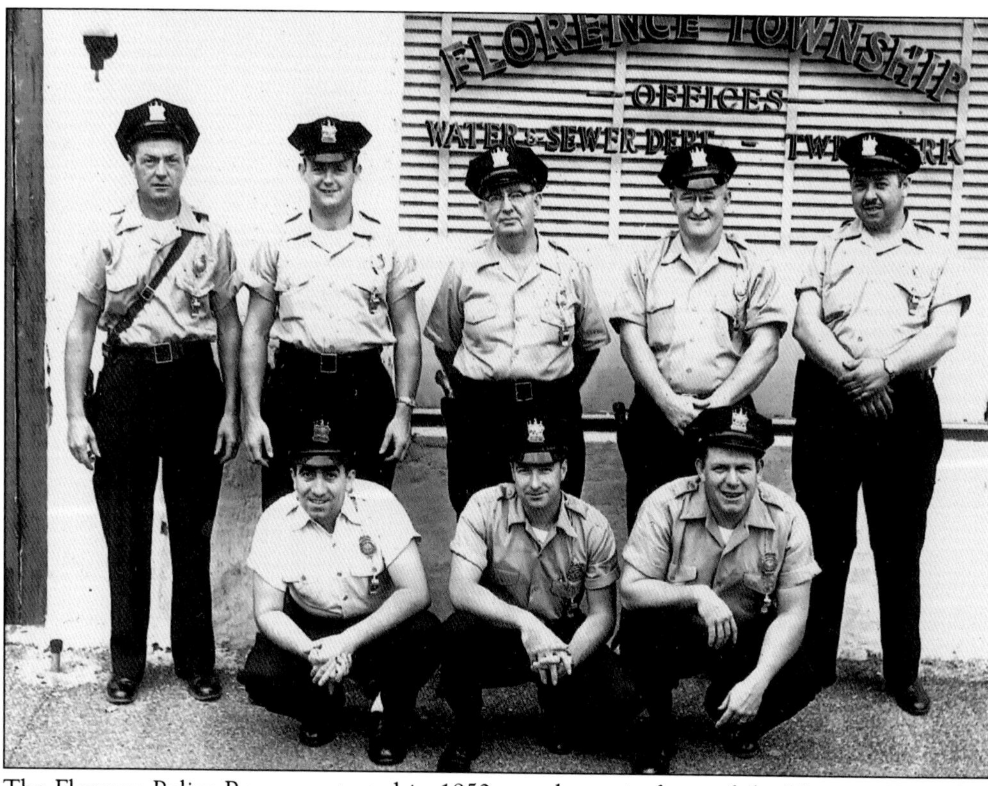

The Florence Police Reserves, started in 1950, are shown in front of the Florence Township Offices (the old Florence Hotel), on Front Street. From left to right are the following: (front row) Robert Filipponi, James Cheesman, and Russell "Icky" Roughton; (back row) Richard Coates, Harvey Worth, James Tapper Sr., Lawrence "Reds" Ingham, and Frank "Blimp" Cicero. (Courtesy of Mary Tapper.)

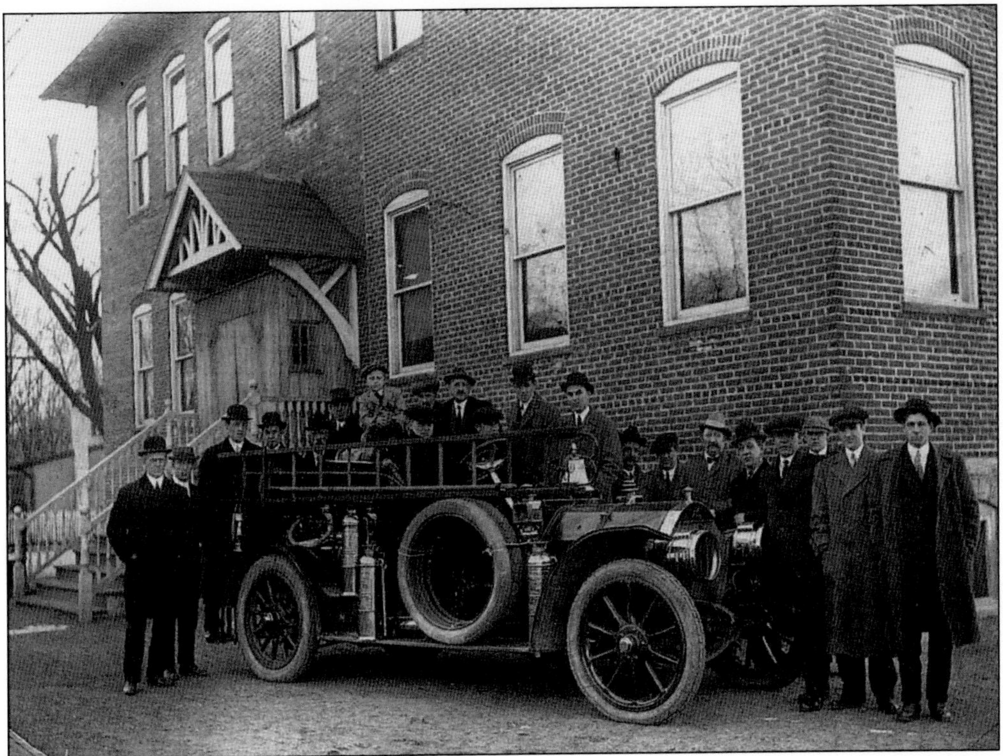

The first motorized chemical fire truck in Burlington County is displayed by Florence Fire Company No. 1 *c.* 1914 near the Second Street School. It was purchased at a cost of $909. (Courtesy of Richard Glass.)

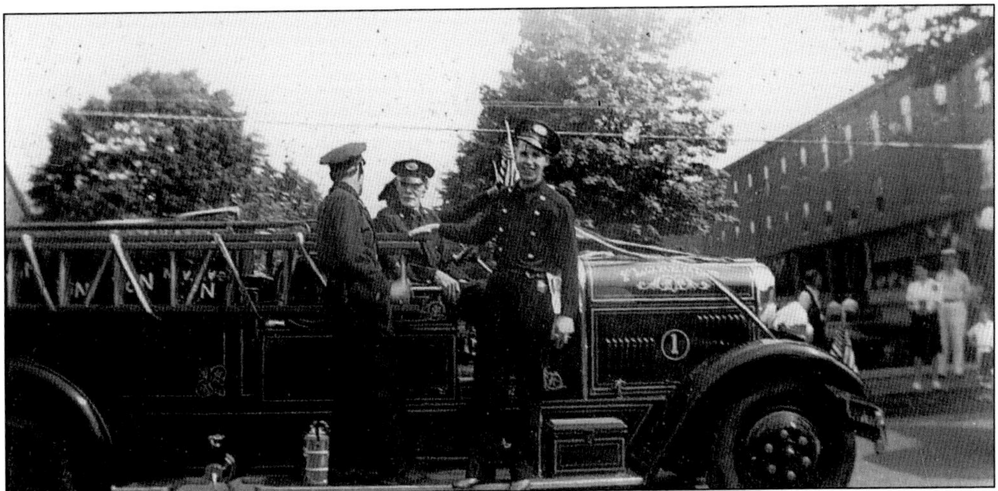

Florence Fire Company No. 1 members and fire truck are shown at a parade in Roebling *c.* 1935. (Courtesy of Albert L. King.)

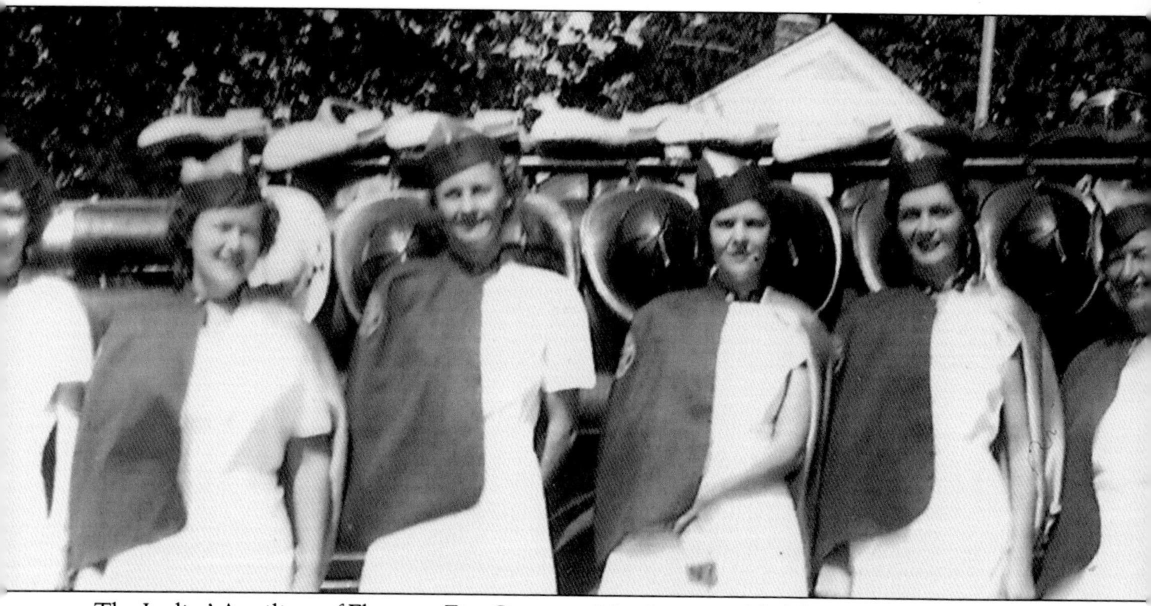

The Ladies' Auxiliary of Florence Fire Company No. 1 is assembled for a parade. Elsie Hughes is second from left, and Nellie Wolfe is third from left. (Courtesy of Marsha Hughes.)

Seven

The River

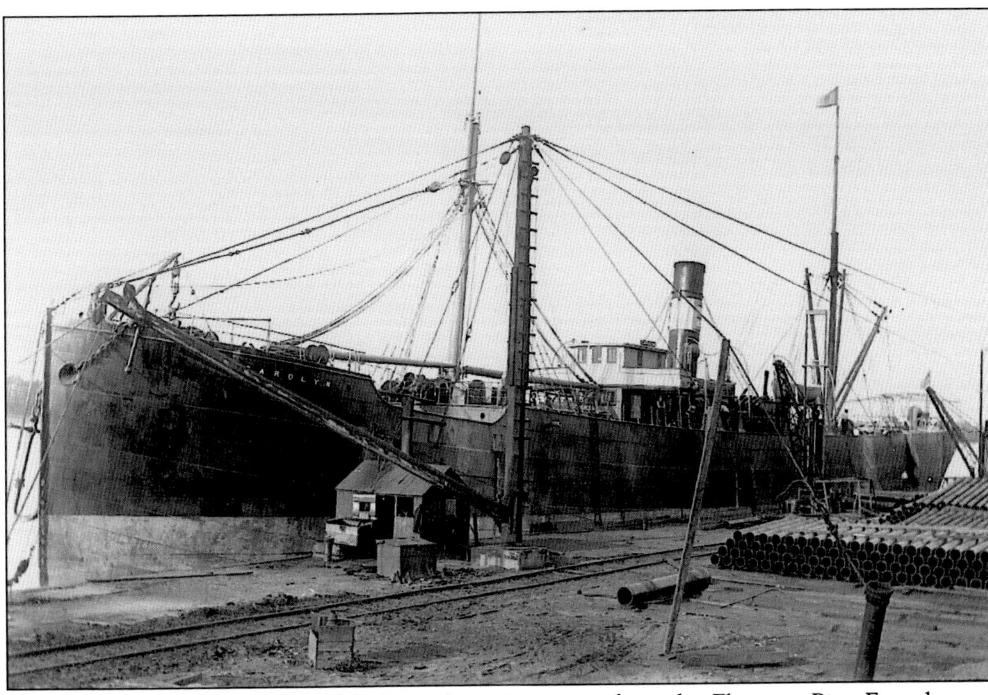

This large ship is awaiting the loading of cast-iron pipe from the Florence Pipe Foundry and Machine Company for shipment down the Delaware River *c.* 1923. (Courtesy of John Pullen.)

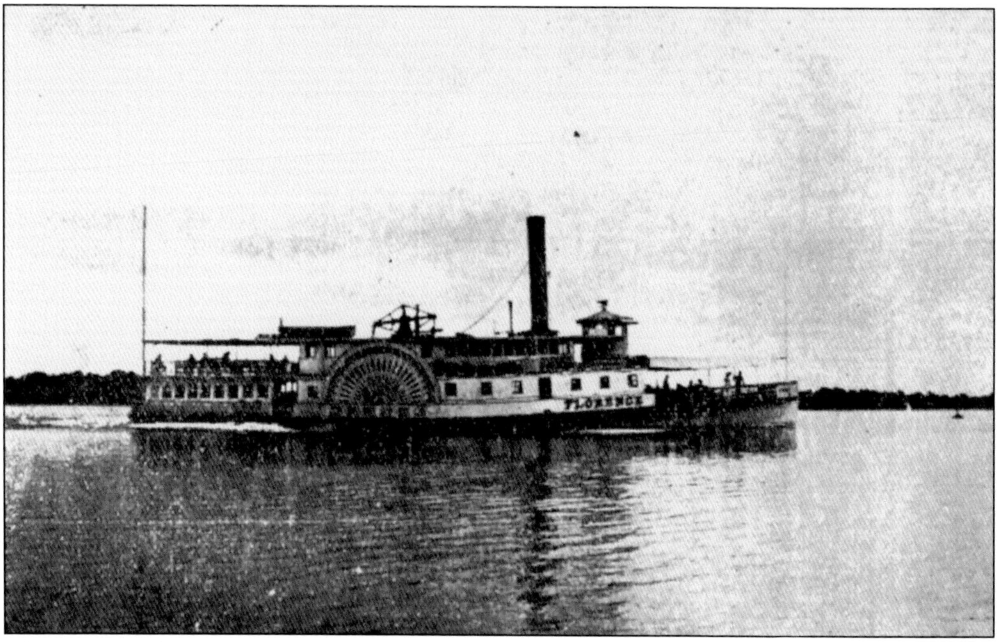

The steamer *Florence*, a side-wheeler from Connecticut, was originally named the *Silver Star*. Used during the Civil War as a dispatch boat, it ran the Delaware River between Philadelphia and Trenton from 1869 to 1902, when it was destroyed by fire in Bordentown. (Courtesy of Florence Historical Society.)

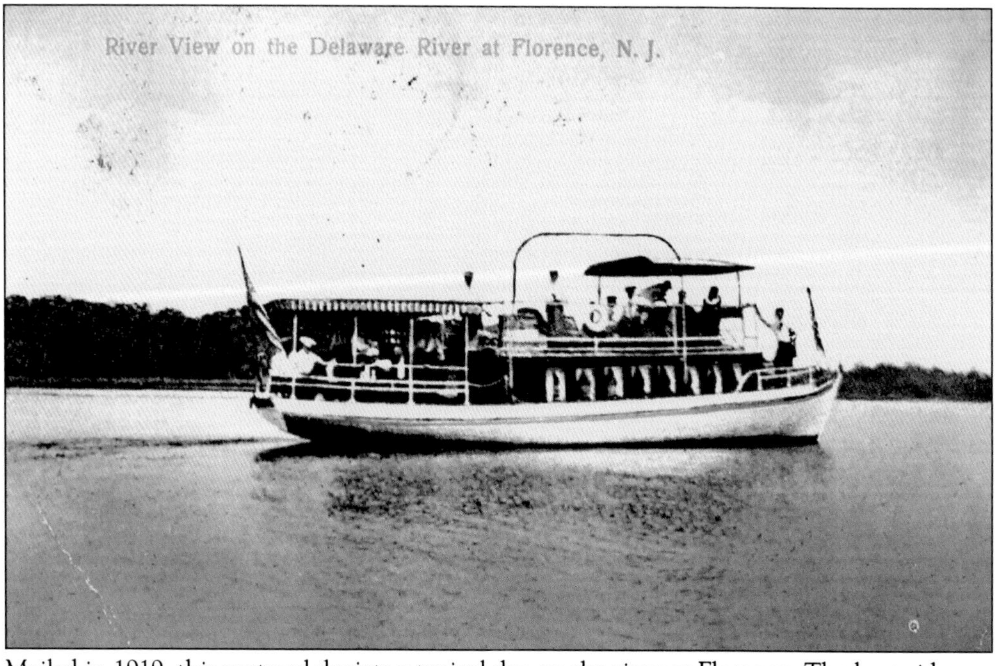

Mailed in 1919, this postcard depicts a typical day on the river at Florence. The boat ride was enjoyed by Austin James of Bordentown. (Courtesy of Florence Historical Society.)

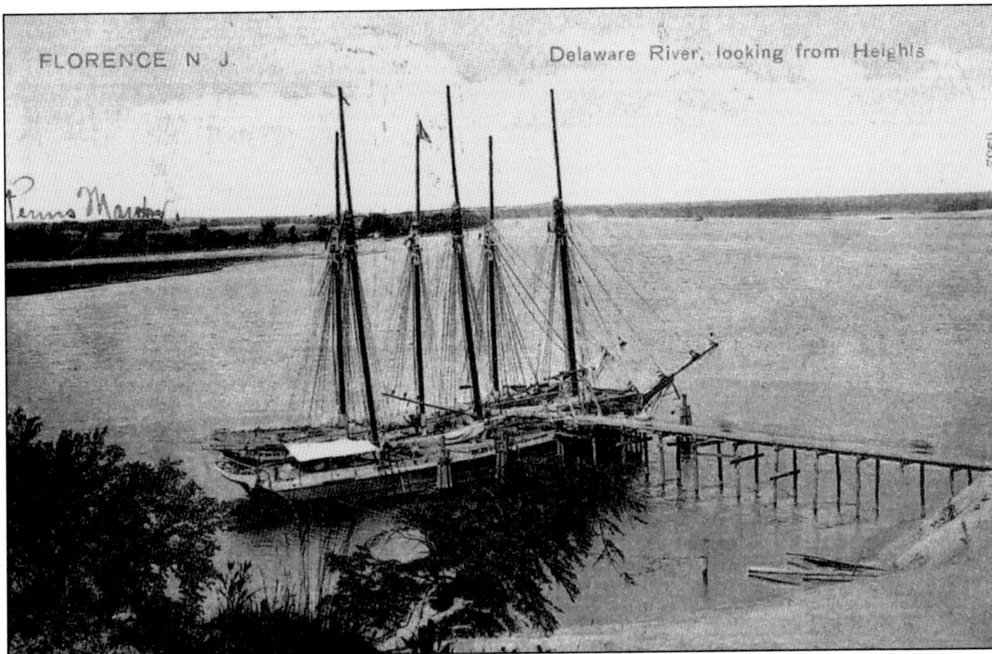

A five-masted schooner is shown *c.* 1906 at Florence Heights, anchored at the claybanks loading platform, opposite Pennsbury Manor. The person who sent the postcard wrote that the ship is being loaded with moulding sand, used in foundries. (Courtesy of Florence Historical Society.)

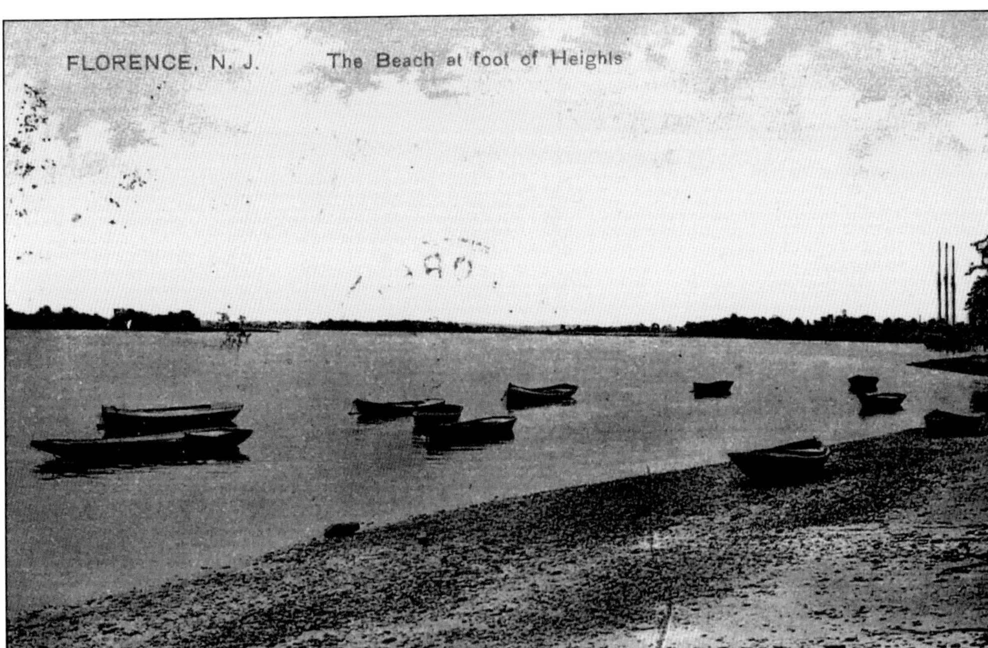

At anchor off the beach at the foot of Florence Heights are rowboats that were rented out by the Clydes as a family business in the early 1900s. The three-masted schooner (far right) is probably at the claybanks for loading. (Courtesy of Florence Historical Society.)

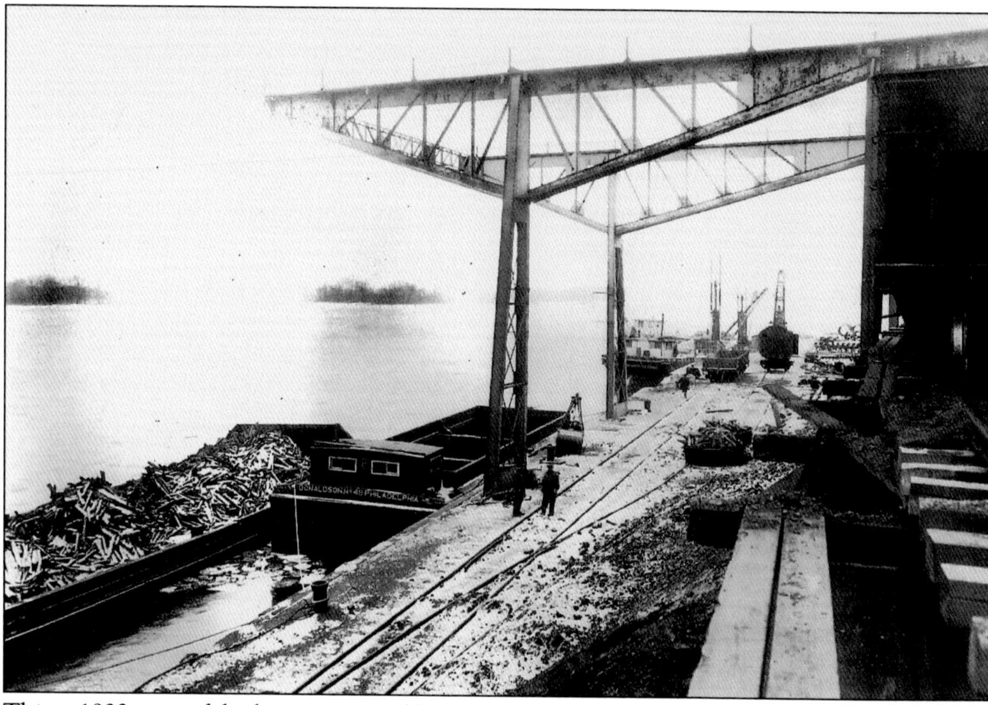

This c. 1923 view of the large crane and loading area on the Delaware River at the Florence Pipe Foundry and Machine Company, on West Front Street, gives an idea of the magnitude of this operation. (Courtesy of John Pullen.)

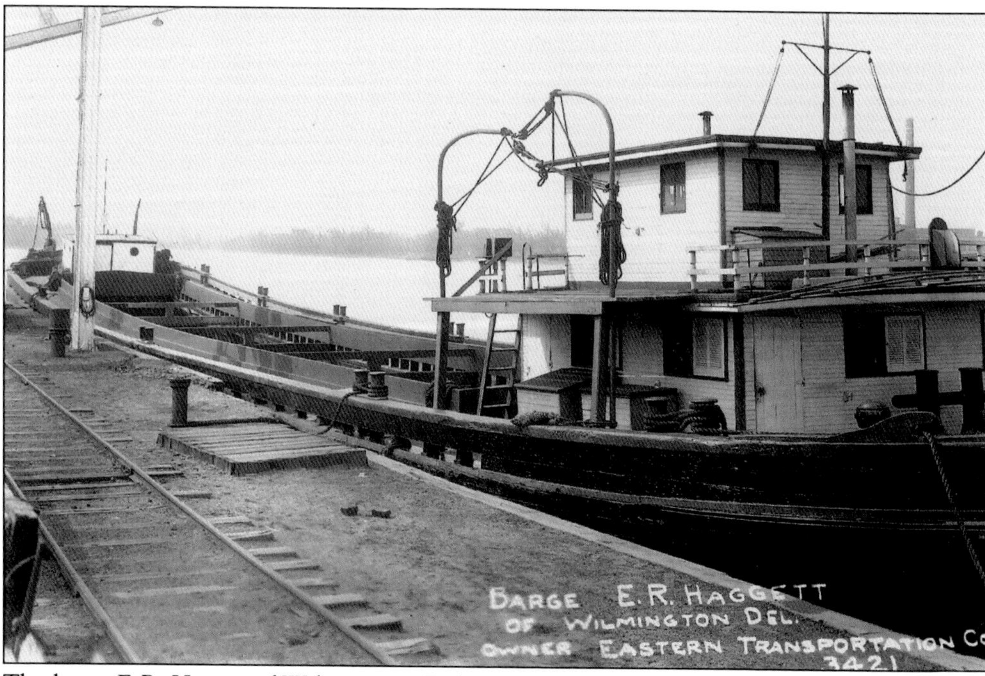

The barge *E.R. Haggett* of Wilmington, Delaware, is shown c. 1932 on the Delaware River at the Florence Pipe Foundry and Machine Company, delivering sand or some other necessity for the manufacture of pipe. (Courtesy of John Pullen.)

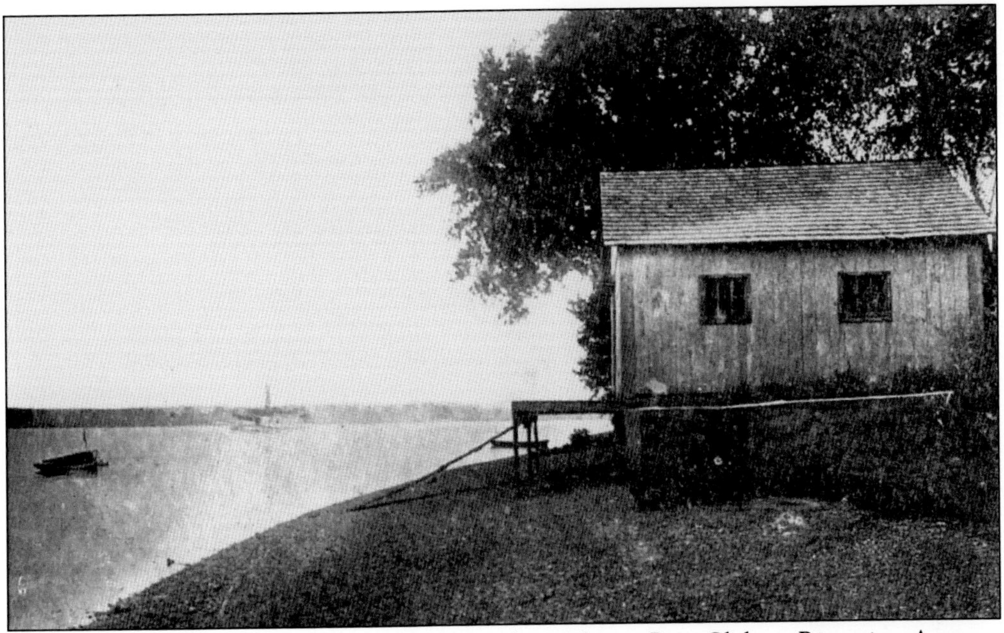

This "river view from boat club" is probably at the Mohican Boat Club on Riverview Avenue, pictured in the early 1900s as indicated by the steamboat in the background. Boats were stored in the boathouse by members, and the dock also served as a diving point for river swimmers. (Courtesy of Florence Historical Society.)

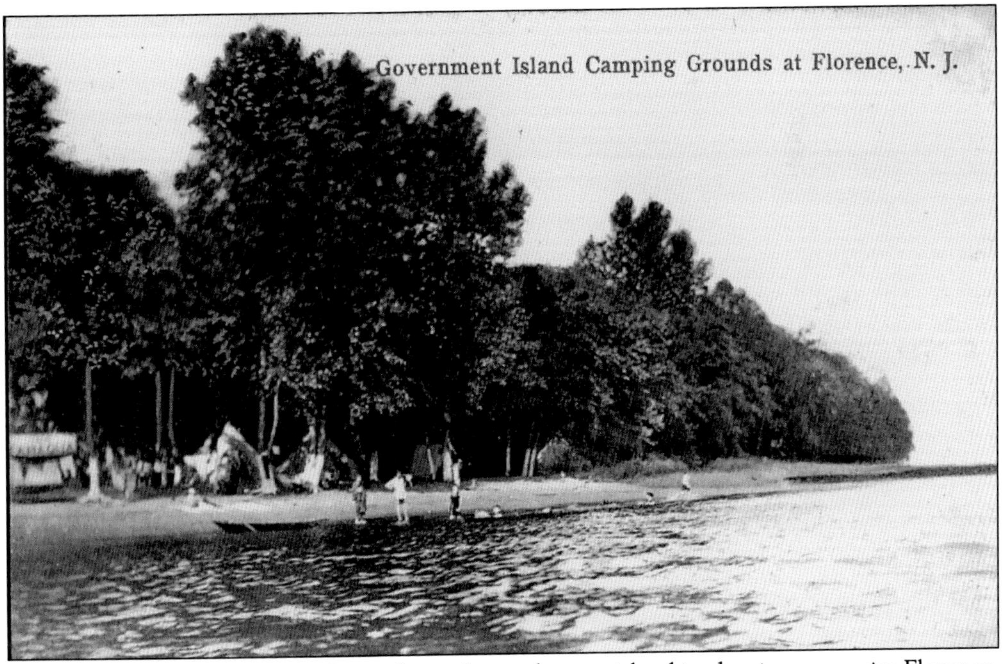

Government Island Camping Grounds was located on an island in the river, opposite Florence. As shown in this early-1900s view, local residents spent summer days here picnicking, fishing, and swimming. The island was removed when the river was dredged. (Courtesy of Florence Historical Society.)

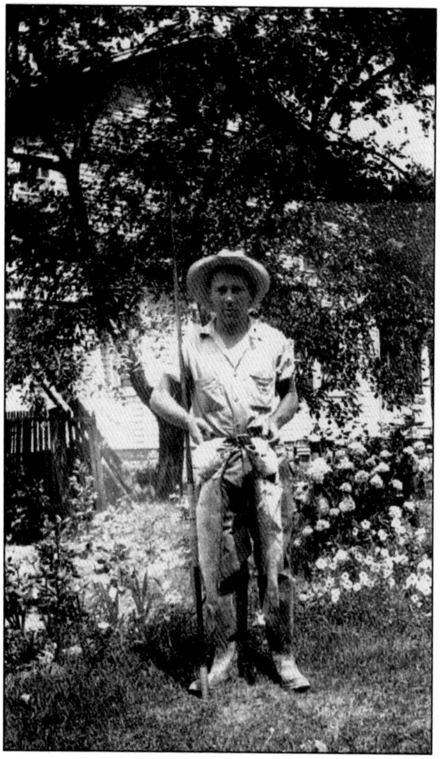

Albert A. King Jr. spent his entire life fishing and boating on the Delaware River, but he caught these weakfish in 1935 at the Jersey shore. He and his catch are pictured in his yard, at East 3rd Street. (Courtesy of Albert L. King.)

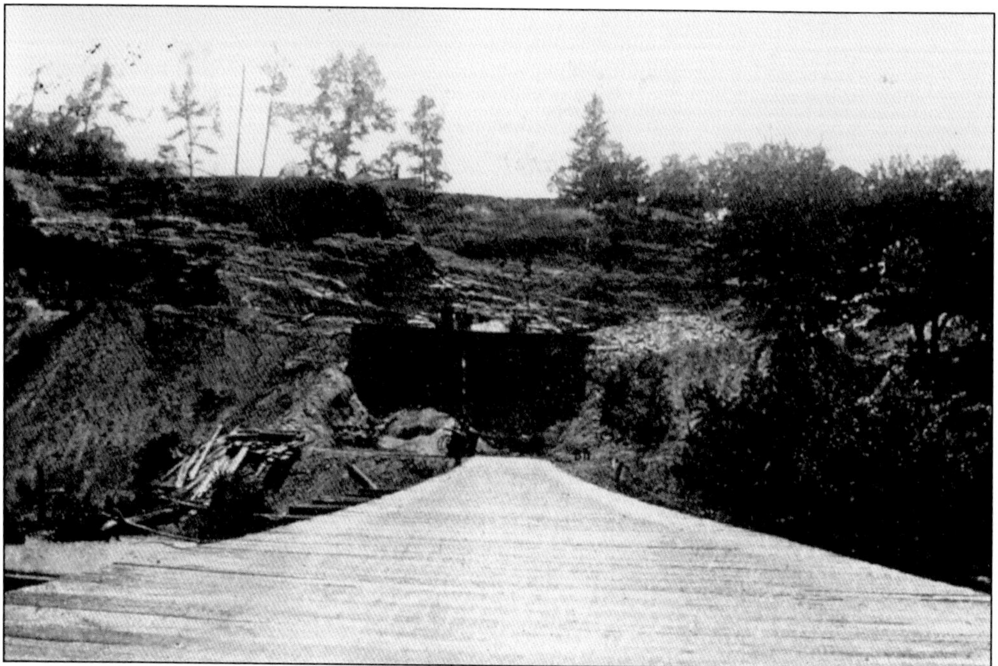

The claybanks at Florence Heights are shown c. 1906, complete with boardwalk for transporting the clay to boats for shipment to pottery factories and brickyards. This area had the finest clay in New Jersey and was, therefore, much in demand. (Courtesy of Florence Historical Society.)

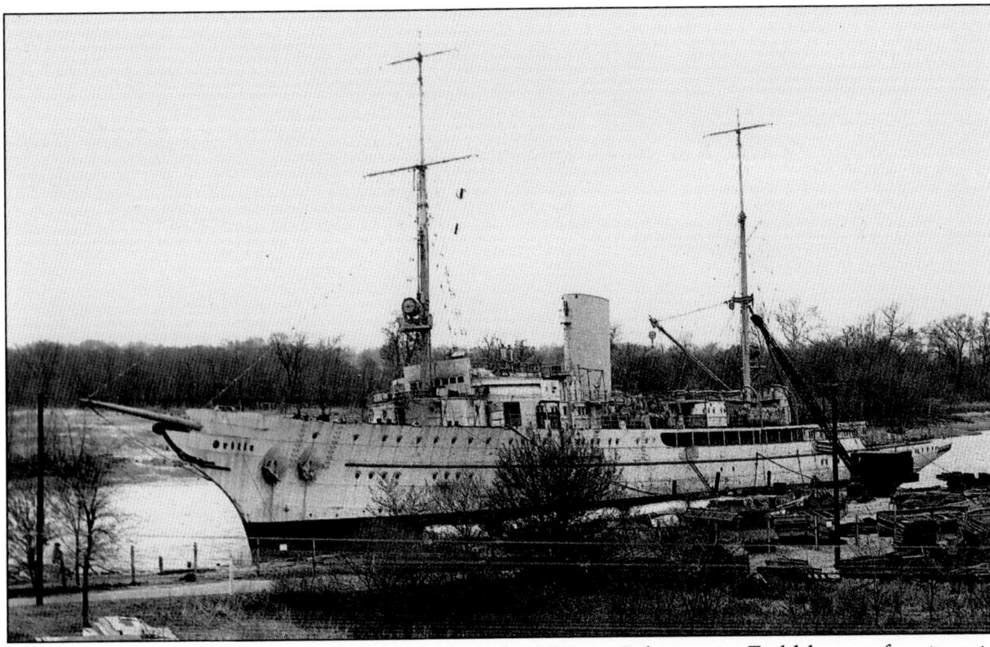

Hitler's yacht, the *Caprice*, is shown anchored at Doan Salvage, in Fieldsboro, after its trip up the Delaware River past Florence in April 1951. Students from Second Street School in Florence were dismissed to assemble at the riverbank and witness its passing. (Courtesy of Albert L. King.)

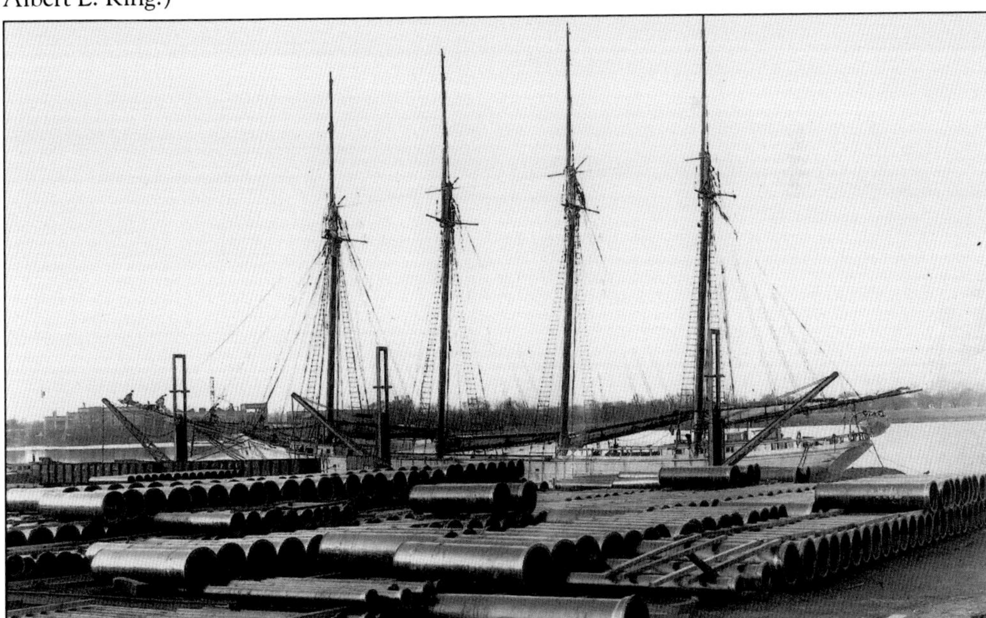

This four-masted schooner is docked on the Delaware River at the Florence Pipe Foundry and Machine Company *c.* 1923, awaiting the loading of pipe for delivery around the world. (Courtesy of John Pullen.)

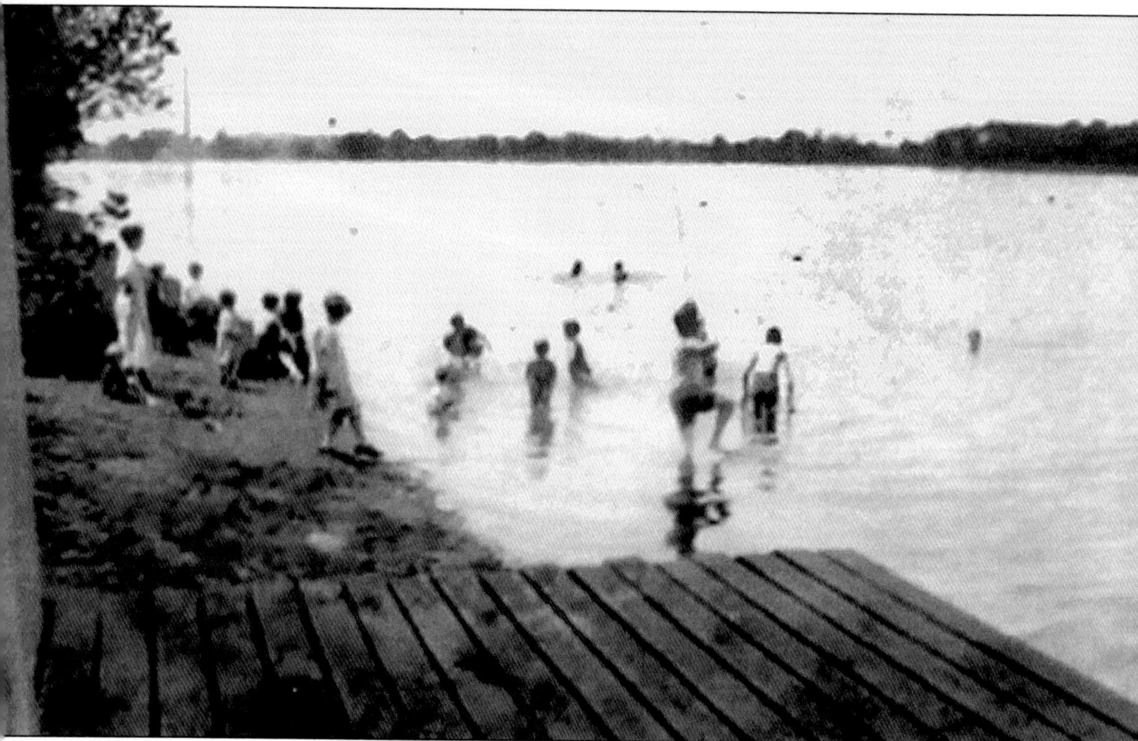

Swimming in the Delaware River was always popular in Florence. The large plank platform was located near the Mohican Boat Club, on Riverview Avenue, and many took advantage of this on hot summer days. (Courtesy of Barbara Bishop Durham.)

Eight

SCHOOLS

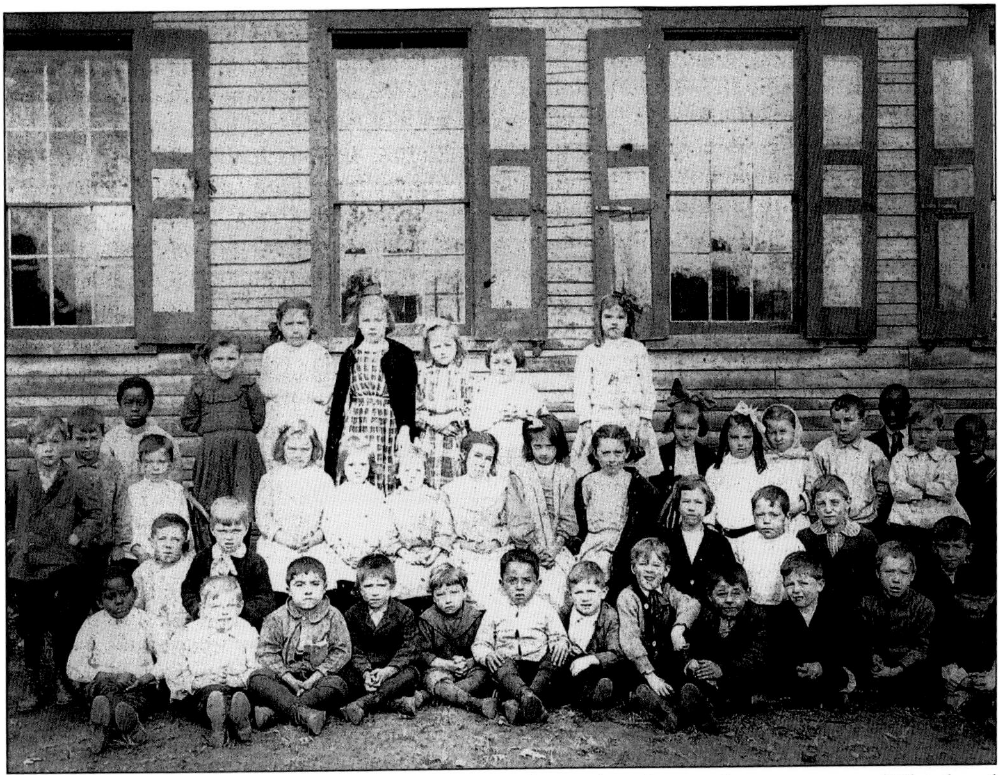

Known as the Foundry School, this building was located at the southwest corner of Third and Foundry Streets. One of the earlier schools in Florence, it was abandoned when the Second Street School was built in the 1890s. The property is now an empty lot. (Courtesy of Barbara Bishop Durham.)

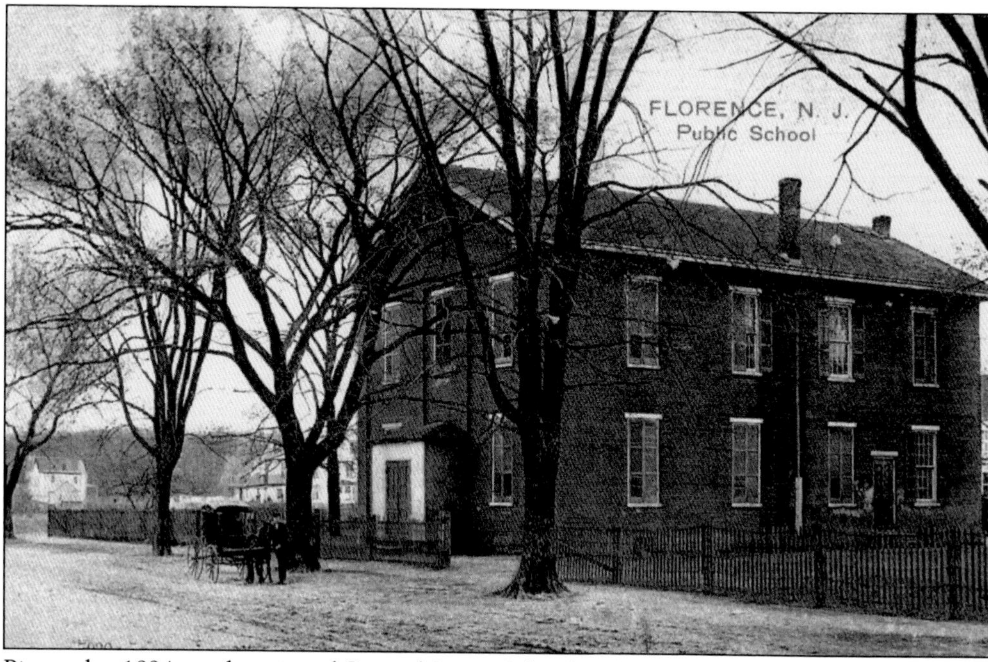

Pictured *c.* 1894 are the original Second Street School and Dr. David Baird with his horse and carriage. (Courtesy of Florence Historical Society.)

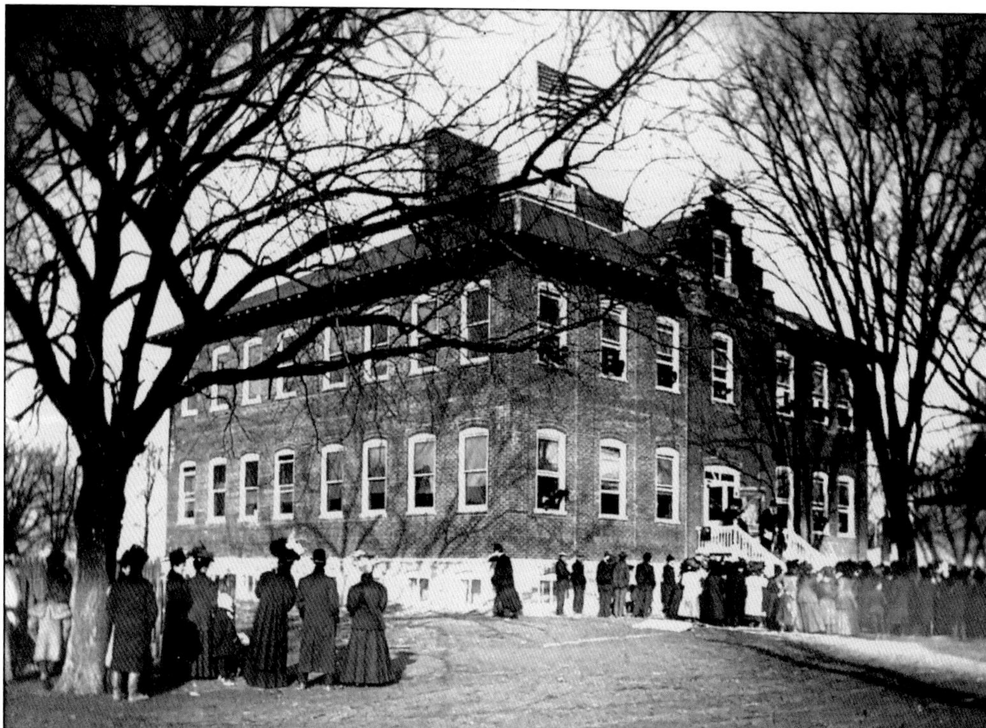

The dedication of the addition to Second Street School is shown *c.* 1905. This photograph was also produced in postcard form. In the group at the lower left, the last woman to the right is believed to be Annie Spencer. (Courtesy of Florence Historical Society.)

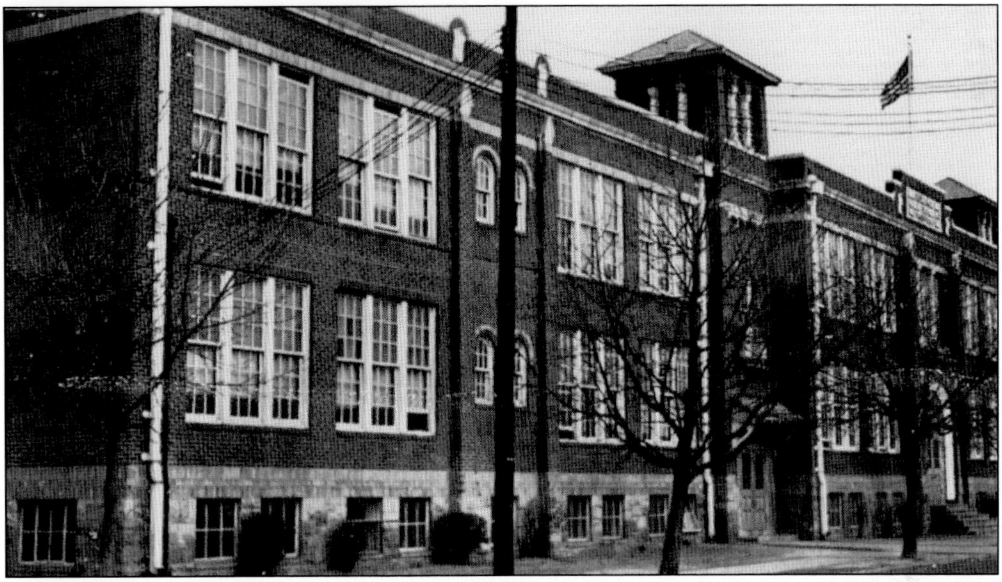

In 1925, Second Street School was renamed Florence Township High School. It was used for first-year high-school and grade-school classes. For the remaining three years of high school, students went to Burlington and Bordentown by bus. (Courtesy of Florence Historical Society.)

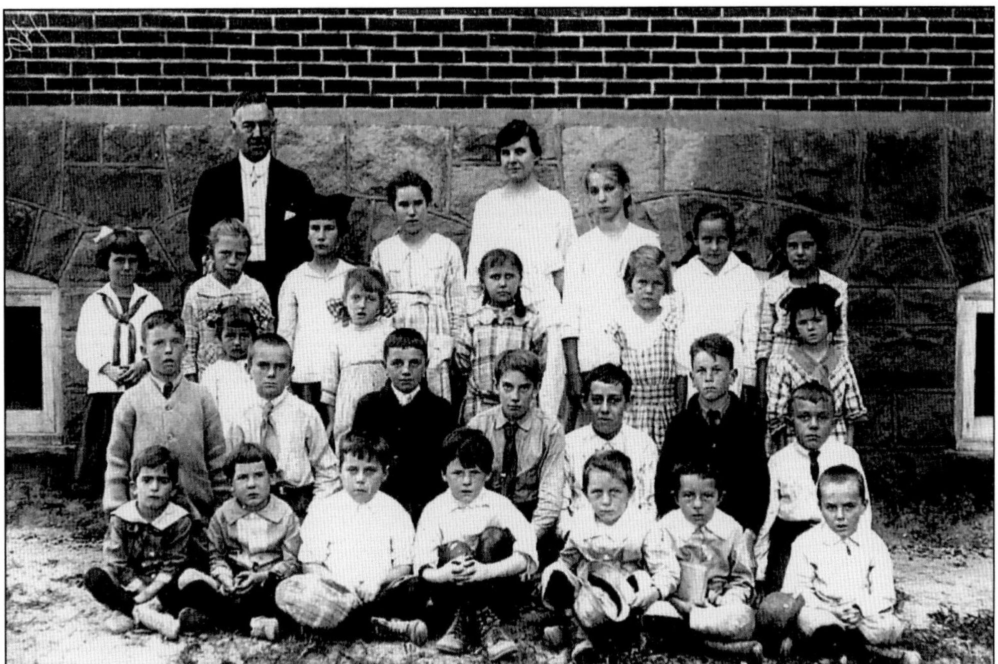

The Florence Station School is shown c. 1917, with principal Maja Mathis (back left). Albert A. King Jr. sits third from the left in the front row. At that time, all young boys wore knickers. (Courtesy of Albert L. King.)

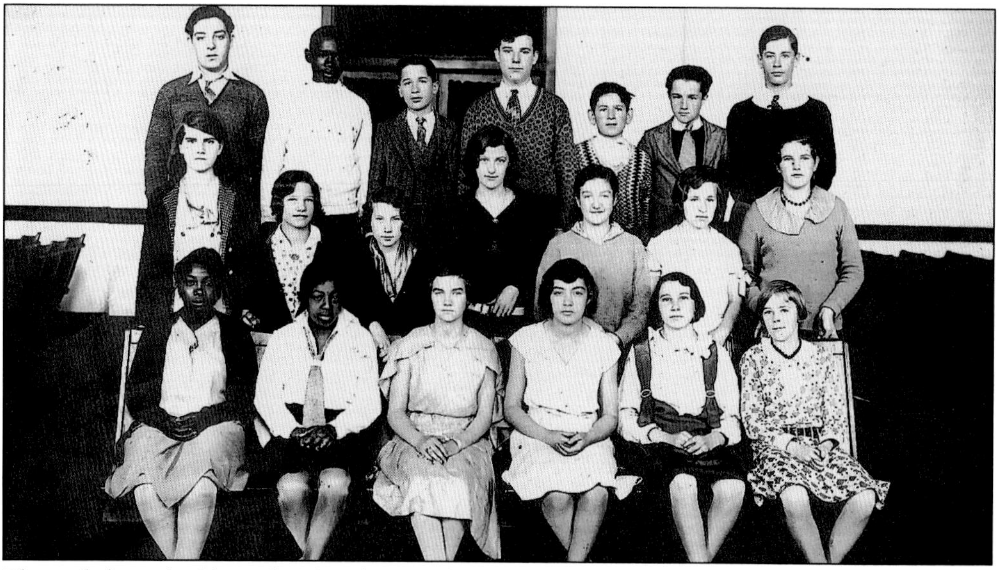

The eighth-grade Class of 1930 of Second Street School is shown. From left to right are the following: (front row) Anna Yonell, Marguerite Dobbins, Margaret Garwood, Nellie Losito, Thelma McHugh, and Mary Stackhouse; (middle row) Catherine Conrey, Fanny Legnaioli, Linian Wilkie, Alice Meher, Viola Frappolli, Pauline Napoli, and Florence Runyon; (back row) Russell Woolston, Leroy Patterson, Attilio Legnaioli, Olin Brinning, Benny Cardi, Elmer Hamilton, and Robert Patterson. (Courtesy of Florence Historical Society.)

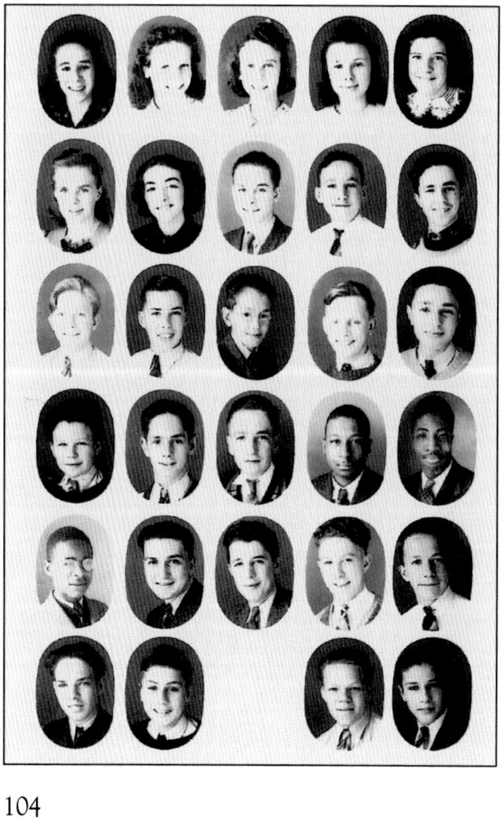

Florence Elementary School eighth-grade graduation class is shown in June 1939. Students are listed as Jennie Fidati, Thelma Kelvy, Betty Moffett, Delores Wheeler, Anne Marie Worthington, Ruth Carlson, Betty Sweeney, Alvin Panaro,Basil Yurcisin, Carl Linda, Douglas Anderson, Bill Dawson, Bob Engel, George Hathazi, Matthew Sparta, Jimmie Gallagher, Harold Delaroi, Baird Barry, Ed Scott, Dempsey Matthews, Hilliard Moore, Alex Rabatin, George Dimon, Steve Tinnick, Mike Timmish, Goodwin Donnelly, Louis Burr, Audrey Markwood (not pictured), John Sunkiskis, and John Molnar. (Courtesy of Mary Tapper.)

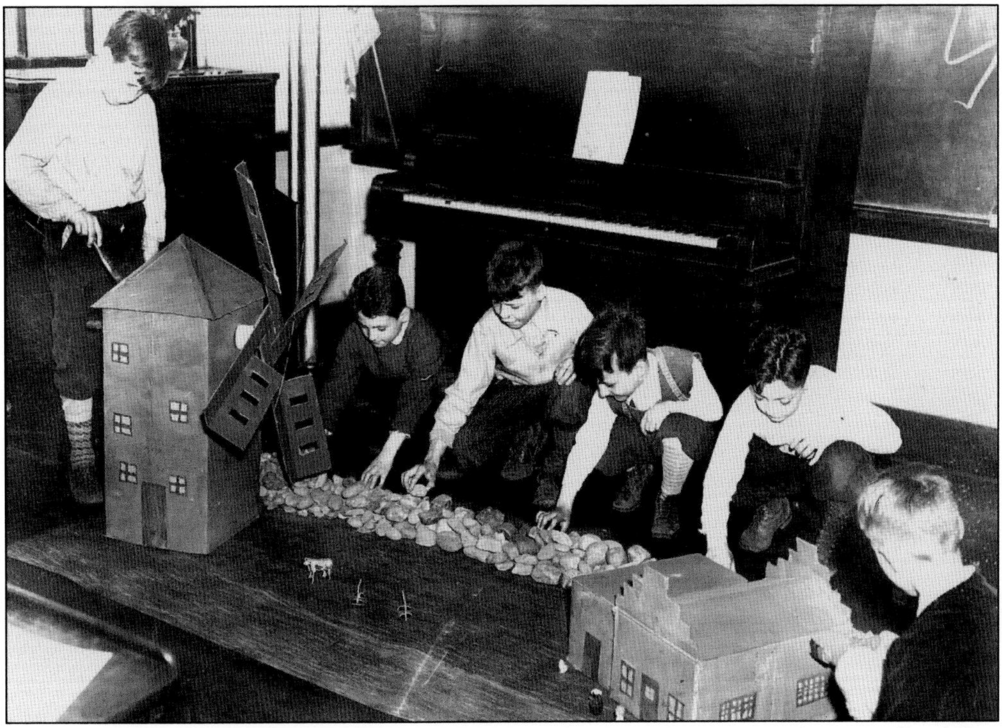

At Second Street School in the 1930s, students are shown with their Dutch windmill exhibit, which is nearing completion. (Courtesy of Florence Historical Society.)

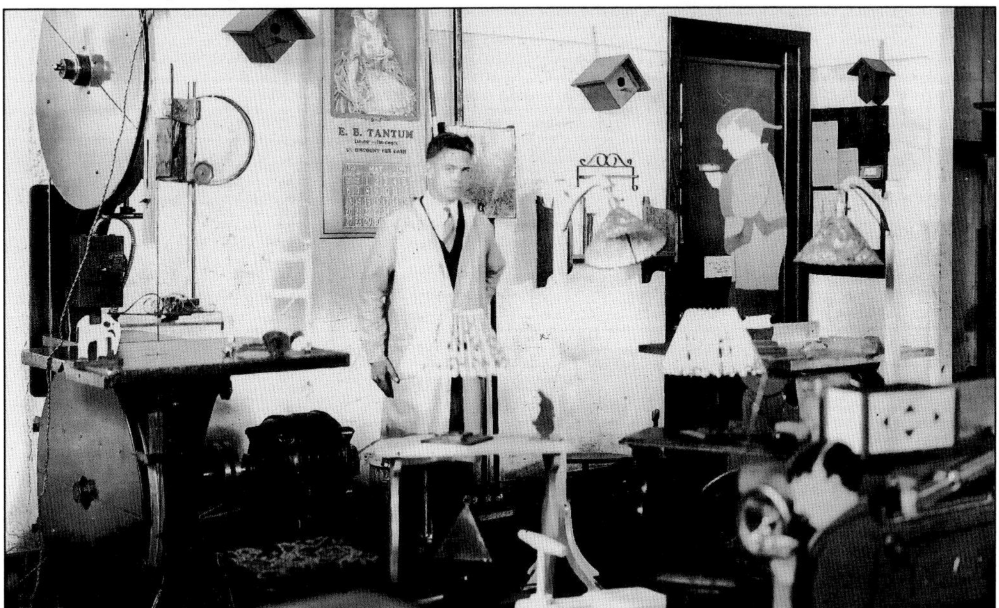

Items finished by students as class projects are shown in the manual training classroom at Second Street School in 1926—dated by the calendar on the wall. The band saw (left) was originally manufactured at Smithville and was old for its time. (Courtesy of Florence Historical Society.)

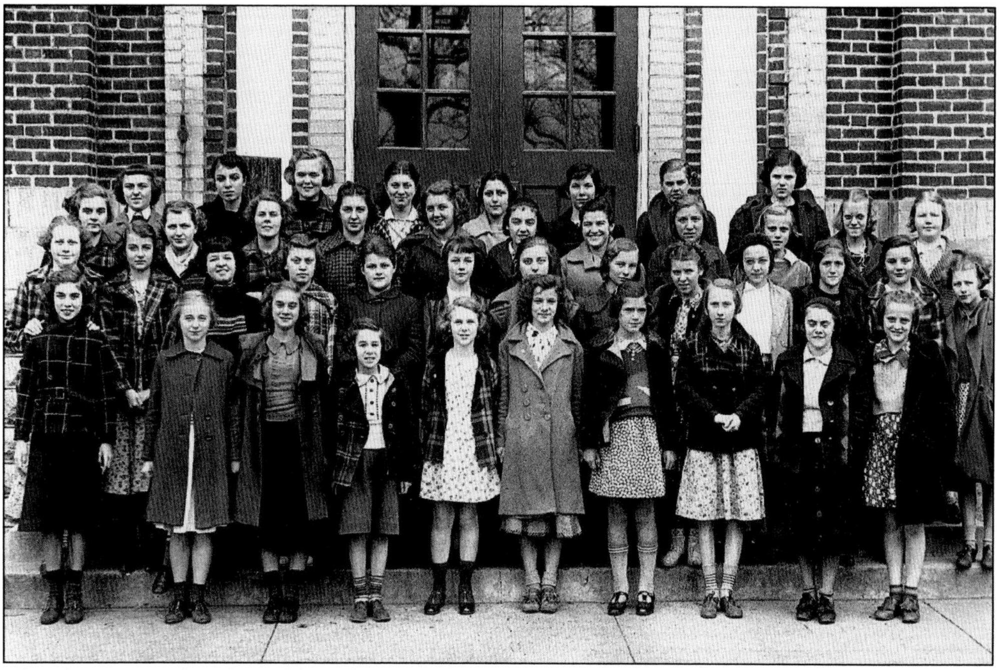

The Florence Girls' Glee Club is shown in front of Second Street School in the 1930s. Identified in the first row at the far right is Doris Lippincott, daughter of Louis and Lillian Lippincott. In the second row at the far right is ? Berryann, and second from right is Nola Sutphin. In the fourth row, second from the right is Thelma (Cheesman) Tapper. (Courtesy of Florence Historical Society.)

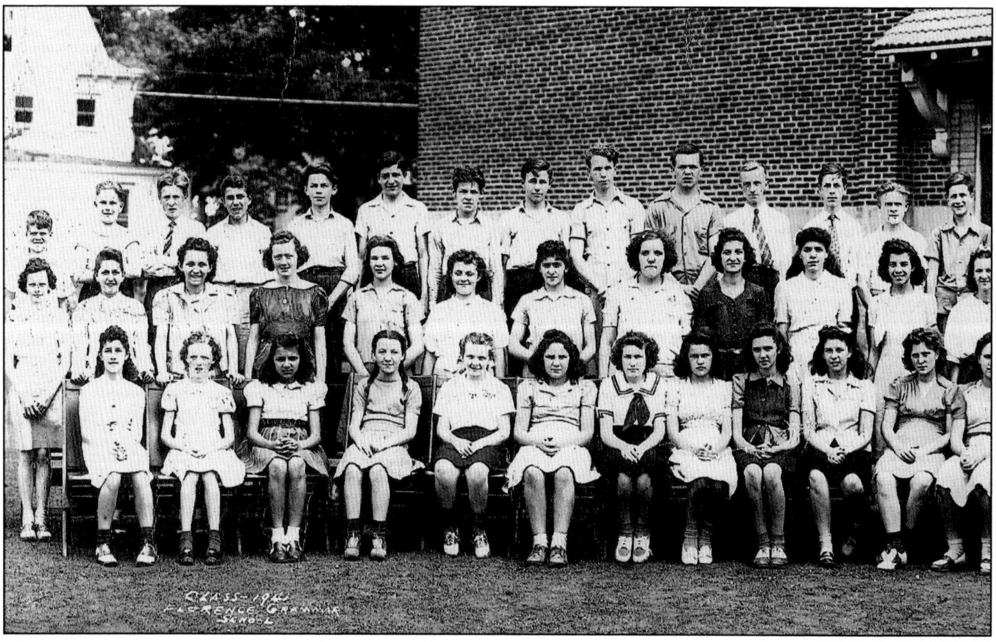

The Florence Grammar School class graduates of 1941 are pictured in the back of Second Street School. Saddle shoes were just coming into fashion for these bobbysoxers. (Courtesy of Florence Historical Society.)

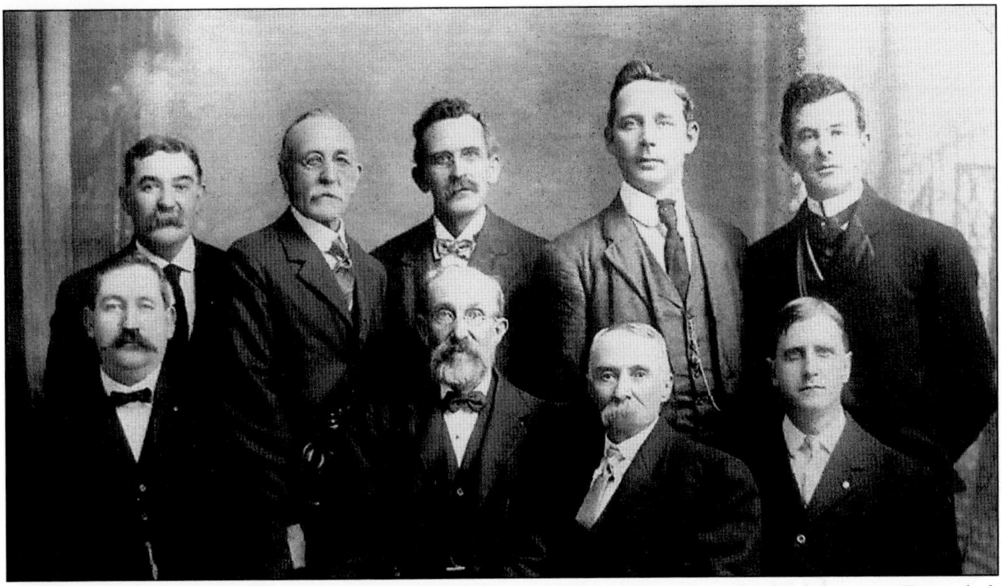

Shown are the members of the 1907–1909 Florence Township Board of Education. From left to right are the following: (front row) Thomas F. Watson, Thomas Rainear, John Adams, and William C. Sturtevant; (back row) James Absalom, William Bisbing, Daniel W. Bishop, Goodwin Donnelly, and Richard P. Hughes. (Courtesy of Florence Historical Society.)

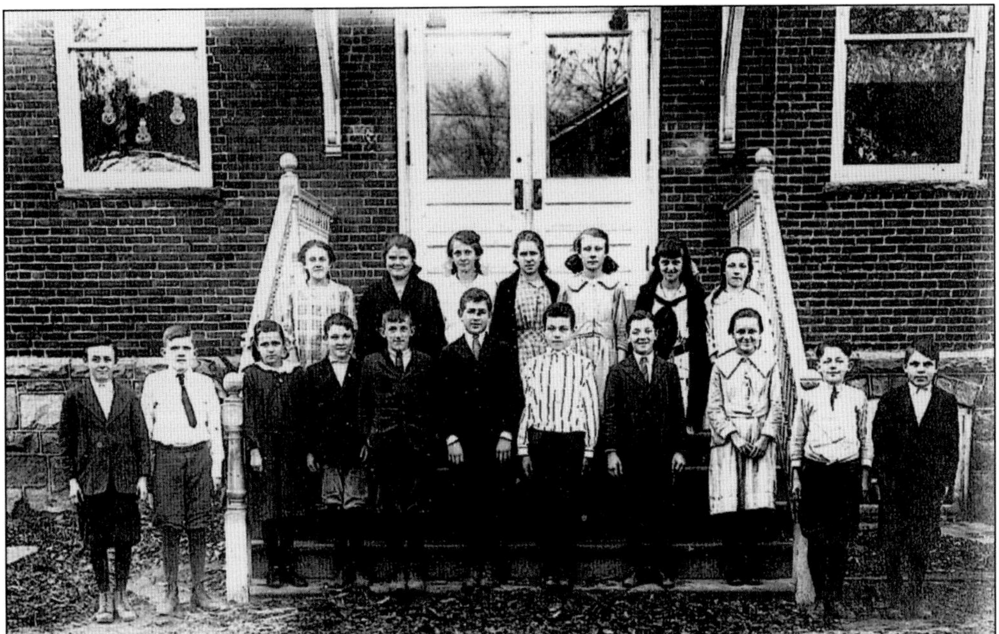

Students pose at Second Street School in the early 1900s. This school was renamed the Marcella L. Duffy School in 1969; it is still in use. (Courtesy of Barbara Bishop Durham.)

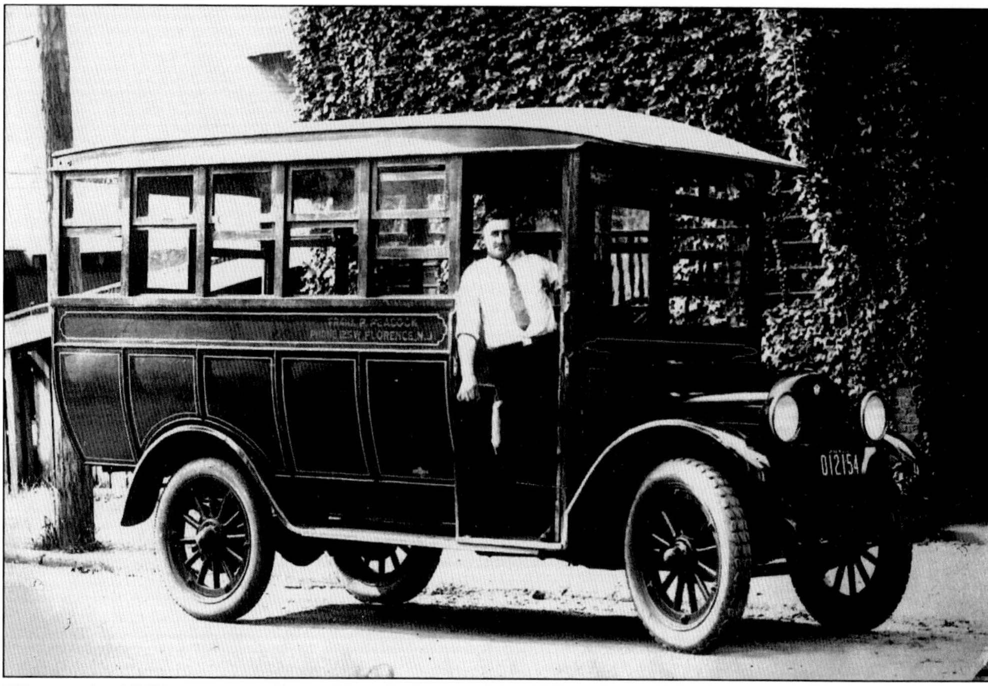

This early-1930s picture shows Frank Peacock and his bus. Charter buses in town were also run by Carty, Peacock, Hamilton, and Paglione for the schools. (Courtesy of Florence Historical Society.)

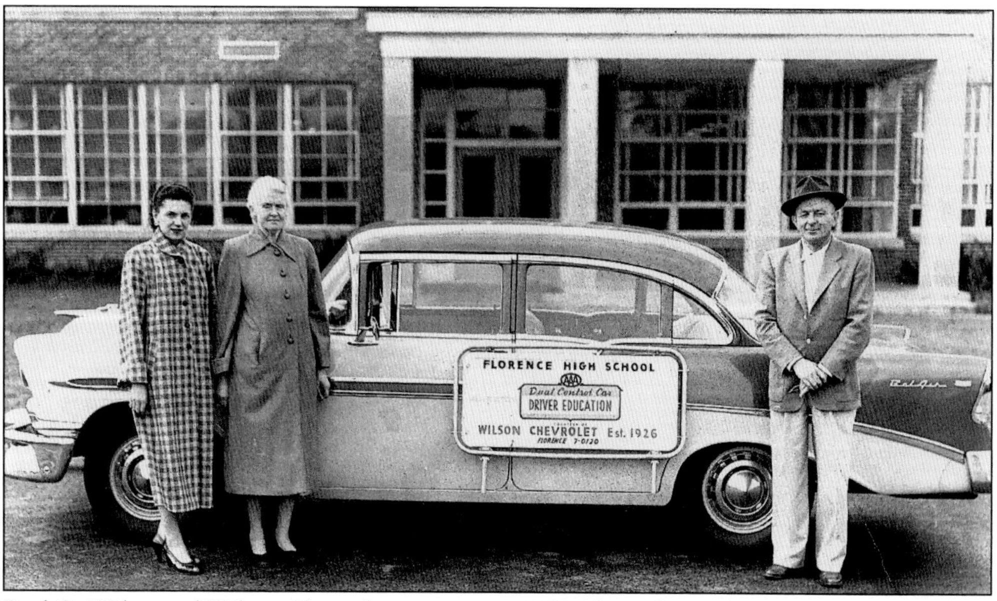

Paul Q. Wilson, of Wilson Chevrolet, presents a 1956 Chevrolet to the Florence High School for driver education classes. Pictured with him are driver education teacher Helen E. Masick (left) and Marcella Duffy, principal of the school, on East Front Street. (Courtesy of Florence Historical Society.)

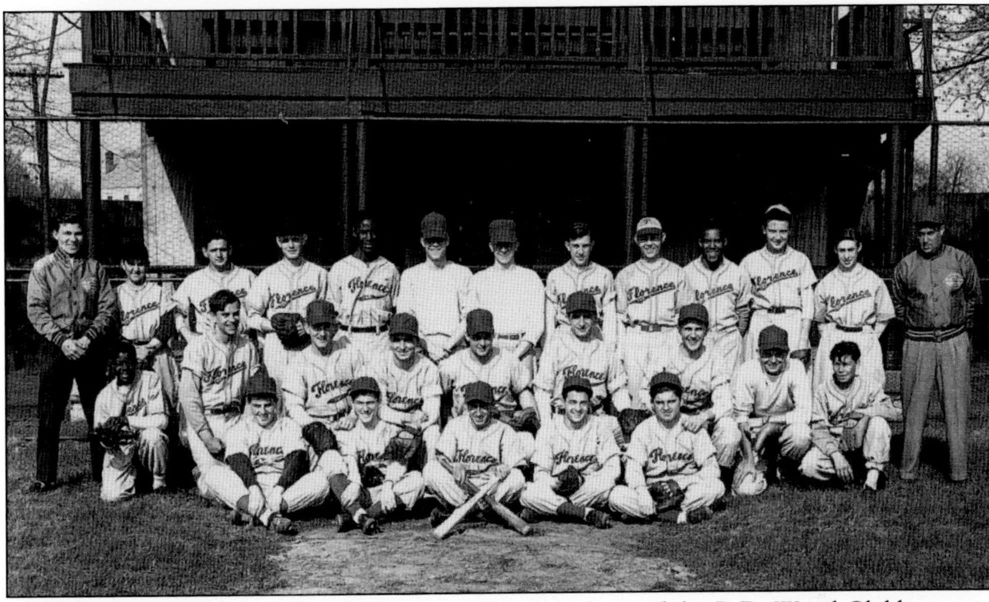

The Florence High School baseball team is shown in front of the R.D. Wood Clubhouse, on West 5th Street in the 1940s. From left to right are the following: (front row) Alvah Smith, Danny Welsh, Sam ?, and William Breza; (middle row) unidentified, Keith Hammell, Dominick Santoleri, Rich Woolston, and ? Yurcisin; (back row) Tebo Csik, John Buccigrossi, unidentified, Norman Spotts, unidentified, ? Everham, unidentified, John Sofchak, Robert Mullen, Roger Morton, Ronald Hoeltz, Robert Page, and coach Marty Fischbein. (Courtesy of Florence Historical Society.)

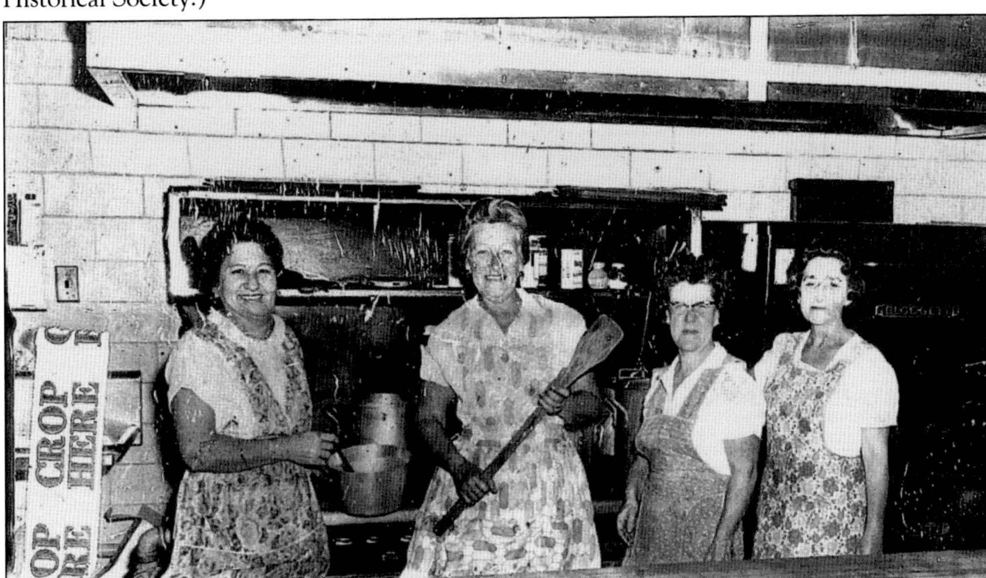

The Florence High School cafeteria women are pictured in the 1950s. From left to right are Violet Sitzler of Florence, Lucille Hague of Roebling, Mary Rossell of Florence Station, and Caroline Wixom of Florence. (Courtesy of Joan Shafer.)

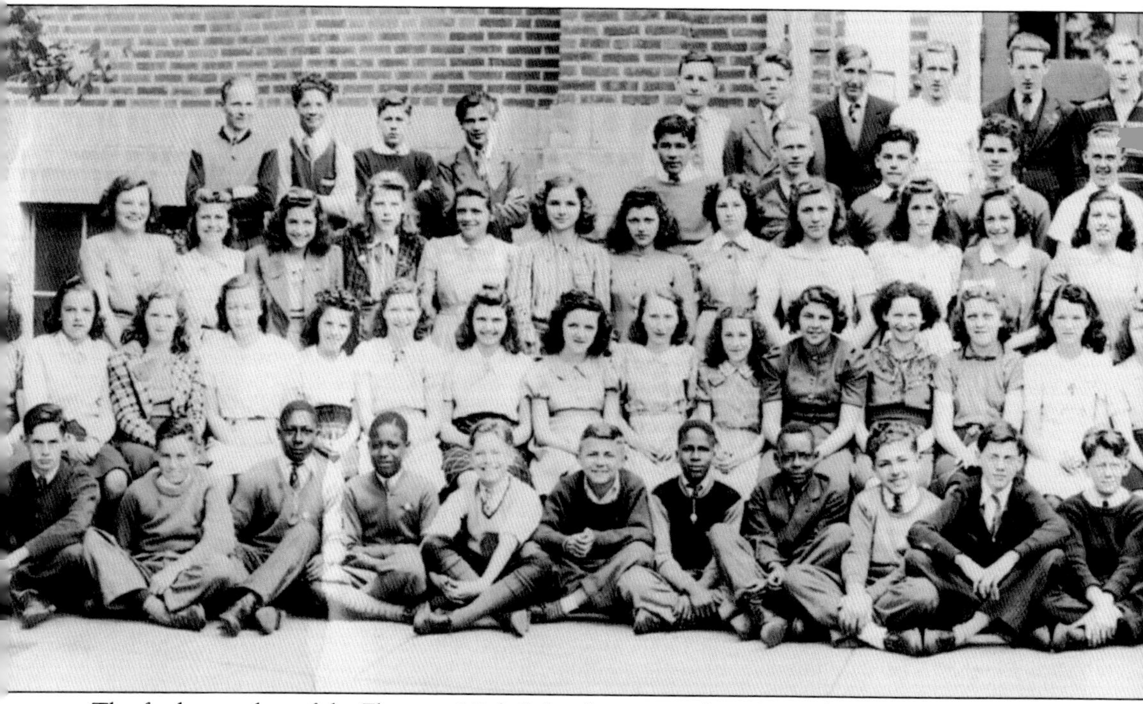

The freshman class of the Florence High School is pictured in 1940. This was the high school's

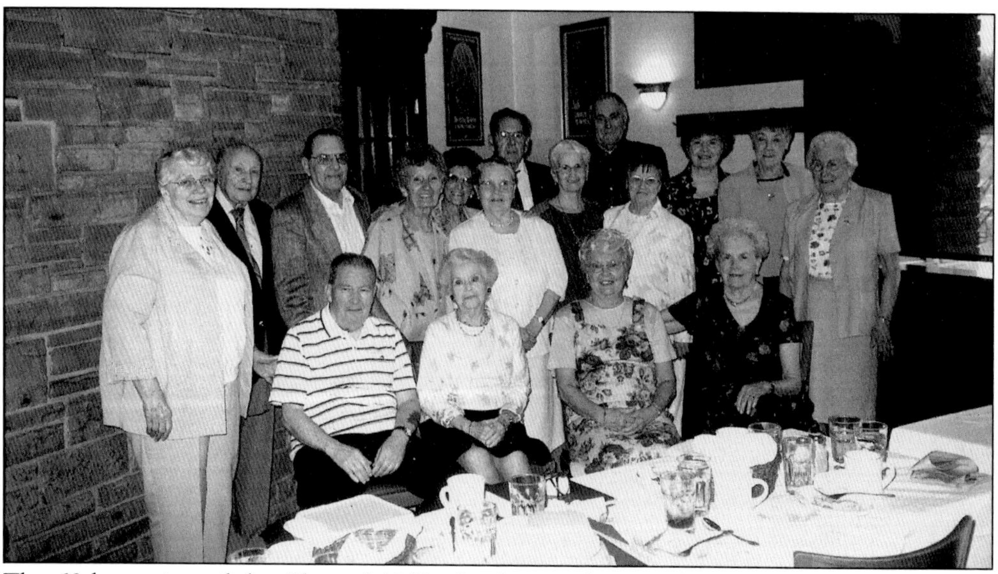

The 60th reunion of the Class of 1943, the first graduating class of seniors from Florence Township Memorial High School on Second Street, was held in June 2003. From left to right are the following: (seated) John Gesemeyer, school nurse Margaret Dougherty, Muriel Sweetman Dougherty, and Ruth Carlson Roe; (standing) Ruth Eels Anilosky, Matthew Sparta, William Gourovitch (Gorvan), Margaret Sahol Buckalew, Margherita Agostinelli Markiewicz, Anna Duffy Rainier, Ralph Foulks, Mary Bago Kern, John Tyira, Nancy Cryan Czaplicki, Nolah Sutphin Forker, Betty Sweeney Breza, and Mary Bombelli Tapper. (Courtesy of Mary Tapper.)

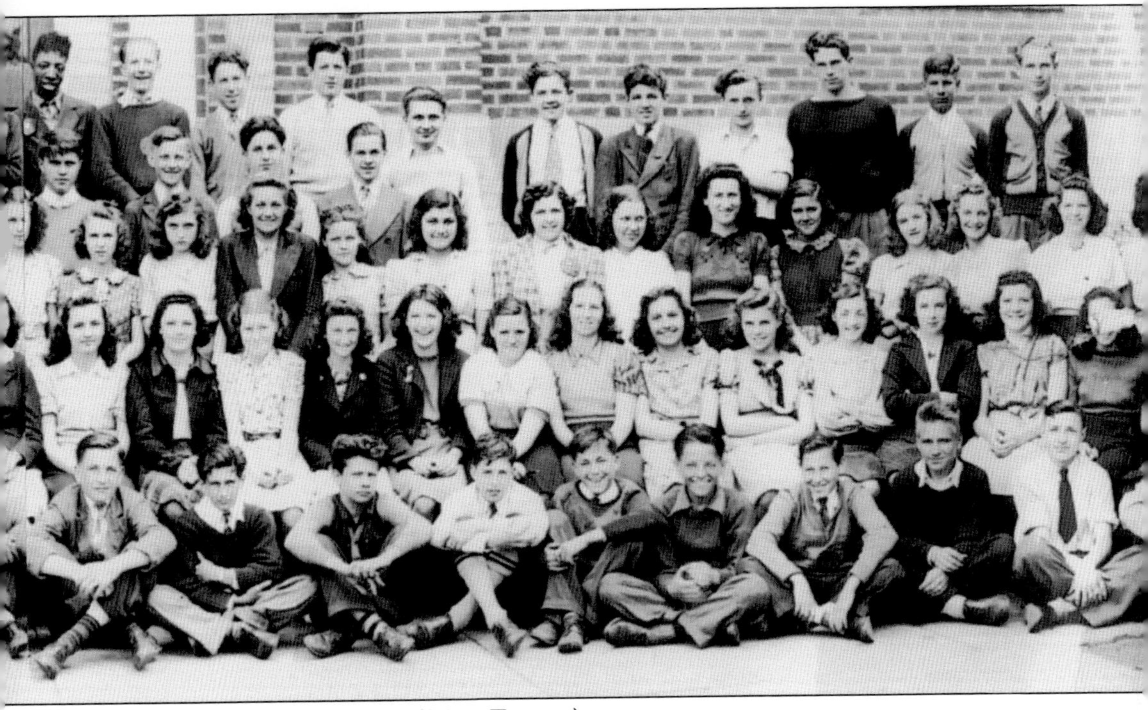

first graduating class. (Courtesy of Mary Tapper.)

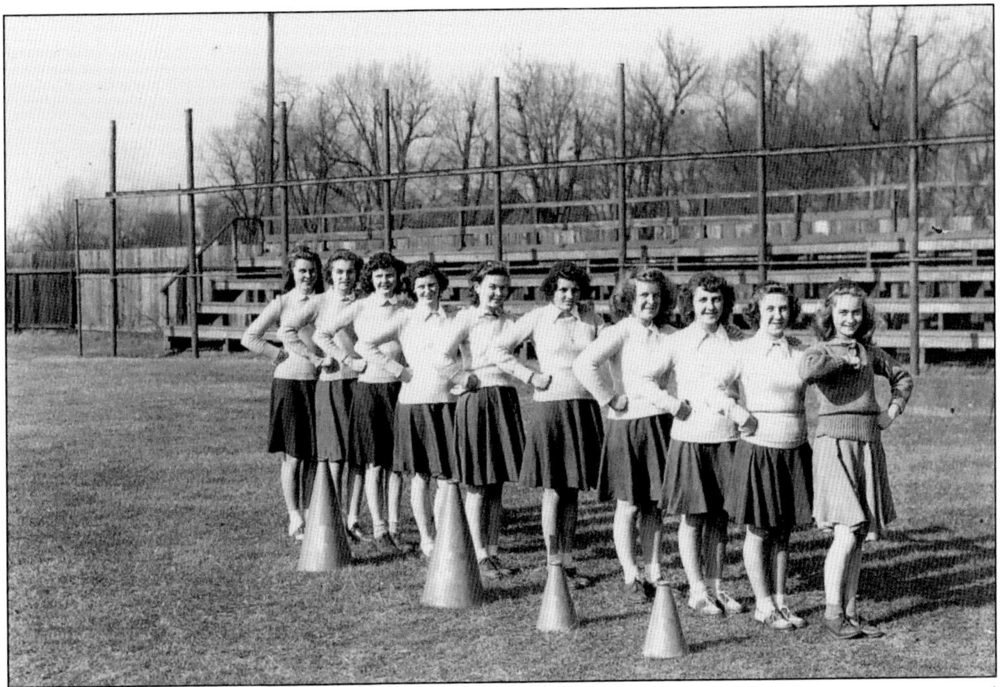

The 1944 junior varsity cheerleading squad lines up in front of the grandstand at the R.D. Wood Field, on West 5th Street. (Courtesy of Florence Historical Society.)

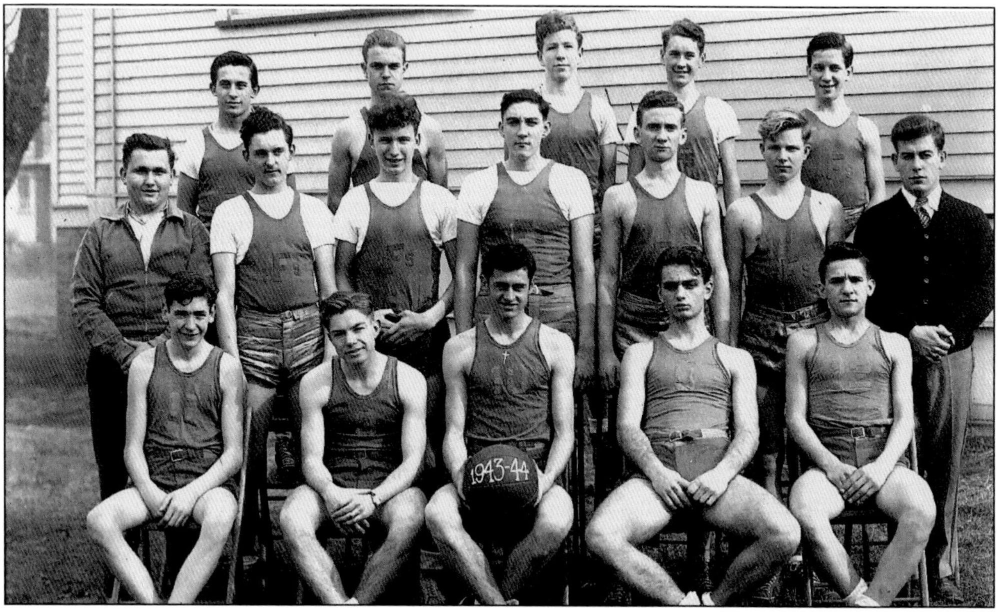

The Florence High School Basketball Team is shown *c.* 1943–1944 in front of the parish hall, where games were played. Owned by St. Stephen's Episcopal Church, the hall stood on the east side of Broad Street in the third block and hosted dances and other social functions. The building was razed to make way for the present-day row of stores. Pictured are, from left to right, (front row) Bob Everham, Milton Hershberger, Jack Quig, John Mazar, and Joe Yurcisin; (middle row) Bill Vash, John Potpinka, Ed Balog, Zoltan Emri, Fritz Wilhelm, Bob Miller, and James Dow; (back row) John Mattis, Fran Bauer, Bill Carter, Tom Adams, and Joe Barta. (Courtesy of Florence Historical Society.)

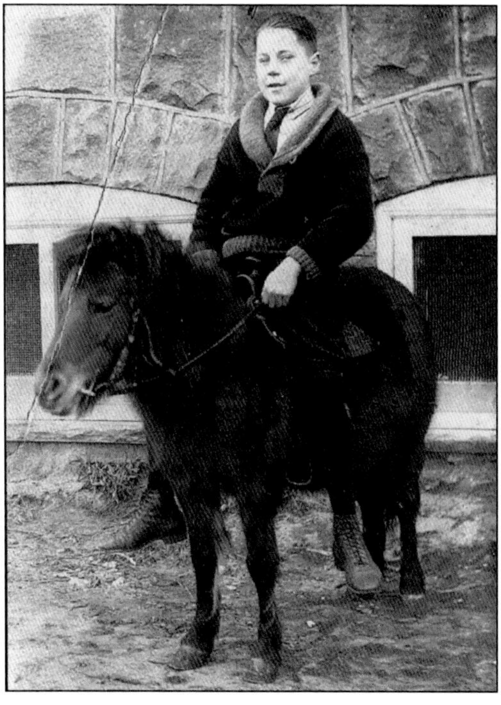

Popular photographs of the time often pictured children on ponies. This one shows Albert A. King Jr. in front of the Florence Station School *c.* 1924. (Courtesy of Albert L. King.)

Nine

SOCIAL ORGANIZATIONS

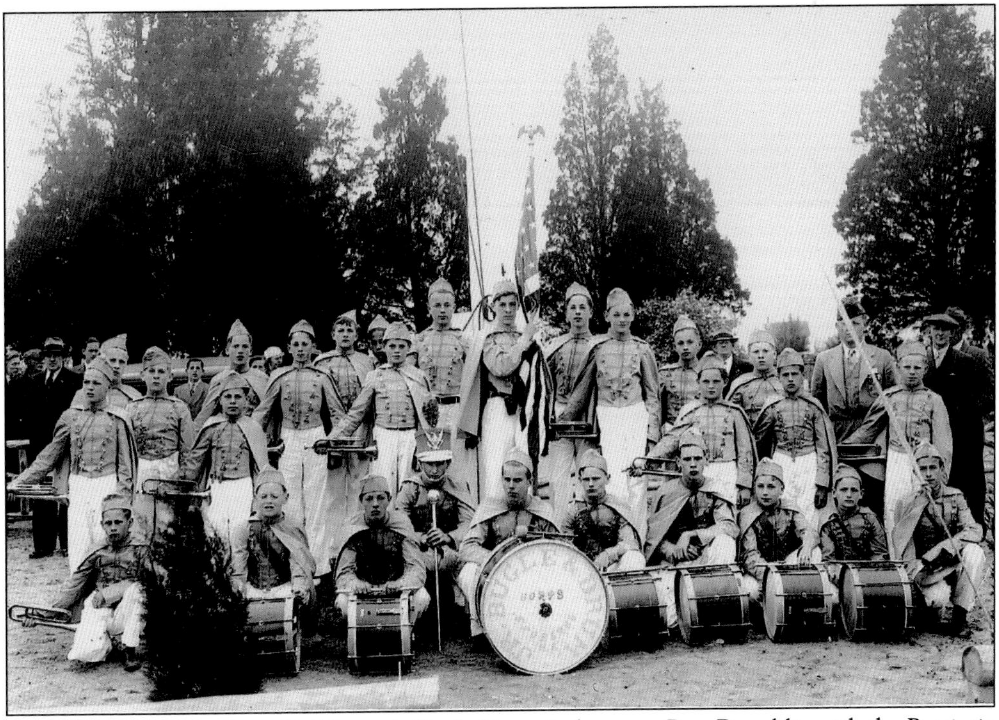

The Francis Robbins Post 194 Drum & Bugle Corps is shown at Port Republic with the Patriotic Sons of America. From left to right are the following: (front row) Jack Gesemeyer, Robert Wilkie, Edward Cryan, James Tapper, Charles Emmons, Arnold Wilson, Harry Everham, Ralph Shuler, Edward Wilson, and James Cheesman; (middle row) Thomas Wilson, Herman Anderson, Richard Spotts, Phil Stone, Paul Phillips, Richard Sweeney, Kenneth Wilkie, "Chub" Cronin, John Molnar, and Andrew Bodrog; (back row) Albert Griffith, Ernest Brown, Jack Ledger, Carlton Durham, John Bodrog, Carl Linda, Louis Kocsis, Shreve Malsbury, and director Harold E. Moore (behind rope). (Courtesy of Florence Historical Society.)

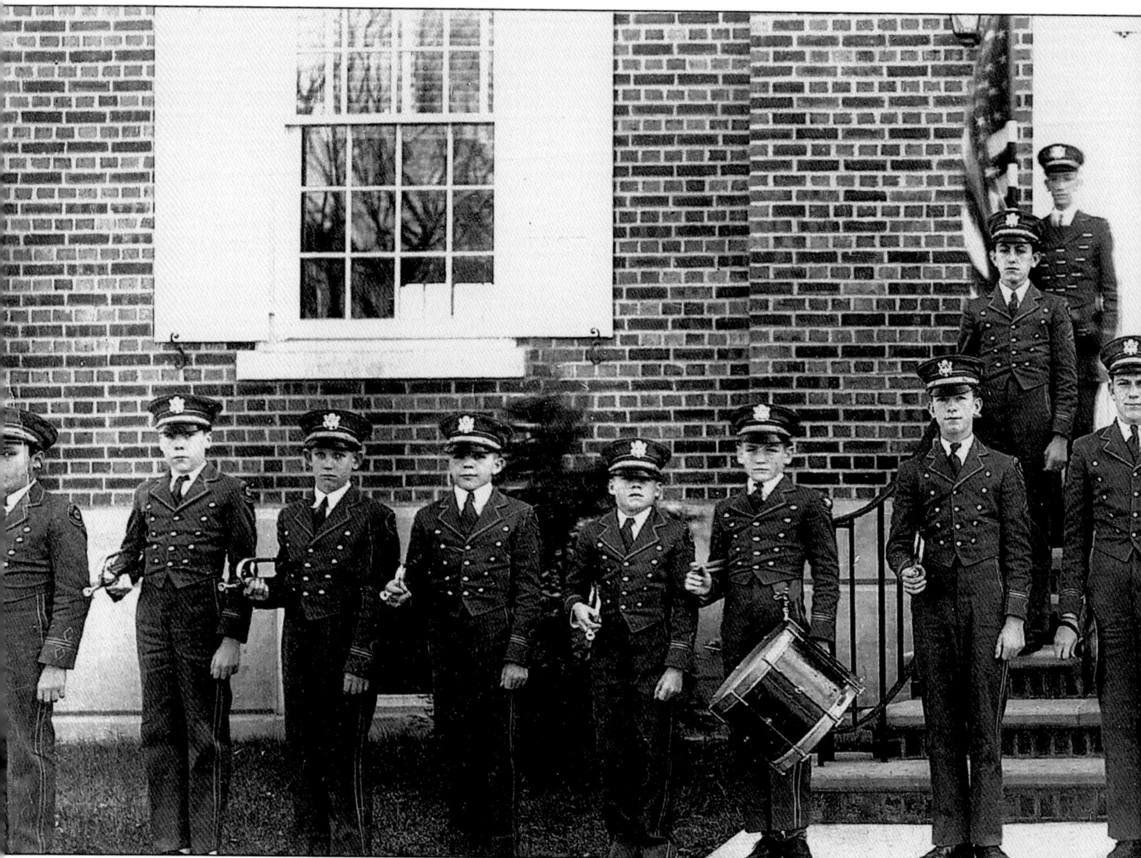

The band of the Francis Robbins Post No. 194 American Legion is assembled in parade uniforms in 1935. From left to right are the following: (front row) Carlton Durham, George Everett, Richard Stark, Peter Capritti, Leon Hamilton, Eddie Wilson, Douglas Anderson, Russell "Icky" Roughton, John Molnar, Arnold Wilson, Ralph Shuler, Ed Cryan, George Nykita,

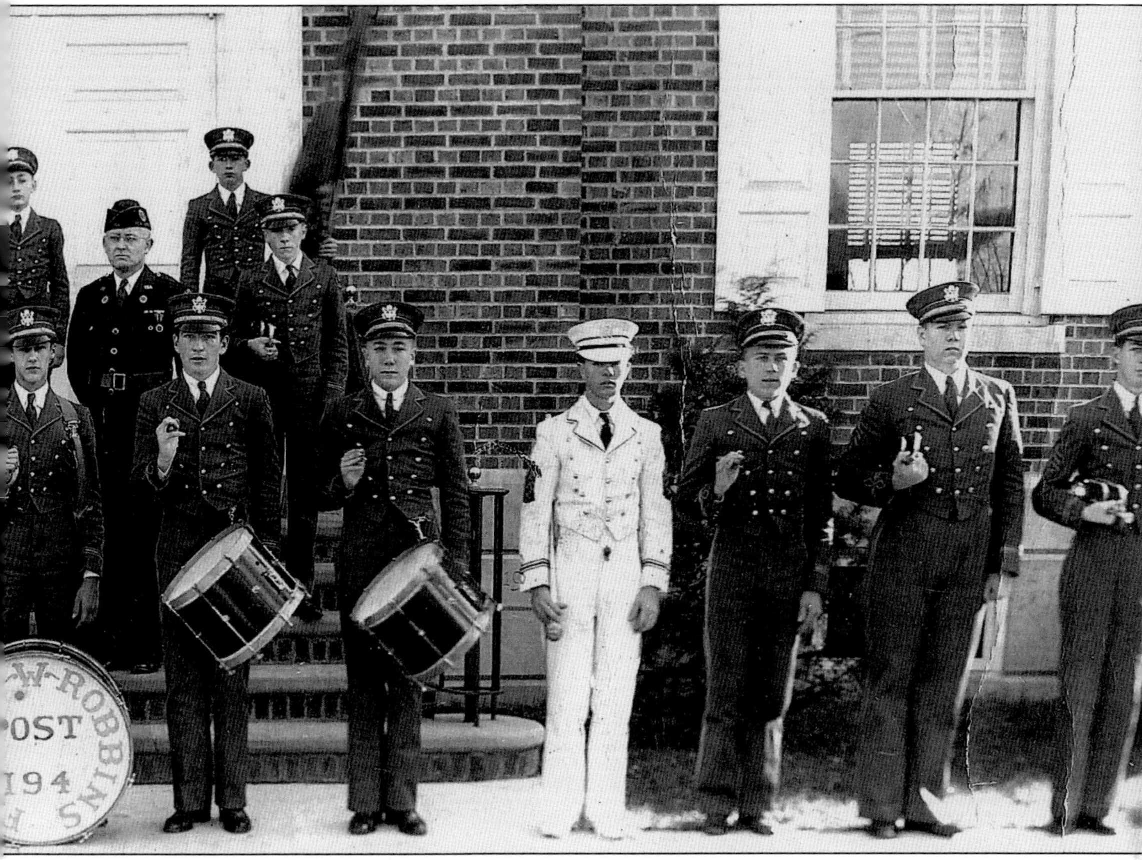

Shreve Malsbury, Thomas Wilson, and Francis McCorriston; (middle row) John Buccigrossi, Bob Everham, Harold Moore, and Linton Everett; (back row) two unidentified people and Donald Matlack. (Courtesy of Joe and Marian Everett Bock.)

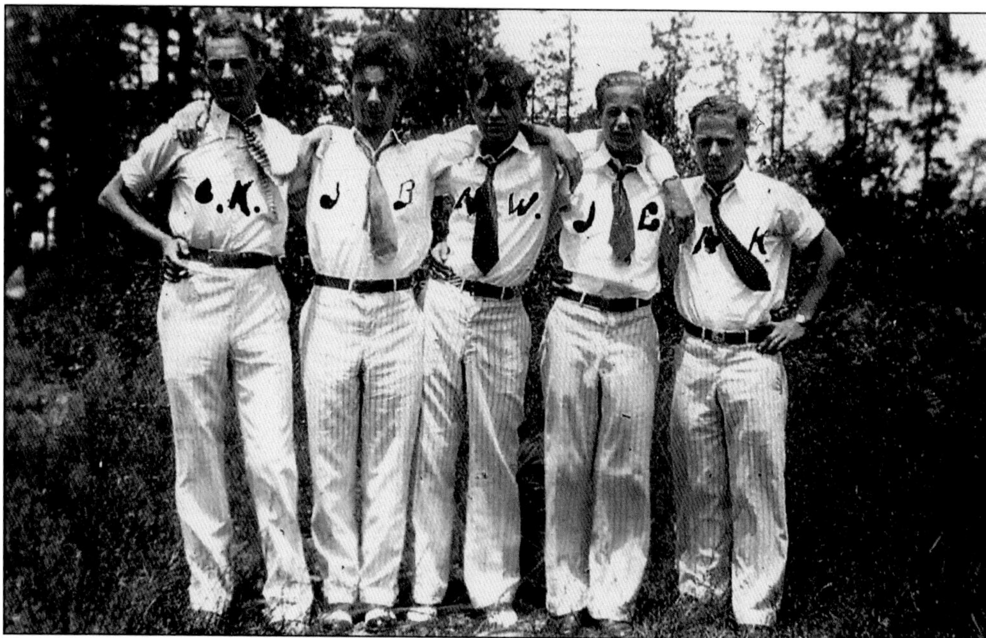

The Midshipmen was a popular band around town. Band members are shown after a booking at Pomona, where they played for an entire summer season in 1933. From left to right are Charles Kimble, John Blakeslee, William "Mimi" Wallace, James Gardner, and Albert A. King Jr. Missing from the group is John Zahorsky. (Courtesy of Florence Historical Society.)

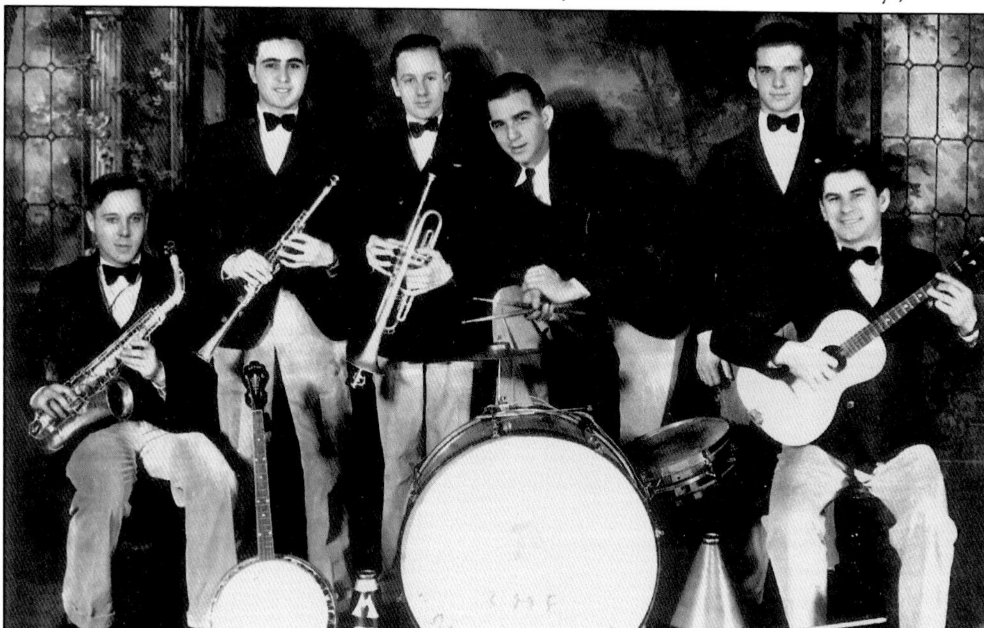

The Midshipmen played at town functions as well as places as far away as Pomona and the Poconos. The band practiced in the gas station at Route 25 and Delaware Avenue late at night, and neighbors enjoyed the music so much they danced in the street. From left to right in this 1930s photographs are Albert A. King, Jr., "Mimi" Wallace, James Gardner, Charles Kimble, John Blakeslee, and John Zahorsky. (Courtesy of Albert King.)

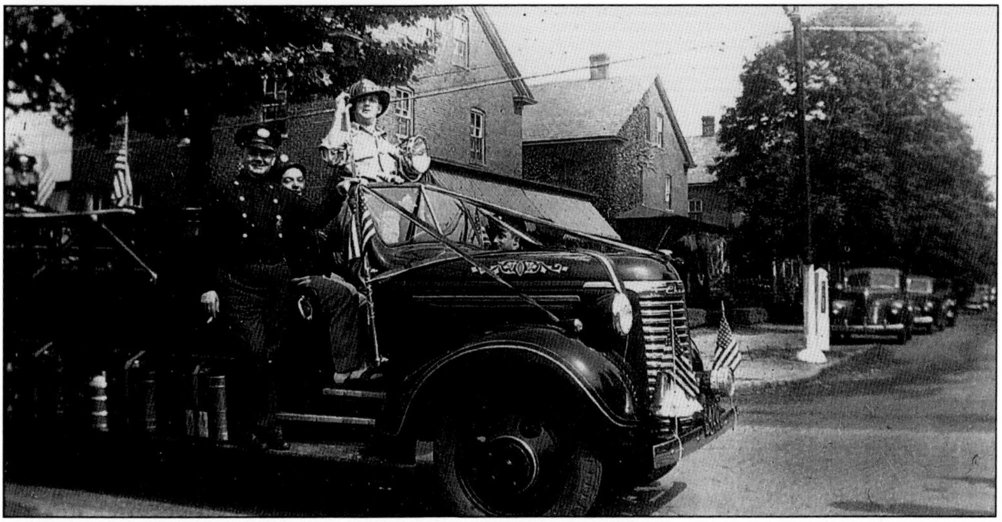

Because of its picnics, carnivals, and parade participation, Florence Fire Company No. 1 is also considered a social organization. Firemen John Baird and Earl Brant are pictured in Roebling on their 1938 Chevrolet in 1942. (Courtesy of Florence Historical Society.)

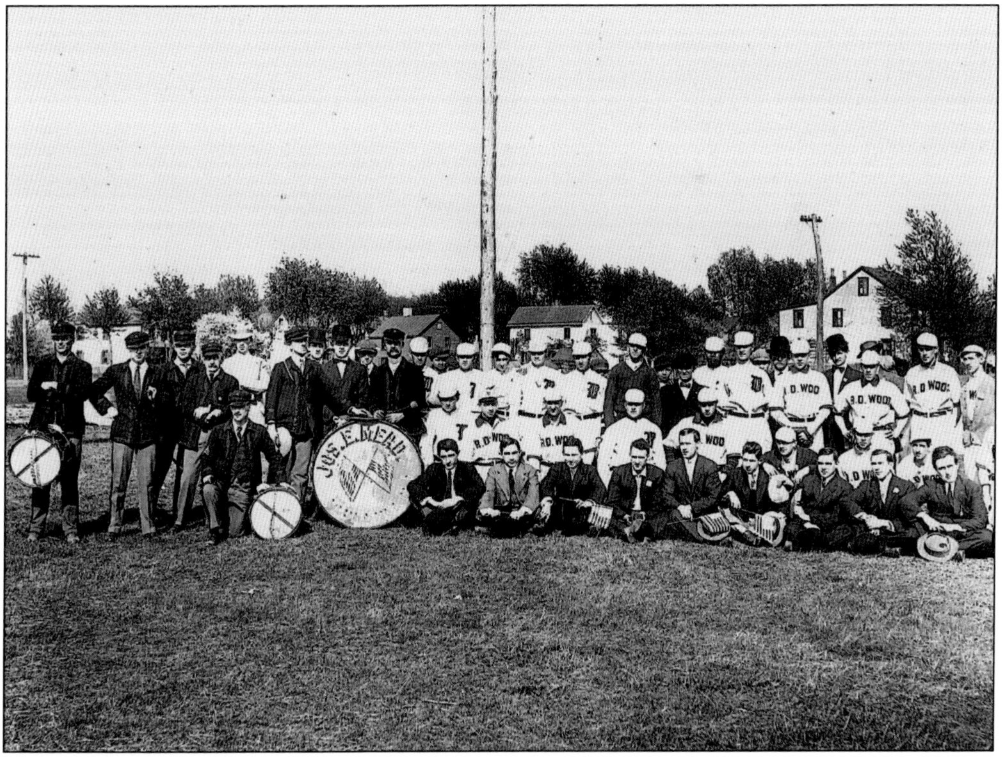

The Joseph Mead Fife and Drum Corps was popular at many town functions—parades, picnics, and baseball games. The group is shown with the R.D. Wood Baseball Team *c.* the 1920s. (Courtesy of Florence Historical Society.)

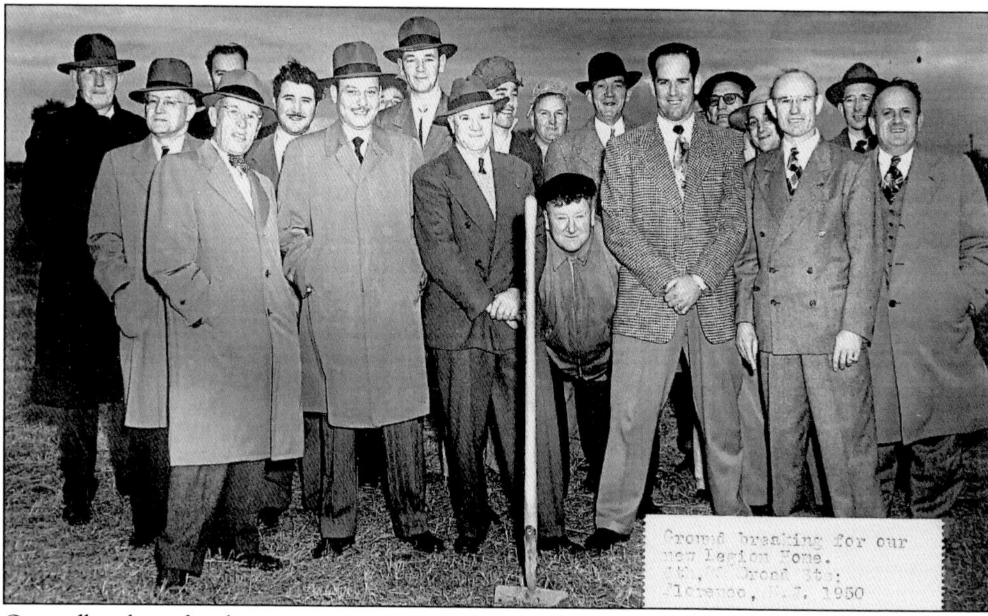

Groundbreaking for the new American Legion Post No. 39 was held in 1950 at the southwest corner of Broad and 6th Streets. From left to right are the following: (front row) unidentified, William Parker, Joe Rue, Grady Walsh, George Phillips, unidentified, and John Baird; (middle row) Harold Moore, Romeo Marinelli, Kenneth Wilkie, Nick DiLullo, and unidentified; (back row) unidentified, Arnold Weeast (directly behind shovel), unidentified, Albert "Nudge" Hamilton (in sunglasses), unidentified, and Charles Adams. The unidentified men on the left may be state officials. (Courtesy of Jim Penacchi.)

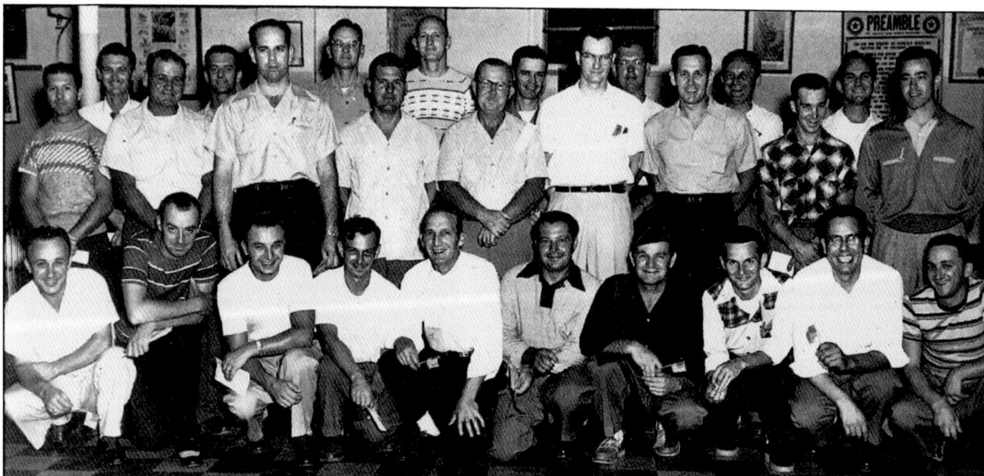

The Francis Robbins American Legion Post No. 194 is shown at a member installation in the 1950s, at Broad and West 6th Street. From left to right are the following: (front row) Carl "Jingles" Lubrano, Richard Sweeney, Mike Talpas, Charles Lowe, Albert "Nudge" Hamilton, Frank Losito, Bill Garwood, Arthur "Corky" Warren, unidentified, and Michael Lubrano; (middle row) Ed Cryan, Alderigo Stefanoni, George Phillips, Howard Gudikunst, ? Sanderson, Arnold Wilson, Neil Mulhern, Robert "Chink" Wilson, and Nick DiLullo; (back row) Steve Molnar, Leon Hughes, H. Kenneth Wilkie, Robert Wilkie, James Doherty, Louis Bushman, Ray Conover, and unidentified. (Courtesy of Florence Historical Society.)

The Improved Order of Redmen was a benevolent organization—at one time the largest in the world—that collected dues for death benefits, as well as for sickness and disability. Florence's tribe was called Minnehaha No. 38. Costumes were not allowed in parades, only in ceremonies. (Courtesy of Mary Tapper.)

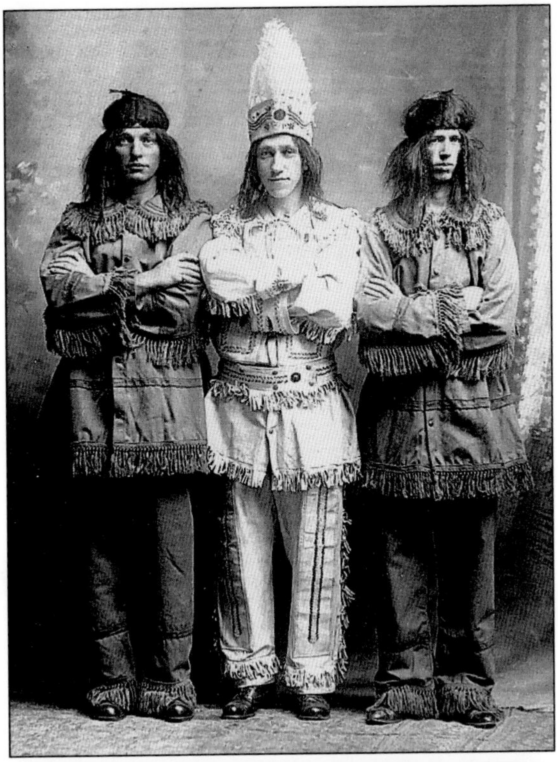

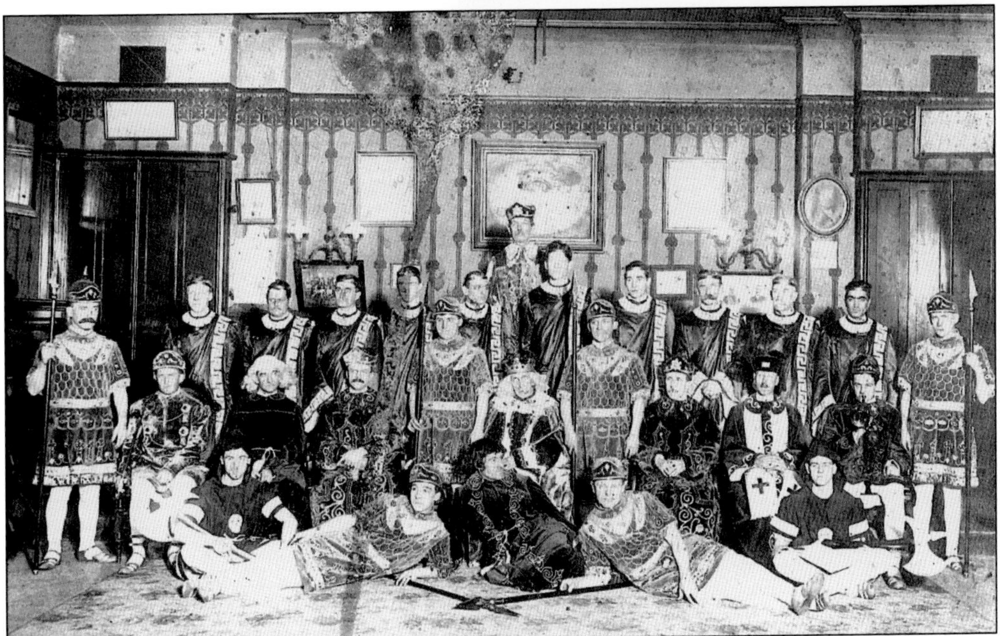

Pictured is the Redmen Minnehaha Tribe No. 38 of Florence in 1929. From left to right are George Ford Sr., Harry Beaumaster, Charles Rodney, Louis Branin, Joseph McCue, George Ford Jr., Harvey McAllister, Raymond Evans, Harry Parker, unidentified, Leslie Parker, John Breamins, Joseph Smith, two unidentified persons, and Howard Wilkie. (Courtesy of Florence Historical Society.)

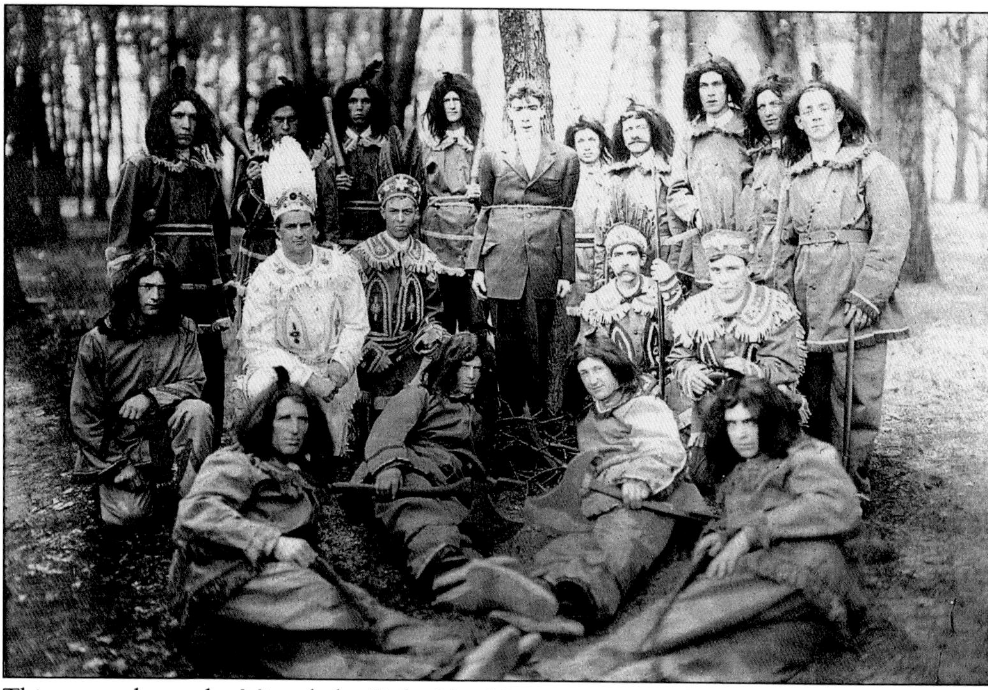

This scene shows the Minnehaha Tribe No. 38 at a ceremonial, or initiation, in which the man tied to the tree is probably a prospective member. In 1927, this was one form of social gathering in the towns around America that participate in Redmen functions. (Courtesy of Mary Tapper.)

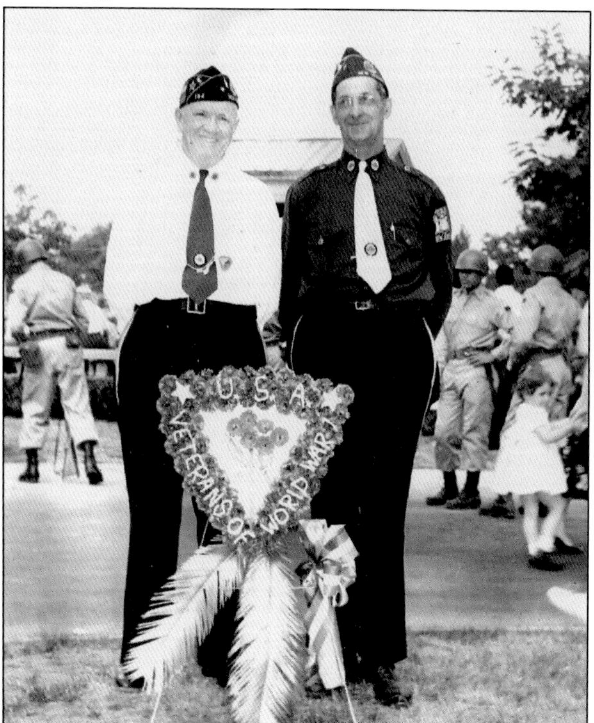

Joe Rue (left) is shown at a Memorial Day ceremony, *c.* 1957. He was a veteran of World Wars I and II and a proud member of the American Legion Post No. 194. (Courtesy of Richard Glass.)

Pictured before a parade in 1940–1941 is Ruth Carlson (Roe), a member of the Florence Girl Cadets. She later became the school and community nurse. (Courtesy of Margaret Lynch.)

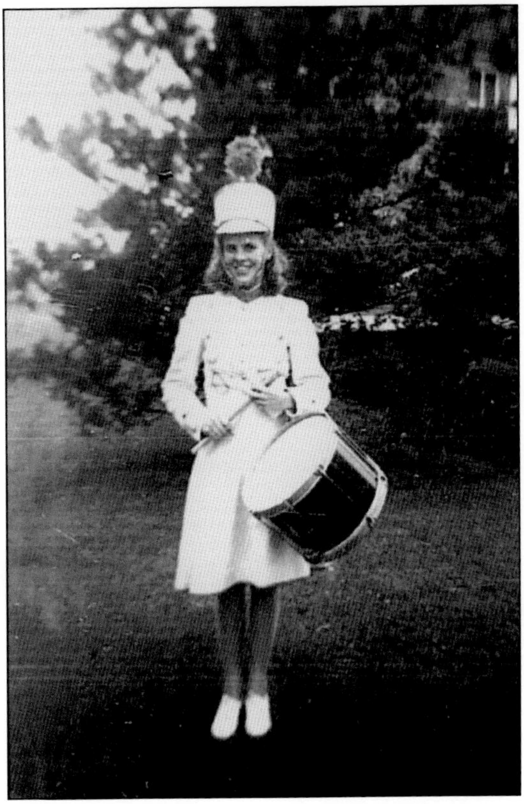

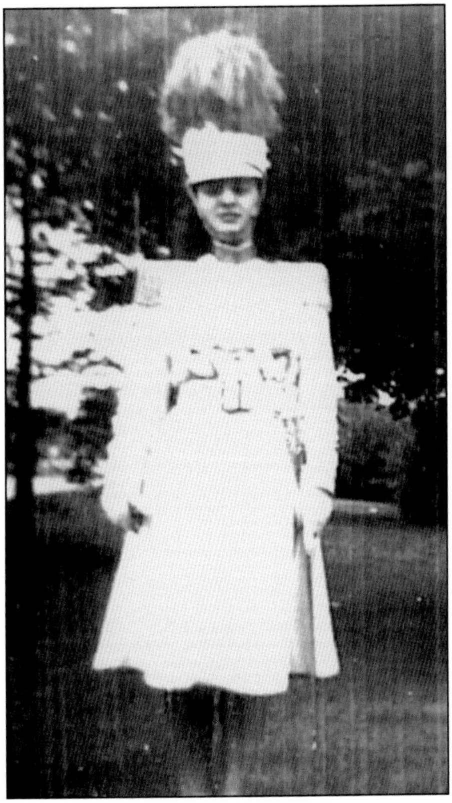

Margaret Nichols (Lynch), daughter of Harry Nichols, is shown before a parade in 1940–1941 as a member of the Florence Girl Cadets. She still lives in the Nichols homestead, on the Boulevard. (Courtesy of Margaret Lynch.)

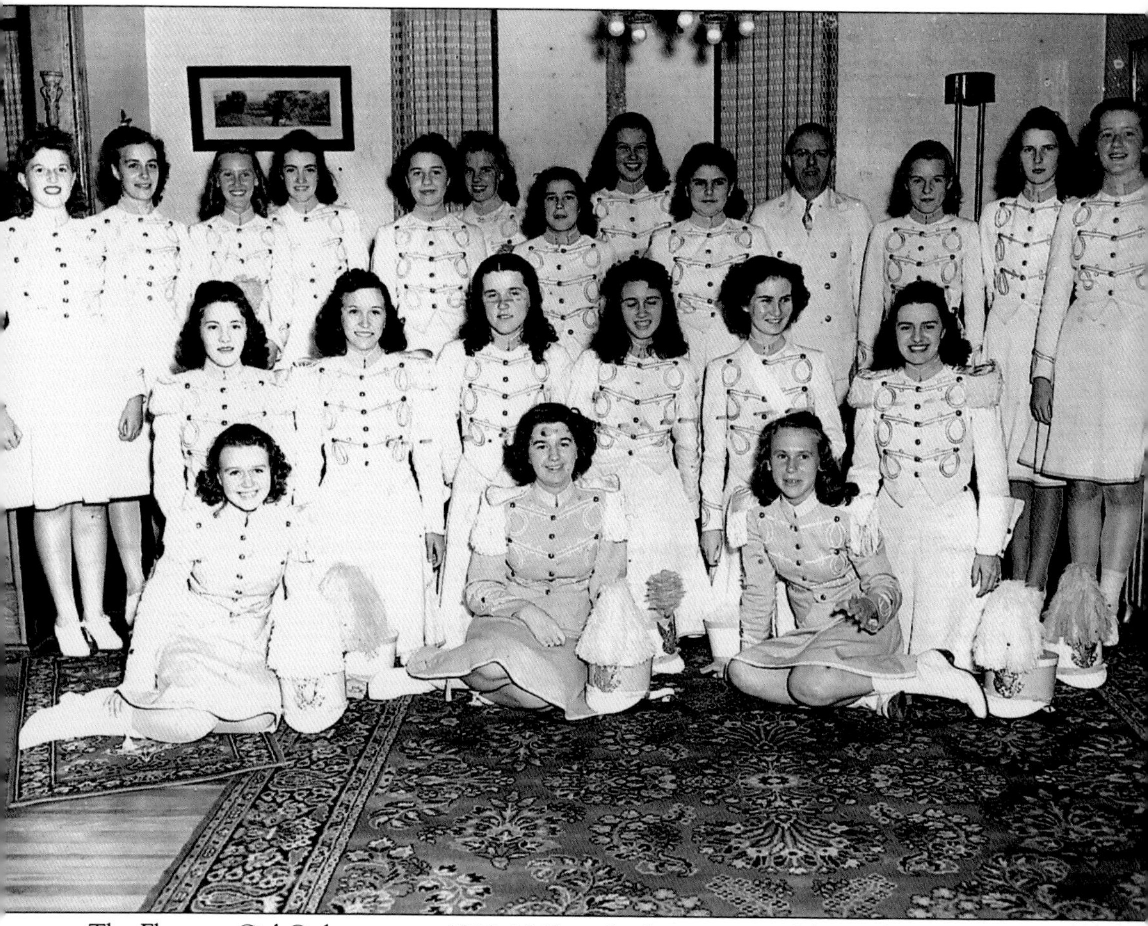

The Florence Girl Cadets pose *c.* 1940–1941 in the living room of the Nichols home, on the Boulevard. From left to right are the following: (front row) Helen Earley, Letisha Nichols, and Betty Moffett; (middle row) Lillian Hamell, Julia Wollman, Doris Durham, Evelyn Rossell, Leatrice Wilson, and Margaret Nichols; (back row) Bertha Smith, Lois Panaro, Florence Adams, Betty Sweeney, Rosemary Regars, Ruth Carlson, Helen Cheesman, Jean McNinney, Thelma Foulks, director Harry Nichols, Laura Jones, Phyllis Keating, and Frances Houlihan. (Courtesy of Florence Historical Society.)

Ten

Sports

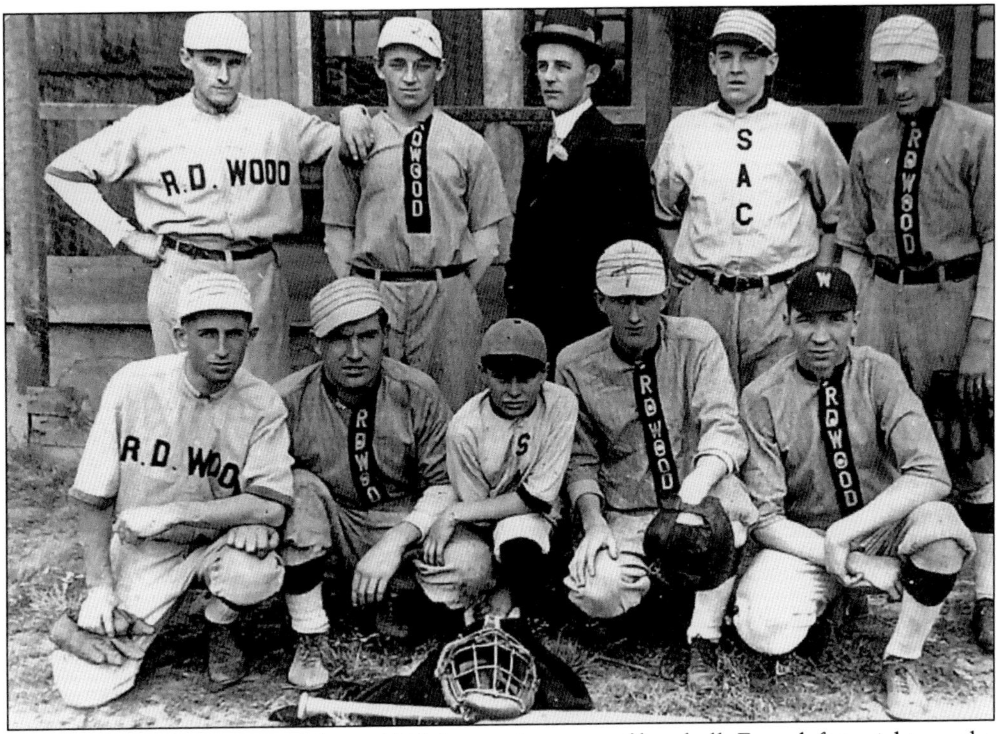

The R.D. Wood team assembles *c.* 1910 for another year of baseball. From left to right are the following: (front row) Lou Kiefer, Bill Sweeney, unidentified, Rowland Elliott, and Emmett Beckett; (back row) Milton Absalom, Harvey McAllister, Bill McGrath, Ivins Camp, and Frank Peacock. (Courtesy of Florence Historical Society.)

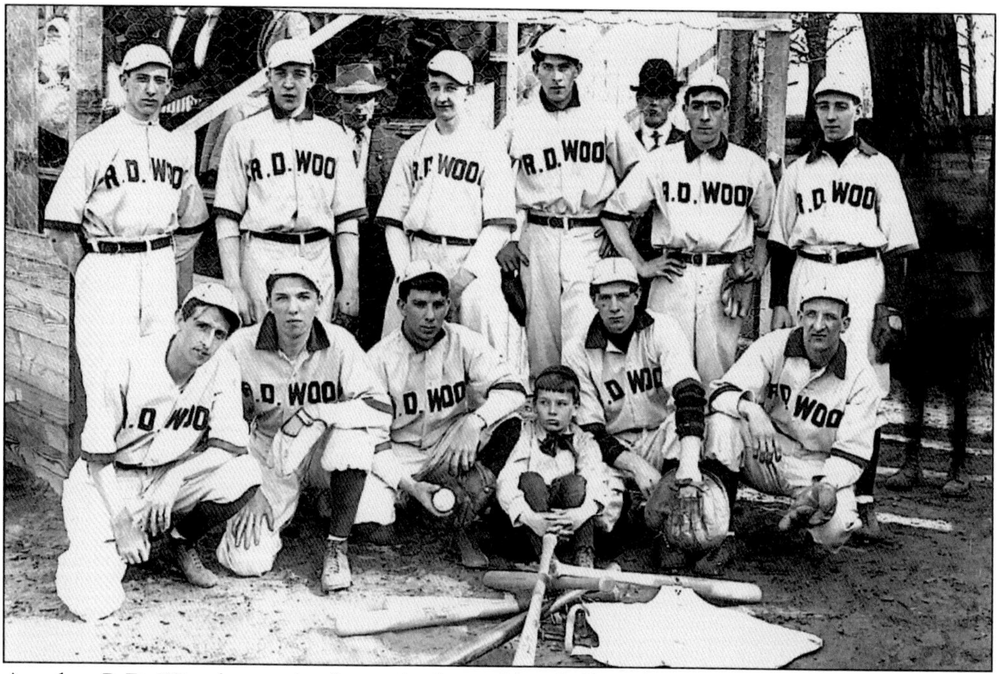

Another R.D. Wood team in the early days of baseball is shown. From left to right are the following: (front row) Charlie Delaroi, Harvey Rhubart, Bill Sadler, Elvin Wilson Jr. (junior mascot), Elvin Wilson, and John Rhoda; (back row) ? Hulehan, ? Beckett, Charlie Peacock, Jesse Foulks, John Cheesman, and ? Baristow. (Courtesy of Florence Historical Society.)

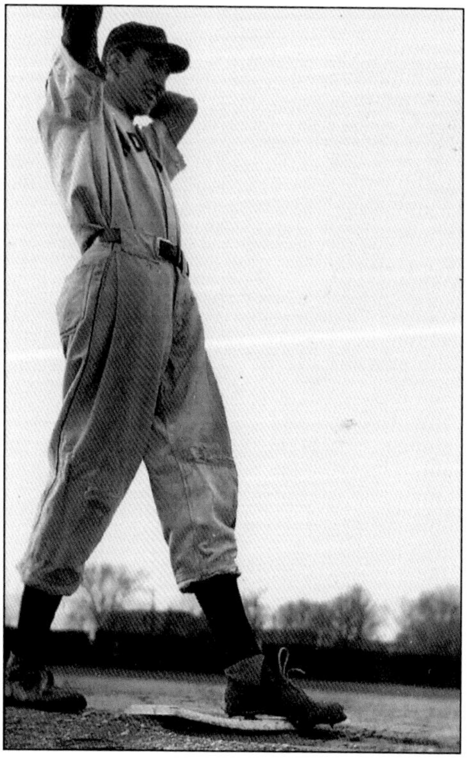

Tom Sweeney is shown winding up for a pitch in 1939 on the R.D. Wood field, on West 5th Street. Brother of Jack Sweeney, he was later recruited for the farm team of the Philadelphia Phillies. (Courtesy of Helen Panaro Henderson.)

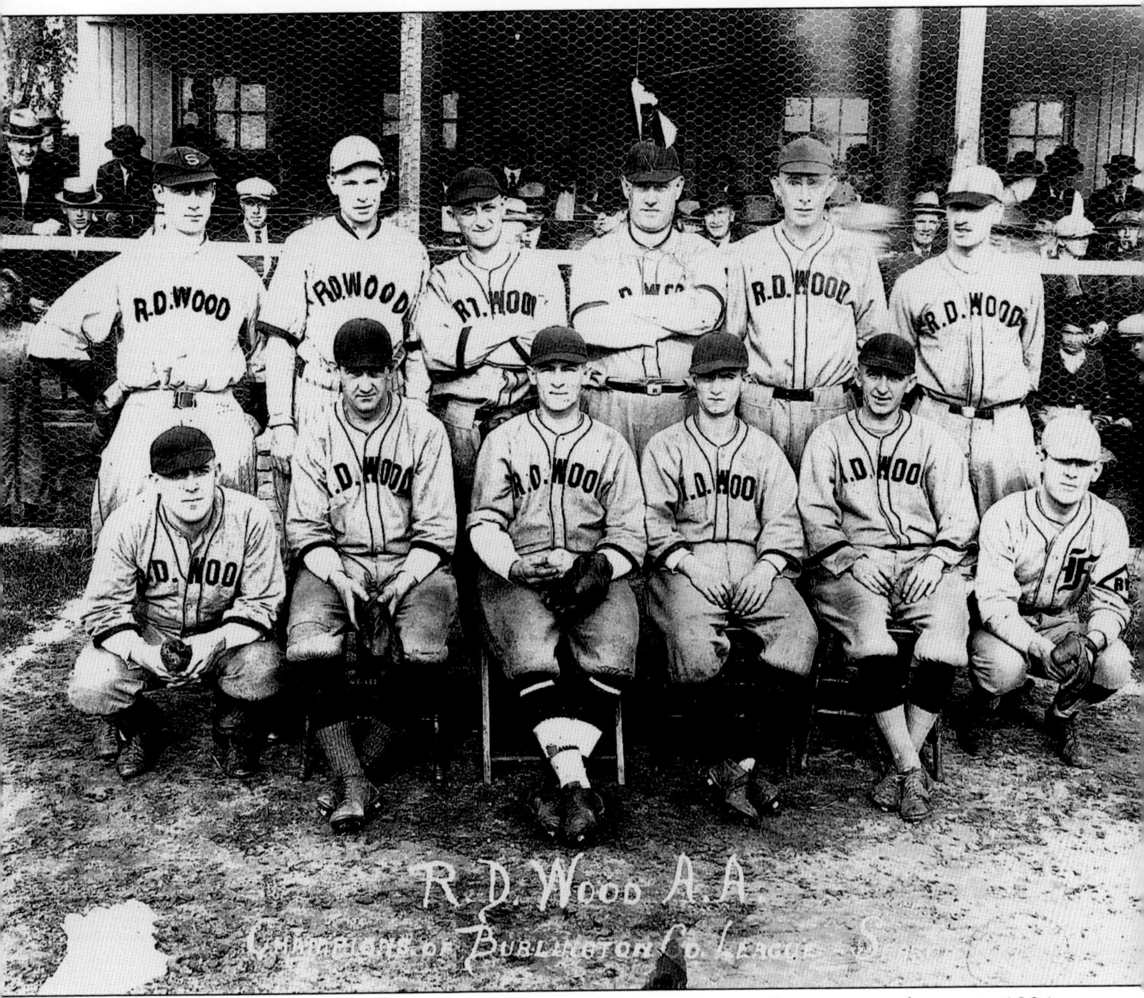

R.D. Wood team members, champions of the Burlington County League, are shown in 1924. From left to right are the following: (front row) "Buck" Beaudry, Charlie Peacock, "Nanny" Woolston, Nick Frappolli, "Ruby" Gilbert, and ? Hafey; (back row) Lou Kite, Bill Everham, John Rhoda, Jack Sweeney, Jesse Foulks, and ? Algie. (Courtesy of Florence Historical Society.)

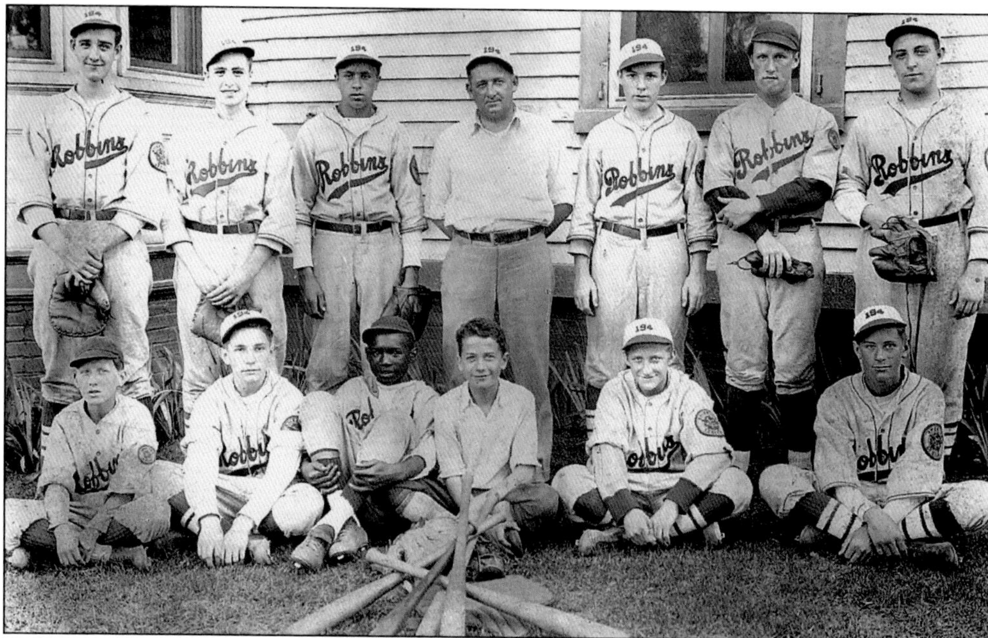

The American Legion Team is pictured in 1931. From left to right are the following: (front row) Albert "Nudge" Hamilton, Bill Britton, ? Patterson, "Tots" Legnaioli, Fritz DeFlece, and "Boob" Patterson; (back row) Hilyard Simpkins, William "Mimi" Wallace, Duder Lynch, Frank Peacock, Olie Brining, Bill Hughes, and Russell Woolston. (Courtesy of Marsha Hughes.)

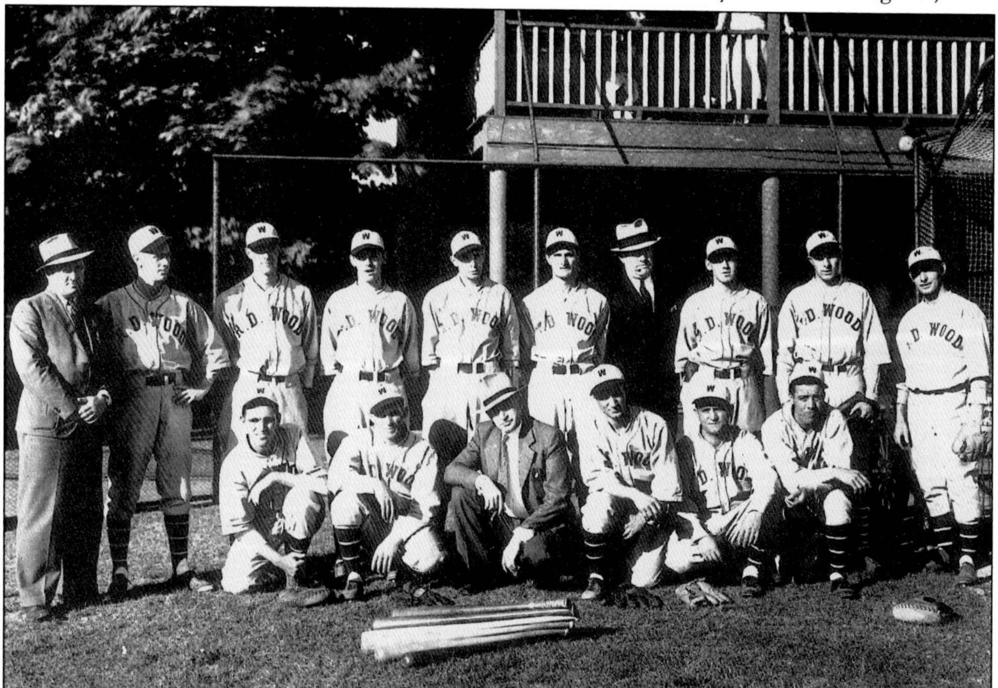

The 1936 R.D. Wood baseball team lines up by the clubhouse, on West 5th Street. Those in the front row, from left to right, are Joe Pasqualine, John Woolston, Ed Robbins, Bart Frappolli, Nick Frappolli, and "Shine" Angelini. (Courtesy of Florence Historical Society.)

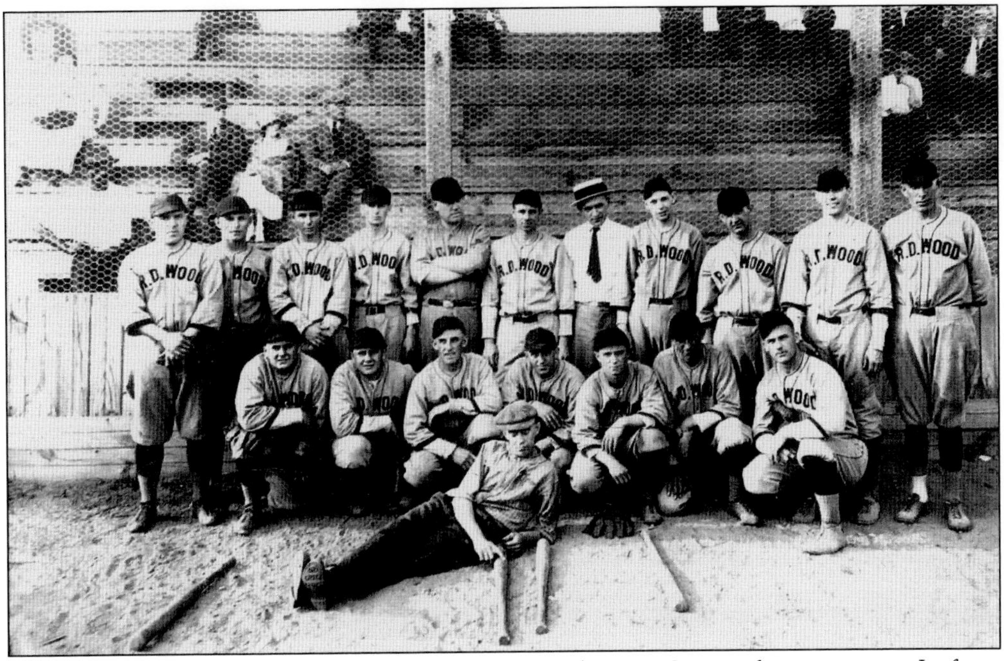

R.D. Wood had a championship baseball team in Burlington County for many years. In front of the R.D. Wood Clubhouse and grandstand are the 1923 champions. From left to right are the following: (front row) Deener, the mascot; (middle row) J. Baird, D. Baird, McGrath, Gilbert, Frappolli, Rhoda, and Moffett; (back row) Beaudry, Woolston, Scully, Parker, Sweeney, Sadler, Ed. Robbins, manager, Everham, Peacock, Fox, and Foulks. (Courtesy of John Williams.)

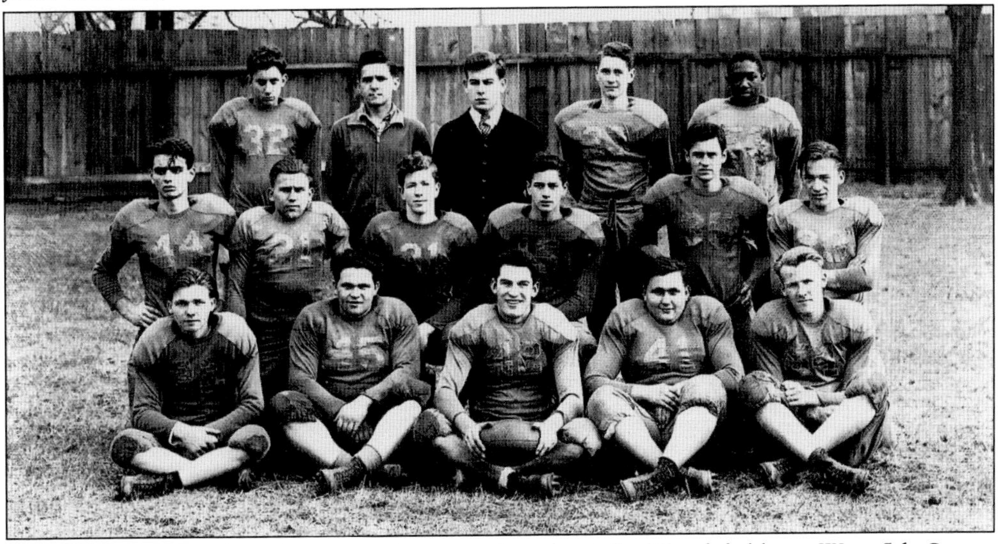

A 1940s high school football team is pictured at the R.D. Wood field, on West 5th Street. Behind the fence stands the foundry farmhouse, a fixture in town until the 1980s. Pictured are, from left to right, (front row) Dave Csik, Ed Cronin, Jack Livercik, Bill Vash, and Rodman Harris; (middle row) John Mazar, George Nyikita, Bill Carter, Bob Quig, Jack Quig, and Steve Steiner; (back row) Al Blakeslee, Joe Yurcisin, Jim Dow, Tom Adams, and Willie Harris. (Courtesy of Florence Historical Society.)

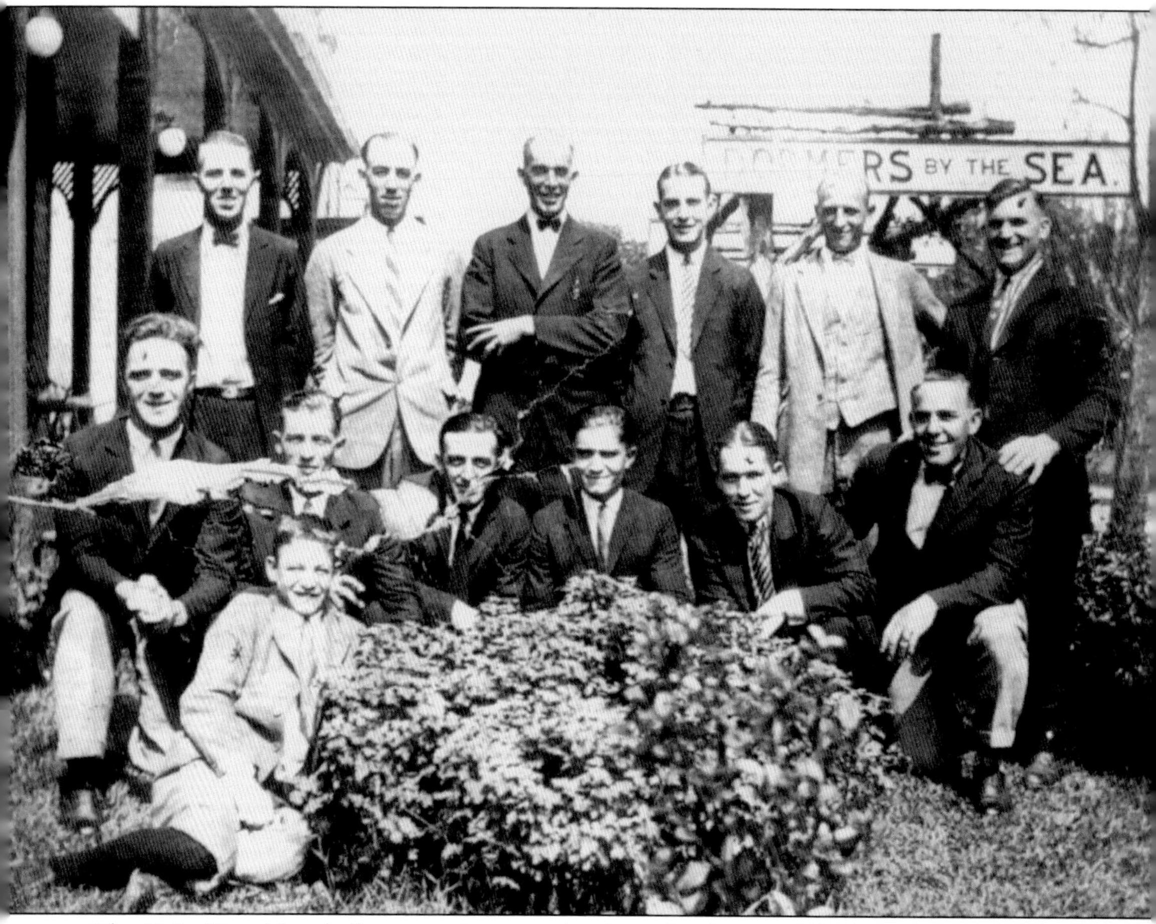

The R.D. Wood baseball team gathers at the shore (perhaps in Wildwood) *c.* 1940. From left to right are the following: (front row) unidentified; (middle row) John Woolston. Ruby Gilbert, Nick Frappolli, Buck Beaudry, Jimmy Moffett, and "Reds" Frappolli; (back row) Marty McGrath, Morris Lippincott, Jesse Foulks, Paul Scully, John Rhoda, and unidentified. (Courtesy of Florence Historical Society.)